PRÁXEDES

WIFE, MOTHER, WIDOW AND LAY DOMINICAN
1886 - 1936

D1471814

PRAYER

Heavenly Father, Thou didst inspire Praxedes with purest charity in her several states of life. Grant that she who served Thee faithfully on earth may be our helper in Heaven. Hasten the day of her beatification, and grant us the favor we now ask, through Jesus Christ our Lord. Amen.

Please report notable favors received through Praxedes' intercession to the Dominican Fathers at:

Postulation
Santa Sabina Convent
Aventino
00153 Rome
Italy

PRÁXEDES

WIFE, MOTHER, WIDOW AND LAY DOMINICAN
1886 - 1936

The Life of the Servant of God
Práxedes Fernandez

By

Father Martin-Maria Olive, O.P.

Translated by
Sister Maria Maez, O.P.
Mount Thabor Monastery
Ortonville, Michigan

*"Who shall find a valiant woman? Far
and from the uttermost coasts is the price
of her."*
—Proverbs 31:10

TAN BOOKS AND PUBLISHERS, INC.
Rockford, Illinois 61105

Approbation of the Spanish edition:

Nihil Obstat: Fray Jose Luis Gago, O.P.
                     Fray Emilio Rodriguez, O.P.

Imprimi Potest: Fray Candido Aniz, O.P.
                     Provincial Prior

Imprimatur: Dr. D. Constancio Palomo
                     Vicar General
                     Salamanca
                     November 26, 1980

Approbation of this English translation:

Nihil Obstat: Rev. John .P. Zenz
                     Censor Deputatus

Imprimatur: ✝Edmund C. Szoka
                     Archbishop of Detroit
                     September 5, 1987

The Nihil Obstat and Imprimatur are official declarations that a book or pamphlet is free of doctrinal or moral error. No implication is contained therein that those who have granted the Nihil Obstat and Imprimatur agree with the contents, opinions or statements expressed.

Translated from the Spanish *Praxedes (1886-1936): Mensajera de reconciliacion,* by Martin-Maria Olive, O.P., translation and adaptation of Gabino Prieto Cienfuegos, published in 1980 by Secretariado Praxedes, Claudio Coello, 141, Madrid 6, Spain.

This translation copyright ©1987 by TAN Books and Publishers, Inc.

Library of Congress Catalog Card No.: 87-50548

ISBN: 0-89555-309-0

All rights reserved. No part of this book may be reproduced or transmitted in any form or by any means, electronic or mechanical, including photocopying, recording, or by any information storage or retrieval system, without permission in writing from the publisher.

Printed and bound in the United States of America.

TAN BOOKS AND PUBLISHERS, INC.
P.O. Box 424
Rockford, Illinois 61105

1987

Letter to the Author
From the Secretary of State
Of His Holiness Paul VI

Secretary of State
N. 200136

The Vatican
December 28, 1971

Reverend Father:

The book that you have just dedicated to "Praxedes Fernandez" has been received by the Holy Father through the mediation of her son, also a Dominican, Father Enrique Fernandez, of Los Angeles, California, and has been received with great benevolence by His Holiness, who has entrusted me with delivering his intense gratitude to the two of you.

The Holy Father is very happy that this biography, so well documented, has been written, and will be presented to the Christian people of God for their edification. He is very desirous that members of the laity who have lived lives of heroism and Christian virtue in obscurity and simplicity will be proposed for the honors of the altar. This is, it seems, the case with this humble woman from among the Asturian people of God, and whose diocesan informative process for her beatification has been completed and presented to the Sacred Congregation for the Causes of Saints.

His Holiness congratulates you for your work and wishes that this work will be well and enthusiastically received by many readers, thus making well known this beautiful woman, daughter, wife and mother of miners.

With all his heart and benevolence, he sends the fortunate son of such a mother, and you, the Apostolic Blessing.

Please accept, Reverend Father, the assurance of my religious affection.

J. Benelli
Substit.

(This letter was received by Father Olive on the publication of his book, Praxedes, 1886-1936 L'Evangile vecu en pleine violence revolutionnaire [Ed. Oeuvres de la Grotte, Lourdes, 1970], of which this is simply an extract originating with the same author.)

CONTENTS

PREFACE

Praxedes Fernandez Garcia was the wife of an Asturian miner. She lived in the valley of Mieres, which has made the headlines as the scene of strikes and disturbances. It is difficult to imagine that in that environment, which is considered revolutionary, a woman has been able to sanctify herself—she who had endured such hardships not only in her home, but in an atmosphere which was considered anti-christian. But nevertheless, in one of the homes in this valley, in this difficult environment, there was a woman who was sincerely growing and maturing in the love of God in a most extraordinary way, leaving a seal of authentic Christianity.

Those were difficult times that Praxedes experienced during the tragic revolution of October, 1934. In Asturias it was particularly violent. And the marvelous thing was not that she did extraordinary things, but that she was able to keep her simplicity and love in the midst of that civil war in her beloved country, where there was such hatred between brothers, sons of the same motherland. She was able to be kind to everyone, preaching more with her example than by word. She was able to give an authentic testimony of her faith, of feminine sensibility and Christianity.

Someone has said that the beatifications and canonizations, especially of foundresses and founders of religious families, are excessive, that they have lost the significance that they had in the past. I do not believe that I can accept that conclusion without distinction—although I am convinced that in our day, in this secularized society, the world needs, over and above those past testimonies that will always have value, other signs that better adapt to its psychology.

Those simple and human saints, who knew how to live a

normal life with others, who suffered the same misunderstand-
ings and injustices, knew how to sanctify themselves through
these very experiences. Therefore, this wife of a miner is a
testimony for Christians of today. She is that sign that the gener-
ation of today needs to help it come closer to God and to the
faith which not only offers future happiness, but has power
to illumine and soften with its charity all the experiences in
the lives of the people of God.

I not only know personally the environment that she lived
in, but I have, as Archbishop of Oviedo, had the pastoral responsibility of those Asturian mining districts. I understand perfectly how Praxedes lived, her greatness and heroic love, and
am inspired that she was able to supersede so much misery
and violence. Much or all of this was blamed unjustly on the
miners, but in reality was instigated by others. They and their
fathers before them had had to work in truly inhuman conditions. Today, thanks be to God, this has changed considerably
in the last few years. These conditions had to be faced, and
those who were provoking a revolution took advantage of the
situation. The miners neither wished nor fomented what happened to their beloved country, at least in the majority of cases.

The publication of the life of this Servant of God, Praxedes
Fernandez Garcia, is fitting because she was one who knew
and wanted to be, in cooperation with God's grace, a living
presence of the Gospel in those difficult surroundings. It is
very interesting, according to my judgment, that for the Church
and for the rest of the world, that through this life, the "black
legend" that has grown around the Asturian miners will be
exposed and disappear.

There were more good Christians among the miners than
it popularly seemed. Moreover, from many of the families there
have been many vocations to the priesthood and religious life.
I can assure you, for I saw it during my years of service in
Asturia, that the priests from these families are more sensitive
to the injustices of this world, and know how to give themselves to the evangelization of all with extraordinary zeal.

God willing, the publication of this biography will help us
see God's plan more clearly through this extraordinary soul,
and at the same time inspire us to be the ferment of Christ,
in family life and in society as a whole. In both, the Church

is present in a special way through her laity who are conscious and responsible, asserting and radiating their faith, especially through love toward all of God's people, so that our society may be more humane and Christian.

May, 1977
Madrid
+Vicente Enrique y Tarancon
Cardinal-Archbishop

Prologue

A PRODIGY OF HOLINESS

Since July 19, 1936 the civil war had bled Spain. The following October 6, around 6:30 in the evening in the city of Oviedo, which was besieged by the miners, a woman belonging to the proletariat world died.

She was the widowed mother of four sons, and was 50 years and three months old. Her name was Praxedes Fernandez Garcia. After the revolution of October, 1934 she had moved to the capital of Asturia with her aged mother, an unmarried sister and two of her sons. They took up residence on the second floor of No. 18, Martinez Vigil Street, not far from the cathedral and between a gas factory and an arms factory. There she lived, never wanting to take refuge in the basement, in spite of the continual bombings of the neighborhood factories.

She was the victim of an intestinal infection, and had been deprived of medicine and adequate treatment because of the war. She had given herself up to God by constant prayer, and especially the Rosary, which had been her special devotion since childhood. While two neighbors prepared her body for burial, her mother, with eyes fixed on her, kept repeating, "This daughter of mine was a saint."

On the following day, October 7, once it got dark, the truck driver who picked up the bodies of those who had died that day stopped to pick up Praxedes in her coffin. No family members were allowed to attend the secret funeral rites. The driver simply left the bodies at the cemetery. It was expected that those in charge of burying them would give them a Christian burial as soon as it got dark. Due to these circumstances it has been impossible to identify Praxedes' body. We only know with certainty that she was buried in what was then called "the old cemetery" and over which is now built the diocesan seminary.

Praxedes lived in Oviedo with her two sons—Celestino, the oldest, who was finishing his profession as a lawyer at the university, and Gabriel, who was in college. She had lost her second son, Arturo, in an accident five years previous. The third, Enrique, had entered the Order of Preachers on October 1, 1933 at San Esteban of Salamanca.

During the first months of the civil war, communication had been interrupted between Oviedo and Salamanca. It was not re-established until October 17, when the national troops had broken through the rebel defense around the capital of Asturia. Thus the notice of Praxedes' death did not reach Salamanca until December 9, 1936. Sometime before that, Enrique had been notified that his mother was very ill. On the 11th, a Saturday, the first solemn funeral rites were offered for Praxedes in San Estaban of Salamanca, where Fray Enrique was a member of the community.

Two days after the services, Father Sabino M. Lozana, the Master of Novices and director of the magazine on mystical theology called *La Vida Sobrenatural (The Supernatural Life)*, met Fray Enrique in the hall and offered his condolences. He added, "Someone told me that your mother was a great and holy woman." The following year, Father P. Maximiliano Canal, professor at the Lateran in Rome, who knew Praxedes and had in fact received her into the Dominican laity in August, 1934, said to Fray Enrique, "Are you Praxedes' son? Your mother is a saint."

Asturias was not completely liberated until November, 1937. In January, 1938 Fray Enrique assisted at another solemn funeral in Mieres for his mother, which was organized by the Passionist Fathers. She had been a member of the Archconfraternity of the Passion. Many of the Passionist Fathers who had known Praxedes assisted at it. They did not hesitate later to hold up her life as an example worthy of imitation.

In the meantime, preparations were being made for Fray Enrique's first Mass. For some reason, totally unforeseen, but providential, he offered his first Mass on the very day of his mother's birthday, July 21, 1941. The preacher of the celebration was Father Jesus Larumbe, O.P., who exalted "the sacerdotal heart" of this mother whose deep desire and dream had been to have a priest son.

Praxedes' fame for holiness grew day by day. Father Enrique's friends often asked him about his mother and urged him to write her biography. Finally, giving in to their requests, he wrote a short, seven-page article on her which was published in the Salamanca mystical theology magazine, *The Supernatural Life*, in the issue of July-August, 1946.

When the article appeared, Father Enrique was serving in Mexico. Immediately following this publication, comments and letters came from all sides. They were from masters of spirituality, theologians, priests, sisters and members of Catholic Action, the laity. He even heard from the magazine editor, who said, "Your mother's biographical sketch was liked and received by many. It did a lot of good. Many letters have been received with this motive."

The article also aroused interest in the General Curia of the Order of Preachers in Rome. The assistant General of the Order, Father Aniceto Fernandez (who in 1962 was elected Superior General of the Order), wrote to Father Enrique on January 10, 1950: "I read the article about your mother in *The Supernatural Life*. Without a doubt your mother was a saint filled by the Spirit of God. I gave the magazine to Fray Antonio, who marvels at her holiness."

All of these instances of interest on the part of his order and many others forced Father Enrique to write a complete biography, which was edited by Ediciones Paulinas of Mexico, in June, 1952 titled *A Mother, Model for our Times*.

The success of the book was outstanding. The newspapers of Asturias, her birthplace, commented on it, showing their admiration for Praxedes. Both theologians and prelates who read the book were amazed at this extraordinary woman from among ordinary people. Father Albert Colunga, professor of Sacred Scripture at the University of Salamanca and author of the most famous modern translation of the Bible, wrote, "I read the book at one sitting and with great pleasure. It is a book of great edification and proves that saints are people of all times and of all circumstances." The Regent of the Theology Faculty at San Estaban in Salamanca predicted, "That book will do much good for souls."

Father Esteban G. Vigil, professor of moral theology in the seminary of Oviedo and twice provincial of the Spanish Dominicans had this to say: "I liked the book very much. I have read the book three times and with the greatest interest and edification, concluding that Praxedes was a saint and of the greatest." Father Victoriano Osende, author of many spiritual works, wrote, "I read the book and it touched me greatly. Upon reading it, it occurred to me to ask God that it reach all those who wish to know the ways that lead to sanctity. I am positive that this book will do an immense good to all who read it."

Father Basilio, a Passionist and professor of theology, Vice President of the Marion Society as well as author of various works declared, "There are saints! This is what cannot escape one who reads the life of Praxedes. My greatest wish is that this heroic and great woman be honored in our day. She is an attractive personality."

Father Sabino M. Lozano asserted, "This biography of Praxedes is certainly worthy of being read. I like it very much. She is God's miracle of grace. Admirable!"

D. Baldomero Jumenez Duque, author of many works on theological spirituality, did not hesitate to say, "The life of Praxedes impressed me greatly. She is truly admirable. She discharged a charismatic and prophetic roll in the everyday life."

At the same time that her biography was causing such great admiration she continued transmitting "the good odor of Christ" among the people of the mining valley. The pastor of Seana, her parish, wrote on October 20, 1952, "It is a great joy and consolation for me to see such widespread interest in this woman who was born here and lived here most of her life in this parish. She was a saint. This is what they called her, call her, and I will always call her."

Another testimony, much like the one above, came from the Superior General Manuel Suarez: "It is of great consolation and edification for me to see that the Lord, in our time, sends us such good and holy people as this mother of a family, gifted with such sublime virtues. May she protect us from her place in Heaven!" (November 17, 1952.)

The year 1953 was the apex in the extraordinary growth and fame of her sanctity. This was when the pastor during Praxedes' time, at Seana, entered the scene. Father Moises Diaz-Caneja was at the time Canon of the Cathedral in Oviedo. When he learned that Father Enrique was at the Dominican Convent in Oviedo, on a visit from Mexico, he invited him to visit him so that he could tell him among other things that the biography of his mother "was very inferior to the reality of what I have known. The greatest grace that I have received after my Baptism is that God placed your holy mother in my path."

The parish in Seana had not yet celebrated funeral rites for Praxedes. Father Moises believed that now was the time to pay their debt of gratitude. Therefore, in accord with the pastor of Seana, a date was set for such a celebration on October 6, 1953. This was the 17th anniversary of her death. It had to be an extraordinary occasion! It was decided that a Pontifical Requiem Mass would be offered with funeral rites and prayers. Father Moises would preach at this Mass. The solemn ceremonies took place in the church at Mieres. The attendance was extraordinary. It included the Archbishop of Foochow, China, Teodoro Labrador, 25 priests representing the Cathedral at Oviedo, the Dominican Community of Oviedo, Passionists from Mieres, the Christian Brothers, numerous religious sisters from the Annunciata Community who were spread throughout the mining valley, and some 2,000 people from all over Asturias as well as civil and municipal authorities.

Among the priests was Father Jose Villar, who had joined Praxedes and Gabriel in marriage in April, 1914. And among the laity was Jose Alvarez, her ex-boyfriend of 1909.

The funeral prayers offered by Father Moises were panegyric. The expression "a prodigy of sanctity" was heard at the end of each phase of her life. At the end he was visibly moved and presented Praxedes as a person worthy of canonization with these words: "It is only normal that Praxedes receive the honors of the altar. You will not have done your job well if you do not do your utmost to accord her this honor. We must place her at the top of the mountain so that she shines for all to see. Asturias expects it. This is your job. It would be treason not to do it!"

The challenge had been thrown out no less than from the Archchurch of Mieres. And it was listened to. Eleven days after that the Archbishop of Oviedo received an official petition signed by the Archbishop of Mieres, the pastor of Seana and all the other pastors of the archdiocese, asking for the introduction of the cause for Praxedes' canonization. The prelate answered right away, with an official letter, on November 4 of the same year. In this official document he said, "I am deeply interested that this process begin at once." He also asked that a postulator be appointed for her cause, right away.

Father Tarcisio Picarri, O.P. was appointed Postulator in Rome and the Vice-Postulator, Father Leocadis Alonso from Oviedo, was named also. The solemn opening of the process of beatification began on November 7, 1957 in the Archchurch in Mieres. On January 10, 1958 the episcopal decree was published ordering the search for all the writings of the Servant of God. All who knew her were invited to testify about anything they knew of her, good or bad.

The newspapers and radio reported this great happening, in Spain and around the world. A Catholic paper in Texas, edited by the Jesuits, praised the cause for Praxedes as "one of the most interesting of modern times." Among the international news agencies that spread the news to the world was the famous N.W.N.C. from Washington, D.C. in its bulletin on January 4, 1958.

From this time on the fame of her holiness grew progressively. More than 300 magazines and newspapers in 16 nations published reports on her in the principal languages of the world. Among the newspapers was *L'Osservatore Romano*. And among the authors was Cardinal Fernando Cento, who not only dedicated an article to Praxedes in a Roman magazine, *Il Cocifisso*, but later dedicated a whole chapter in one of his works, *All'ombra della Croce* (Rome, 1960), to her also.

In France, the *Revue du Rosaire* dedicated the September, 1961 issue to her. An authentic flood of letters came to them from France, Spain, Belgium, Cameroon, Italy, Marruecos, Canada, Argelia and from the Mauricio Island in the Indian Ocean. These letters indicated favors received and asked for more details of her life within a complete biography in French.

In a visit that I paid to Asturias in April, 1964, I was able to gather many testimonies, and these were later published in the February issue of 1965 of the same magazine. The whole issue was then dedicated to Praxedes.

In the meantime the diocesan inquiry process was completed in September, 1960, in St. Dominic Church of Oviedo. Many attended, including the Bishop and the Archbishop of Foochow and the Bishop of Salamanca.

The writings on Praxedes were approved with high praises by the censors appointed by the Sacred Congregation for the Causes of Saints. One remarked that solely by these writings she qualified being a "soul adorned by great Christian virtues, and could justly be called a saint." Pope Paul VI decreed on March 30, 1967 that there was "nothing opposed to Praxedes' cause" and that it could proceed.

The Postulator General of the Dominican Order received permission from the Sacred Congregation to form a new process to get more facts on the Servant of God. They were to be presented to the same Congregation on May 11, 1975 together with other documents.

In June, 1976, there was constituted in the capital of Spain, Madrid, Claudio Coello, 141, Madrid 6, a "Secretariat on Praxedes," directed by Father Jesus M. Rodriguez Arias, O.P. He is the new Vice Postulator of the Cause. It publishes a bulletin periodically.

The biographies so far published are two in Spain, one in Colombia, two in Mexico, one in El Salvador and now one in the United States. In France I myself published this one that is now being translated into Spanish in a shortened form.

From all parts of the world news of favors received through the intercession of Praxedes is being received. The pastors of God's people are anxious to have her raised to the honors of the altar for the edification of all. Nine Cardinals, one Patriarch, and more than 100 Bishops and Archbishops from 26 nations and four continents have sent letters to the Pope requesting that Praxedes be canonized a saint. The letter of the Cardinal-Archbishop of Compostela, Quiroga Palacios, deserves special mention, for he states that even while Praxedes lived he heard of her goodness. "I myself, while she still lived, heard of her virtues."

Is it not permitted then, to hope that the voice of the Vicar of Christ be joined to the many that are now asking that she be solemnly proclaimed a saint. "Yes, this woman is truly a saint!"

Chapter 1

IN THE HEART OF THE MINING VALLEY

Praxedes was born in the Municipality of Mieres, in the heart of the mining valley of Asturias in Spain. There, at the time of her birth, was found a harmonious unity between ancestral traditions and the most modern developments in the soft coal and metallurgy industries.

Asturias, as it is well-known, was the last bastion of Iberian independence during Roman rule. It was conquered in the year 25 B.C. by the Emperor Augustus. Centuries later the Asturians formed part of the Visigothic Kingdom. When in the year 711 the Moors destroyed this civilization in Spain, Asturias, thanks to its mountainous isolation, preserved its independence. Commander Pelayo, a descendant of a royal dynasty, founded a new monarchy.

He defeated the armies of Mohammed in the year 718 in the foothills of Covadonga, aided by the Virgin of the Cave and a handful of brave men. This was the deciding point of stopping the Arab invasion and the beginning of the Christian reconquest of Spain under the symbol of the "Holy One." This is why Pelayo and Covadonga symbolize the religion and nationalism of Spain.

Proud of its glorious fatherland and of its faith, the Asturian is equally as proud of the natural riches of its land, agriculture and mining. The principality is mountainous with summits in some parts which reach 2,600 m. in height.

Mieres is at the bottom of a valley crowned by lesser heights. It is crossed by the River Caudel, which descends from the Port of Pajares and follows the course of the Cantabrico River.

Due to abundant rainfall and the mild climate, the humidity

1

favors luxuriant vegetation and rich cultivations. The gardens produce all kinds of vegetables and cereals, especially corn, which is strung and hung from the pillars of houses to dry. This gives Asturias its quaintness and a very original and picturesque appearance.

Numerous apple orchards produce cider in such an abundance that it constitutes the main drink of Asturias. It is cleverly served by pouring it from high above the table into a delicate glass. In this process it becomes a foaming, delicious drink. With this beverage are offered the toasts for all occasions, and it is served with daily meals as well as for all kinds of gatherings. Praxedes' in-laws were owners of a wine press where this popular drink was produced.

Over and above agricultural products, the valley of Mieres has the most incomparable riches in its subsoil: mercury, iron, cinnabar, magnesium, calamine, sulfur, and above all coal. Her mines had been worked for a long time in times past, but it was only in the past century when the European industrial movement gave this region such an impulse that it made it the first and most important region for soft coal production, and made Mieres the capital of the mining valley.

When Praxedes entered this world in 1886, Mieres was at the peak of its development. Without losing any of its traditional customs the region became one of the most active centers of industrial development, as well as of soft coal mining. A net of railroads unites all these mines. The manufacturing installations raise to the heavens the great chimneys of their high furnaces, while inside powerful machinery produces iron and steel and utilizes all their byproducts. Hundreds of perforations can be seen in the mountains in all directions. It is through these holes that rich deposits are extricated. While qualified engineers direct all this activity, more experts in mining are being trained in the School of Engineers of Mieres.

It was at this precise moment that Praxedes appeared in this mining world. Her father was a graduate of the School of Mining Engineers of Mieres. Her three brothers also received the same formation and education as their father did and worked in the mines. She herself later married an electrician who was employed by one of the most famous mining companies of Spain, Hulleras Turon, S.A. (Soft Coal Turon). Two of her four sons also became miners. We can almost say that she was born in the mines. Even the name of the place of her birth has the name of one of the mines, La Luisa.

In order to better situate Praxedes in the midst of her environment we shall underscore her many ties with the famous steel mill of Mieres, La Fabrica. It was the pride and "mother" of the land in this region. Here her father and brothers worked and contributed to its growth and development. Moreover, she was educated in the school of La Fabrica. It was staffed by the Dominican Sisters, whose goal was the formation of the daughters of the miners. Praxedes also attended the equally famous chapel of La Fabrica all her life.

Rafael Fuentes, in his work *Industrial Asturias* (published at the beginning of the present century) has described in great detail all that was relative to this manufacturing industry. "In 1848," he wrote, "an Anglo-Austrian enterprise established in Mieres the first foundry in Spain which produced ingots. In turn it produced coke under the direction of Engineer Lambert. However, not having obtained the expected results, he ceded it to a Numa Guilhou, who from 1870 on had great success in the development and preparation of filtered iron, wrought iron and laminated iron. On March 22, 1879 Numa Guilhou formed a corporation with capital of 16 million pesetas. Besides the manufacturing of steel and iron on a grand scale, he developed the mining of soft coal, iron, magnesium, mercury, calamine and lead sulfate."[1]

When Praxedes was born, Numa Guilhou, of French origin, was the proprietor of the factory and Engineer Jeronimo Ibran the foreman. Jeronimo Ibran was later her sponsor of Confirmation.

For 46 years Praxedes lived on the borders of the Mieres municipality, in different small towns. She lived in Oviedo for two years but was still linked to mining. For another two years she lived in Andalucia, but all those on her father's side of the family still worked in the mines.

On all sides, then, were the mines. On all sides too were the chimneys, factories and coal. These were the familiar and human surroundings so dear to Praxedes.

There is a famous proverb that comes from Asturias that says, "All comes from the mines." Clearly, it refers to the coal and the daily work of the miners. But who knows, God willing, someday we will be able to add, "and also a saint!"

Chapter 2

FAMILIAR SURROUNDINGS

Praxedes' parents formed an ideal and exemplary marriage. The father, Don Celestino Fernandez Fernandez, who was born on February 18, 1854, was an important figure in this farming and mining country. "He was someone," Sister Pilar Vila, a contemporary of his, told me in April, 1964; and she added, "He was a little authoritarian but very good. He was a great man." One gets the same impression from a picture taken of him when he was in his forties. He was a handsome man with a certain air of majesty about him. He had a high forehead and noble, dominant look, from which emanated great kindness. His oval face was adorned with a short and well-groomed beard.

He was a descendant of a family of small landowners who lived in Sueros during the 18th century. While continuing farming, his father, Enrique Fernandez (1822-1901), successfully practiced law without a legal title. His mother, Florentina Fernandez (1833-1883), was well-known for her beauty and virtue.

Celestino had inherited the ability of his father as well as the goodness of his mother. He was the second oldest of 13 children, and turned out to be the most intelligent of all. He was a tireless worker who greatly improved his heavily indebted land inheritance, turning it into a profitable and successful farming enterprise. He also became the owner of forest land in the mountains, which he used to produce lumber.

Members of Celestino's family worked in the mines and for the mines. But he wanted to study at the School of Foremen in Mieres, to make it possible to be more successful in the mining business.

His nephew-in-law, Jesus Antuna, told me in 1966 that he

5

was considered the "father of the village." All the testimonies that I gathered in my four visits to Asturias support this comment. He was a gentleman all the way, of an untouchable honesty and an unquestionable prudence. The neighbors constantly asked him to arbitrate their differences, always depending on him to restore calm and peace in family arguments. His daughter Florentina claims that "They came from the farthest points of the municipality of Mieres."[1]

If he was esteemed and loved by the neighbors, Celestino was, without doubt, immensely much more loved by his own family. This was precisely what I heard said of their father from his two daughters, Celestina and Florentina, in April, 1964: "Very intelligent, very upright, very charitable, very religious."

"My father," said Celestina, "was a very good Christian and was gifted with all the virtues—especially charity—giving many alms but always secretly, even from mother. He served breakfast to a young man for over a year. He sent money to the pastor to help out in the carrying out of the liturgy. During Lent he gave up smoking, which must have been a great sacrifice, as he loved to smoke Cuban cigars. He was concerned that we all attend Mass every Sunday."[2]

Celestino was a lover of books. He also enjoyed composing verse, which he read at weddings and birthdays. He also played the guitar fairly well. "Papa was a very happy man and everyone loved him," Celestina told me.

"Celestino," affirmed a neighbor who was an intimate friend for many years, "was a very honest and upright man who was never in the least unjust with anyone. That is why when he was the foreman of the coke plant, when socialist anarchy was beginning, his workmen never protested. He never gave any reason for anyone to be disturbed. He was very generous and a very good Christian."[3]

Amalia Garcia Suarez, the mother of Praxedes, was born in La Pena, Mieres, on June 10, 1858. Her parents were Jose Garcia (1825-1897) and Vicenta Suarez (1819-1902). They were owners of much property and many houses, and owned a store. Amalia was the third of ten children, of whom only five lived to adulthood. Florentina has left us this "picture" of her. "My mother was very good, a hard worker and always busy. She even set up a bakery in which she herself tended the ovens and sold the bread. She was more thrifty than my father. She was very kind and pious."[4]

Celestina added the following details: "My parents were both very religious, especially my mother, who assisted at all the novenas at the Seana Parish and never missed the Marian May devotions. She also belonged to the Association of the Perpetual Rosary. The Rosary was prayed at home every day. It was led by mother and sometimes by father."[5]

The neighbors admired her greatly. Julia Suarez put it very well: "Amalia was a great worker and an excellent administrator. When she worked, one could not distinguish her from the hired help, but when she rested she was 'the lady.' She did not like to waste anything, not even in the running of her household, teaching her children to take only as much food as they could eat. But she was also a very charitable almsgiver. She had great patience with her hired help and was very diplomatic in cutting off conversations when someone was speaking ill of someone. Many times she was the peacemaker in marriage problems, above all between her tenants who came to her with all their problems. She listened to each party separately, and with her gift of persuasion she managed to bring them together to live in peace."[6]

Her picture, beside her husband, shows us a lady of dignity, with beautiful features and the look of one who is not easily duped. She looks very open, with a bit of shrewdness and good practical sense.

There was an admirable understanding between the two. Each one in his way was charitable and pious. They participated in the Sacraments regularly and had family prayers. He was generous and joyful, she very generous with the poor and thrifty by nature, and was so even with her daughter Praxedes' children. One of them told me in 1965, "She never gave me one penny to buy candy."

Celestino and Amalia got married on January 7, 1880 in the parish of Seana. She was 21 and he 24. They had 12 children, four boys and eight girls, of which five died in infancy. Celestino died on December 27, 1914 and his wife on September 25, 1946. They are buried in the interior of the parochial church of Seana, beneath a white marble tombstone that says, "Here rest the fortunate parents of Praxedes."

Chapter 3

BIRTH AND FIRST YEARS

Praxedes entered this world at nine o'clock in the morning of July 21, 1886. She was born in a small country house on the outskirts of Sueros, named "The Bridge of Luisa." Two baby boys and a baby girl had preceded her. Later on she was followed by Consuelo, Celestina, Celso and Florentina, besides four others who did not survive her. They were all "blessings from God," as Amalia wrote in a letter to her oldest child dated July, 1919.

Five days after her birth she was baptized in the parish church of Seana. She recieved the name of Praxedes, the saint of the day on which she was born. Her godparents were Robustiano Fernandez, her father's brother, and Elena Garcia, her mother's sister. Robustiano and Elena both became her favorites and she never failed to give them her loving attention. Her godfather died in 1912 and her godmother in 1933. Both received her loving care during their last illness and death.

Praxedes' devotion to her patron saint is reflected in the following prayer that was found in her worn-out prayer book: "O glorious St. Praxedes, who reigns with God in glory, remember me in the presence of the Lord, so that I may never bring disgrace to your name with my faults and failings, and pray that I may one day be with you and partake of that glory that you already enjoy. Amen."

One curious and strange incident marked the child's infancy. She was already 20 months old and she had not yet learned to walk. Her little brother was born at this time. The poor mother was overwhelmed at having two babies to carry. She confidently turned to St. Rita, who was highly venerated in her parish of Seana. She had a Mass offered in her honor to ask for her intercession in this problem. Upon returning home from the Mass, what did she encounter but little Praxedes running up to meet her mother with open arms!

This episode became famous and was the talk of the neighborhoods. As for Praxedes, her gratitude to the saint for the favor granted to her never wavered. Father Enrique, one of Praxedes' sons, has told me that she had a picture of St. Rita hanging at the head of her bed. She was popularly called "the lawyer of the impossible."

In 1891, when Praxedes was five years old, her family home became too small, so they moved to the little town of Ablana. They lived in a two-story home, provided by her father's Fabrica in the section called *El Puente de la Luisa.* They still belonged to the municipality of Mieres and the parish of Seana.

At the age of five or six Praxedes began her schooling in the public school. As she grew up she also developed a tender care toward the poor and the sick.

Her parents had a young servant girl named Josefa Solis living in their home. On November 2, 1964, when Josefa was a nonagenarian, she told Father Enrique how his holy mother had had such a great concern and love for her when she lived with them during her youth. Memory guards what the heart has felt profoundly. One cold and rainy day Josefa came in trembling with cold after several hours of washing clothes in the river. Upon seeing Josefa all wet, Praxedes was full of compassion for her, and anxiously asked if she were hungry and cold. Immediately she began to plead with her mother to give her a good hot meal.

At about this time a similar significant episode took place in Praxedes' life that the author of a biography of Praxedes, Father Paul Albiol, recounts. It was also taken from an interview with Josefa Solis: "She [Praxedes] was four or five when this happened. One day one of the poor of the area knocked on the door of the Fernandez home. I was about to tell her that the lady of the house was not in when Praxedes took a knife and began to cut some bread. She was so small that the piece of bread looked quite mutilated. The poor woman took it and said, 'Your kindness is enough for me.' "[1]

Praxedes was a true daughter of her parents. "No poor ever

came to our door," said her brother Ovidio, "without being taken care of by her."[2] And the oldest, Ismael, added, "From a very tender age, she showed a special concern for the poor and sick. One evening someone came to ask for some milk for a sick person, and she, not having drunk hers yet, offered it immediately."[3]

Her piety was as great as her mercy. "Her religious inclinations," affirmed Ovidio, "were awakened in her at a very tender age."[4] Her cousin Benigna Fernandez agreed to this, saying, "She was very pious even in her early childhood. She was born with this gift, but she also had the example of her mother, who was also very religious."[5]

Praxedes' greatest joy was to pray the family Rosary. "I know that Praxedes was the most fervent in praying the Rosary," her sister Celestina testified. "Yes, I remember that sometimes she would fall asleep and she would tell us that it was the devil who tempted her."[6]

Praxedes was always lovable with her parents and obedient at all times. "She outdid all of us in her obedience to our parents,"[7] said Celestina. Ovidio for his part wrote, "She was always obedient at home."[8] Old Josefa affirmed this when she said, "She was very obedient. Never did she question her duty on this point, either with her mother or anyone else."[9]

Pious, good, always serving others, a model of obedience and respect for her parents, affectionate with them and with her brothers and sisters, is what all her family and Josefa and all who knew her in her childhood said of Praxedes.

She then began to show her qualities as a good housekeeper. She helped her mother around the house and in caring for her younger brothers and sisters. After all, she was the oldest of the girls.

On May 13, 1894 Praxedes received the Sacrament of Confirmation in her parish church, La Rebollada. But it was above all her first Holy Communion that she was anxiously awaiting. Here we have Josefa's remembrance of the great joy Praxedes experienced as the day of her first encounter with Jesus approached. "How happy I am that soon I will receive my first Holy Communion," she repeated over and over. Wondering at this often-heard "sing-song," her sister Consuelo asked Praxedes one day, "Why do you repeat that so often? I am also going to make my first Holy Communion and I don't say anything!"

Dressed in white, Praxedes approached the holy table on the feast of Corpus Christi in 1894, in her parish of Seana. Upon her return home, overflowing with joy, she was heard saying, "I feel so happy for I have received Holy Communion today."[10]

At this time, Praxedes' maternal uncle, Jose Ramiro, from far-off Cuba, wrote to his sister Amalia saying, "It would please me greatly if you did not ever again subject my dear nieces and nephews to the ridiculous practice of confession."[11]

A month after her first Holy Communion Praxedes received the first of many shocks of her life. The first shock was the death of her little brother Higinio, who followed her in age, and whom she loved tenderly. He died of diphtheria at the age of six. It was then that she began to see the vanity of earthly things.

In 1895 her family moved again, this time to Sueros, Celestino's birthplace. They moved into an old house at first, on property of the family. While living there they began to build a two-story house with a basement. When it was finished a delicatessen was opened in the basement. To the side of this the ovens to bake bread were installed. The whole village bought their bread there. For this reason their home soon became the heart of Sueros.

At the age of 11 Praxedes was her mother's "right arm," in the housekeeping chores as well as in running the store. Besides this she helped in the two gardens her parents had, took the sheep to pasture, helped her mother knead the dough and bake the bread, as well as cared for her little brothers and sisters like a little mother.

In spite of all this, her parents were careful about her education. She, together with her brothers and sisters, went to the public school of Seana every day. She was also very faithful in frequently attending Mass at the parish church on top of the mountain.

Her family consisted of nine persons: the parents, three brothers, Ovidio, Ismael and Celso. The four girls were Praxedes, Consuelo, Celestina, and Florentina, who was just born that same year of 1895.

Ovidio, two years older than Praxedes, has given us, in a letter, some of Praxedes' personality traits that help us understand her as the years went by. "Your holy mother," he wrote to one of his nephews, "was always obedient at home. She never wasted time in useless playing and dancing. When she wasn't yet very old she helped with many tasks that she took upon herself. She never missed Mass on Sundays and holy days."[12]

Her sister Celestina has made the same observations. "Since Praxedes was but a child and as long as I can remember, I know she was very obedient, helpful, and loving toward our parents. I don't remember having heard my parents complain about her in any way. On the contrary, they were always pleased with her and loved her very much."[13]

A little incident related to Praxedes' childhood reveals her beautiful disposition of generosity in sharing not only her belongings, but herself as well. Father Jacinto of St. Paul, a Passionist, has told the following: "Recently, in one of my visits to El Valleto, a palace belonging to Valdecuna, Mieres, from where I am, I heard a very old lady by the name of Dolores Blanco tell of this incident. Praxedes and a group of her friends were celebrating at a fair during one of the feasts of Valdecuna. The girls wanted to buy some candy, but had no money. Praxedes gave them all she had, ten cents. In those days one could buy a lot of candy with ten cents. This she told about Praxedes to show that even at an early age she had a kind as well as detached heart, even as a child."[14]

It was clear that the poor, the sick, her family, strangers, all were a special concern of Praxedes' solicitude. Her spirit of self-giving and service is what stands out in this good child.

It was during her father's fatal illness that Praxedes' loving care for her sick parent stood out. Ovidio said of her at that time, "The delicacy that she had for our parents was extreme, especially toward my father, who suffered from a chronic stomach ailment. It hurt her so much to see him suffer like that."[15]

Praxedes' father was so greatly touched by such attention and kindness that he found in his daughter that he began to show favoritism toward her—but without ever provoking jealousy from her brothers and sisters.

"My father," confessed Ovidio, "always showed a special love for her because he saw the nobility of her soul."[16] And Celestina remembered a poem composed by her father in which he referred to Praxedes without ambiguity: "I love her unto madness." This was a poetic exaggeration, perhaps, but it proves exactly the place that she held in his heart.

If Celestino could assert what he did about this favorite daughter of his without causing jealousy among his other children, it was because Praxedes had already won their affection with her goodness and concern for them. Ovidio gave us a clear witness of this: "I love my sister with a very special love, and I have always admired her for the extraordinary way in which she always excelled us in everything."[17]

Chapter 4

IN THE DOMINICAN SCHOOL
(1898-1901)

Praxedes was close to her twelfth birthday when, in January, 1896, the Dominican Sisters of the Annunciation founded a school in La Fabrica in Mieres. Their intention was to educate the daughters of the miners. In the village of Mieres a similar school was founded for the boys, directed by the Brothers of Christian Schools.

Celestino immediately enrolled all of his daughters in the Dominican school, anxious to give them a good education both intellectually and religiously.

The sisters were careful to give the girls a formation that corresponded to their future rolls of mothers and wives. In the morning they were taught general culture, such as grammar, mathematics, geography and history. In the afternoon they were taught sewing, cooking and embroidery.

Praxedes, who had always been very good when it came to housekeeping, took advantage of these classes to perfect herself. Florentina made reference to this in a letter she wrote to one of her nephews on October 3, 1949. "Your mother was a model of everything. Her cooking was an art, and certainly there was no equal to her in her housekeeping. Everything seemed to always be in her favor. When she served a special dish, it was a marvel. In sewing, too, she was prodigious, as she could take any piece of cloth and make beautiful things. She embroidered very well. She was what one calls an outstanding lady."

Praxedes also loved culture. She wrote well and expressed herself with elegance and clarity. We have her letters that show that she was gifted along this line. She esteemed the learned, "those who know" as they say in the villages. Later on she firmly encouraged her sons to be learned, and she inspired each one to set high personal goals, each according to his ability.

The moral and religious formation of the Dominican Sisters was no less profound. These excellent teachers did their utmost to inculcate the love of God in their students. They grounded the students' piety on a solid, filial devotion to the Blessed Virgin Mary.

Fortunately, we have direct testimonies where little by little one can see the character traits of Praxedes' personality. Of exceptional value is Sister Pilar Vila's testimony. "I knew Praxedes from 1900 to 1934. When I met her for the first time, she was 14. I came to the school on July 7, 1900. At first, I did not have her in my classes because I taught the retarded. But even so, I remember that she was always neatly and modestly dressed. She was always very proper. And I know that all the teachers held her in high regard. She wore her long hair in two braids which hung down her back, tied with ribbons. In her adolescence and later as a youth, she showed a great love for her mother and helped her at home with whatever had to be done. She was her father's favorite. Her sisters were good, too, but she had something special about her and was the best one of them all. Even at that young age she proved to be very pious. She was willing to do everything. With her, everything was a willingness to help. She attended all the worship services in the chapel at La Fabrica. She was very upright. She was always very attentive to the sisters, and her friendship for them went on into her widowhood and until she moved to Oviedo in December, 1934."[1]

Praxedes was an exemplary young lady, irreproachable and very delicate in all that concerned her personal life. Praxedes was her parents' pride and joy. She greatly enjoyed attending worship services and with that "something special" that she possessed, she clearly excelled in many other areas. This is the picture that her teachers give of her.

Her classmates have even more to say, as they are able to recall incidents more precisely. One of them, who later became a religious sister in Cintruenigo, Navarra, Sister Covadonga Espina (1892-1962), gave the following written

testimony upon being interrogated officially by the Vice Postulator for the cause of Praxedes' beatification, D. Leocadio Alonso.
"I feel very honored at being given the opportunity to contrib-
ute my little grain of sand toward the elevation to sainthood
of my fellow countryman, Praxedes. It is true that we knew
each other as pupils of the school run by the Dominican Sisters in El Cano. But because we came from opposite directions,
she from Sueros and I from Mieres, we just saw each other
in class. Perhaps because she was so good and humble she went
unnoticed. This is why I did not form a friendship with her.
I know the following detail about her: We were in class once
when one of the girls who sat next to me told me in a mysterious voice, as though she were relating something grandiose,
'The girls from Sueros that come to school with Praxedes say
that she often gives her lunch to the poor or to one of the
girls that come to school with her. They say that when they
scold her or try to quarrel or even blame her, she remains quiet.
And if they hit her she lets them hit her.' I remember she told
me this full of admiration."[2]

Praxedes' cousin and classmate, Benigna Fernandez, confirmed
this attitude of peace in Praxedes that Sister Covadonga has
described. "Praxedes accepted everything as if it came from
God's hands, and she never became irritated by anyone or anything. She was like this even from her childhood. She was always calm, very tranquil, peaceable and smiling. I never saw
her angry, not even as a child."[3]

Another classmate of hers, Maria Paton, had this to say: "I
knew Praxedes at the Dominican Sisters' school and what I
know of her dates from that period. Already at that time I
noticed her virtuous conduct. I love her very much because
I am convinced that even as a child she was so good. She fulfilled her duties, religious and otherwise, so well. She was often
at Mass. I never saw her angry. Just by her ways one couldn't
help noticing her humility."[4]

A third alumna of the sisters' school summed up in a few
words her schoolday memories. "I got to know Praxedes from
our schooldays. I also knew her parents, who were exemplary.
No amount of praise could ever measure up to the reality of
her goodness, for she was of a very religious character, very
joyful and extraordinarily humble."[5]

Finally, Adela Fernandez has told us in vigorous terms what is one of the dominant characteristics in the life of Praxedes—namely, her total application to whatever she did. "I knew Praxedes when we both attended school at La Fabrica. She was so good and always performed her duties in a most praiseworthy fashion. She was a person of faith and was outstandingly religious and pious. Her refined conduct and goodness were remarkable. She was also very humble, as her school life at that time proves."[6]

In another more detailed testimony she continued, "Praxedes was very serious and quiet. She never joined in games that were very active such as running and jumping. She always went straight home from school and from home to school without ever entertaining herself along the way. If you were to ask me if she were that way even as a child, I would have to say that she was not only good, but very good."[7]

"From home to school, from school to home." In these few words can be seen Praxedes' total dedication to duty. And this, in the long run, was her way of living throughout her life. She was all to all, always attentive to the needs of everyone, especially of the poor and the sick, and not ever excluding those who had contagious diseases. Her brother Ismael confirmed with a sworn statement an outstanding act in which prudence accompanied a heroic act of kindness. "Once when she was still an adolescent I overheard my uncle reprimand her for taking care of a woman who was tubercular. My sister explained to him that she took all the precautions necessary to avoid contagion and that she would continue her care of the woman."[8]

Praxedes was also outstanding in her piety. "My sister," declared Celestina, "was the most fervent of all. In spite of the fact that there was much to do at home, she always accompanied our mother to the novenas of St. Rita and St. Anthony in Seana, over bad roads and at six o'clock in the morning."[9]

The path continues to be in a bad condition even to this day, as I made the trip on foot in 1966 with Father Enrique Fernandez, her son. But Praxedes did not seem to mind the steep hill that is part of the walk. This hill separates Sueros from the Seana parish. "She always returned with a bouquet of wild flowers. She loved flowers with a passion," said Celestina.[10]

Praxedes loved the temple of the Lord and wished that His commandments would be faithfully kept by all. One particular incident at this time of her life reveals to what point the zeal for the glory of God consumed the heart of this fourteen-year-old. One Sunday on the way to the ten o'clock Mass at the Fabrica, Praxedes met two of her friends, Maria and Josefa Iglesias, blood sisters. She invited them to Mass, which was just about to begin. They told her that they did not have their veils, which were a must at that time. "Just a minute and I will get you some veils," she said and ran home to get them. Her friends did not miss Mass. This was told by Maria, who witnessed her zeal, which was never held back under any circumstances.[11]

These years were marked by a series of events that accentuated Praxedes' precociousness in dealing with life and her awareness of the vanity of worldly things. This seriousness, that was not in keeping with her age, was the admiration of her classmates, but was also considered strange. As was said before, the heart of this oldest sister and "little mother" had already bled at the death of her brother Hijinio. On August 9, 1897 she mourned the death of Jose Garcia, her maternal grandfather. On October 5, 1899 her little sister Cecilia, aged two, also died. The following year, 1900, two of her first cousins who were her godchildren, Maria de Mercedes and Maria de Jesus, also died. The following year on January 13 of 1902, her maternal grandmother, Vicenta Suarez, passed on to eternal life to join her husband. Praxedes, who was so attached and loved her family so much, suffered much because of the flood of deaths.

At the end of 1901 something unforeseen happened that gave a new direction to Praxedes' life. It had been a life that was so peaceful and placid in the school run by the sisters, where she was so happy.

Celestino, always anxious about advancing, took advantage of an offer of a magnificent job. He left in June of that same year to become manager of some mines in the province of Cordoba. As the state of his health was very precarious, he returned to Sueros at the end of that year to take Praxedes with him so that she could take care of him.

Even though she was only 15 years of age, Praxedes went to care for her father because of her housekeeping skills and her exceptional qualities in nursing. She remained there for two years. During this time father and daughter became even closer to each other.[12]

In 1904, after leaving Praxedes in Sueros, Celestino went to work in the mines of Guardo, Valencia. But alone and without the care and attention of his daughter he soon fell gravely ill. It was necessary to bring him home in an ambulance. The whole town went out to meet him when he arrived in Mieres.

Celestina told us that when Praxedes returned from Andalucia she never returned to school. But she never stopped helping the sisters and thanking them for the wonderful formation that they had given her. Their formation left such a Dominican imprint in her person that later she joined the Dominican laity, then known as the Secular Third Order of St. Dominic. This happened in 1934, near the time of tragic developments, during which time her authentic Christianity was proven.

Chapter 5

IN THE NEIGHBORHOOD OF JOY

When Praxedes returned home to Sueros from Andalucia in 1903, her family numbered only six. Besides herself, who was now 17, there were her mother, Consuelo who was 13, Celestina 11, Celso 12 and the youngest, Florentina, who was 8. Ismael left home when he turned 20 to work in the mines of El Palmar in Almeria. Ovidio was at home. He left Sueros in 1904. Celestino had just been transferred to Guardo, Palencia as foreman in some mines there. He returned from there so very ill that he was never again to work.

They all lived in the new home that was built on a hill and was accessible from two different directions. One entrance was from the ground floor that faced the railroad. The other faced the main street and went out into the main square, which made it easy for the people to come and go. On the ground floor they had opened a general store where food, clothes, home utensils and drinks were sold. In the same compound Consuelo opened a Sewing Center in 1907 where many of the young women gathered to work. To the side of the home a bakery was opened that supplied the whole town. With the Sewing Center, the general store and bakery, their home soon became the heart of Sueros.

After Celestino returned from Guardo he was confined to his room most of the time and could not even leave the house, but was always the first one to start the fun. He was respected as the patriarch of the family and never failed to maintain a happy mood at the family reunions where song, accompanied by guitar, was enjoyed by all. They also enjoyed the recitation of verse. Amalia, the mother, besides singing very well also

20

received applause for her manner of retelling Aesop's Fables. Their beautiful daughters, too, contributed to these joyous occasions and were greatly loved and respected by all.

Praxedes was the most elegant of all of them, as well as the most beautiful. However, it was Consuelo, the sewing teacher, who was the life of the party. She was so lively and friendly that her jovial and pleasant conversation attracted the handsome young men. Celestina had to leave home to accompany her brothers to Andalucia in 1907. She kept house for them until she returned in 1910. When she returned she could play the guitar very well, and was able to accompany the singing and dancing that they had in their home. Florentina, the youngest, had a marvelous singing voice. She was coquetish and conceited, as Julia Suarez affirmed, and also somewhat lazy as she was pampered by her parents.

In this family everyone had received a gift from the muses. Many of the poems that Celestino and Consuelo composed are still preserved. Celestina used to write letters in verse. Praxedes has left us a four-line congratulatory verse by her. She played the guitar quite well, but could not sing like Florentina. When it came to dancing, she did that to perfection.

We can see that to her poetry, song and dance, Praxedes added her love of flowers. On a piece of uncultivated land by the side of the house, Praxedes made a most beautiful flower garden, the most beautiful in Asturias. "She was very fond of flowers," said Celestina.[1]

Because joy reigned in their home, the neighbors consequently named the Fernandez home the Neighborhood of Joy (*Barrio de la alegria*). Celestino was the first to welcome the new name. In a letter to one of his daughters around that time he wrote in the heading, "Joy, February 1, 1908."

Yes, joy reigned in that home. The Christian understands that joy accompanied always by modesty, temperance and control of the emotions creates perfect harmony. Celestino discreetly saw to it that this was the case in his domain. The phrase comes from St. Paul, "Let your modesty be known to all men." This was the case with Praxedes in this radiant period of her life.

The testimonies that confirm this are abundant. The impressions of Praxedes in all that met her at this time are very precise. Upon reading them one cannot help but come to the conclusion that that young lady truly possessed a very proper and winning personality. Let us not forget that the memories of youth are indelible, especially if they are pleasant.

"She was extremely pure," affirmed Ovidio, "and didn't start going out until 1904, this being an example for the rest of us. She never enjoyed going out to parties and other entertainments. She was happy to be at home with her parents."[2]

Celestina added, "Praxedes was a very happy person who liked to entertain herself at home dancing the jota, a Spanish folk dance, and singing, but with moderation and modesty. She fled excessive reveling and spent the greater part of the time at home. However, because of the store, the sewing center and the bakery, she did mingle with many people, among them young men who liked her. She conversed normally with them and even allowed some of them to court her."[3]

One of Consuelo's best friends, Olvido Estrada, has given us even more details. "In Celestino's home all was joy, a good time. Since Praxedes didn't like to go out to public places for entertainment, we used to plan folk dances and parties and had a good time. Frequently, it was Celestino who played the guitar while we danced. Once in a while Praxedes played the guitar too, as she learned when she was in Andalucia, even if it wasn't the best. She was always laughing and radiated joy and happiness."[4]

Another friend, Aurelia Gutierrez, testified that there was a beggar who was accustomed to come to the Sueros park which was in the Neighborhood of Joy to play the flute. As soon as Praxedes heard that he was there she would run out and begin to dance.[5]

Because the winters of Asturias were so humid and very bitter, the Fernandez girls got the idea of dancing before going to bed, and in this way they warmed up. They danced the "Muneira," a Galician dance that requires much jumping. This was a quick way of bringing on the heat.

There is no doubt that Praxedes loved to dance, but only at home and under the watchful care of her parents. She abhorred dance-hall dancing and all public dances in general. "She did not lose time in public dances," asserted Ovidio.[6] And Teresa Alvarez, one of her teenage friends, gave us another interesting view of her repugnance for public dances. "When I was young I lived in Santullano, where Praxedes had an uncle by the name of Nicanor, who loved her very much. Every year on the feast of Our Lady of Mt. Carmel she and her sisters went to Santullano, where this patronal feast was celebrated. They stayed at their uncle's home.

"Together with the religious aspect of the feast, a carnival with very lively dances was organized. Her sisters went to these but Praxedes didn't care to even go near the place. She spoke very little. I used to say to my friends that she was never going to get married, because she didn't go to dances and spoke very little to the boys. She was a very beautiful girl. She had red hair and clear blue eyes. She was very formal and so refined. She didn't put on airs, nor was she vain. She wasn't interested in keeping up with the latest fashions, either. She was always smiling and a very happy person. I heard her uncle say many times that she was a saint."[7]

Praxedes' holy diversions, however, did not get in the way of her duties. She was up at dawn and sanctified the day with daily Mass and Holy Communion. Her brother Ismael wrote, "She always went to Mass whenever she could, which was every day except on rare occasions."[8]

"Ever since she was a child," said Celestina, "Praxedes was forever occupied with the housework, helping our mother. There was always so much work to do, as we had the general store, with customers to be waited on. We also had the cows that had to be milked and an ass that had to be taken out to pasture. The stables had to be cleaned, too. Besides this there was the cooking to be done, and the sewing, too. We had a servant, but each of us girls still had to shoulder part of the responsibilities. Praxedes was the oldest and she was always the first to do her share and more, always so willingly. When I was away, 1907-1910, and Consuelo managed the sewing school and Florentina was in Oviedo studying to be a teacher, it was Praxedes who stayed with our mother to help out in all these chores."[9]

There are still other occupations that Celestina did not mention that Praxedes held herself responsible for. For example, there was the hard work in the bakery and the garden. She plowed, sowed, weeded and finally harvested the produce. "She worked hard," said her cousin Benigna Fernandez, "but not only in the house. She worked out in the fields and with the animals. I used to see her from time to time, carrying a basket on her head full of potatoes, onions, and other vegetables from the garden."[10]

Another of her friends of that time tells us that Praxedes took her turn at pasturing the two cows and two or three sheep. "I knew Praxedes when she was about 18 years old. She was admired by all. She worked as no one else did. My family had property adjacent to theirs and so I used to see her pasturing the cows and sheep. She took her spiritual reading along and some sewing to do as she pastured the animals. Sometimes we would just talk and she gave me some very good advice."[11]

Praxedes was housekeeper, cook, baker, gardener, shepherdess and seamstress. She never drew back from work. Later on when she had children of her own, she instilled this philosophy of work into them and taught them that laziness is the mother of all vices. She never knew what it was to be idle.

During all this time Praxedes was also committed to some very serious and time-consuming religious exercises. While still quite young she became a catechist both in her parish of Seana and in the chapel of the Fabrica. In 1977 one of her pupils of that period was still living. She related the following: "From 1905 on Praxedes was a catechist in the chapel of the Fabrica where Father Luciano Fernandez was chaplain. I was one of her pupils then, and at the same time she was a catechist in the parish of Seana. She taught with such dedication that we often prolonged the class past the time allotted. The other young ladies found other Sunday evening diversions. At times some of us would accompany her to her second class in Seana. She did this for many years. I remember that when I was a teenager I invited her to go with me on a Sunday evening and she said, 'I can't accompany you, as I have a class of catechism for the children.' "[12]

In 1912 there was a Mission in the parish of San Juan in Mieres. A very important part of the Mission was the journey from Sueros to Mieres. There was no other road except a very narrow path that followed the riverbed alongside the railroad. Not only did Praxedes attend, but she became a veritable missionary, and took along with her all the young ladies of the town. One of them, Aurelia Gutierrez, testified, "Praxedes attended every day and we with her, as she had invited us. It was night time when we returned and all the way back all we talked about was the sermon."[13]

But Praxedes was attentive not only to the children and teen-agers, but also to the materially as well as the spiritually poor. Paulina Mohojo recounted the following, full of gratitude: "Prax-edes, before she got married, used to visit my mother, Olipia Solares, often. She was elderly and suffered much because of sickly knees. My mother received much consolation and joy from her visits. I saw her give money to my mother, as well."[14]

Fidel, a fourteen-year-old boy, a servant who had developed ulcers on the sole of his foot, was taken care of with tender care before he went to bed. "I used to admire her," said Benig-na, "as I watched her wash and bandage his feet with her beau-tiful white hands."[15]

On the bridge that separated the banks of Seana and Mieres sat a beggar every Sunday. His legs were excessively swollen. On the way back from Mass, Praxedes would stop to give him the alms sent him by her father. Ovidio Estrada, who accom-panied her on some occasions, referred to the visit thus: "The poor man knew Praxedes very well, and when she approached he would say, 'How I missed my angel.' "[16]

In spite of all her occupations, Praxedes still found time to care for the needy. From 1906 to 1914 the Countess of Mieres with Sister Marta, the Superior of the hospital of the Fabrica, founded the so-called "Sewing for the Poor" to provide clothes for the poor of the area. She then proceeded to invite all the young ladies of the town to gratuitously give their services to this work for the poor. Maria Cloux, a religious of the Secular Institute, "United for Jesus," and a native of Mieres, has told us that they sewed from 2:00 p.m. until 6:00 p.m. They worked it in such a way that all those who volunteered took turns during the week so that there was always a good number sew-ing every day.[17]

Herminia Perez wrote, "One day Praxedes was late in com-ing to the sewing room. One of the girls said that she probably would not be in that day. The Countess, who also came to sew, was there and commented that she was sure she would because she never missed. And sure enough, shortly after that in came Praxedes, excusing herself for her involuntary tardiness.

To be sure, the only thing that kept her from attending was inclement weather, like the heavy rains that are so common in Asturias. While she was there she spoke little and was always so pleasant."

Happy, joyful and good, always radiating with the many gifts God had given her, Praxedes fit the description of the true apostle: "...he that giveth, with simplicity; he that ruleth, with carefulness; he that sheweth mercy, with cheerfulness." (*Rom.* 12:8).

When Consuelo opened her Sewing Center in the Neighborhood of Joy, Praxedes used to work there also at times. Those happy and beautiful young ladies could not help but attract the attention of the young men. One of the admirers, Jose Alvarez, who was still alive in 1977, recalled those happy days. "It was in 1909 that I was employed in the Fabrica of Mieres in one of the mines, 'Nicolasa.' At the same time I was pursuing my studies in the School of Superintendents. On my way to Mieres I had to go through Sueros, and on Saturday nights I had to go by the Sewing Center that was near the main road. One day I asked if I could come in and rest. All the girls were there, and Praxedes as well. At first they were all alike to me, but soon Consuelo stood out because of her jocularity and inquisitiveness as to the reason of my visit. I answered her questions and I found myself being studied by the whole of the fun-loving, noisy and lively seamstresses. I had not even noticed Praxedes amid all this."[18]

Chapter 6

DEVOUT YOUTH
(1901-1914)

Praxedes left school at the age of 15 because of having to go to Andalucia with her father. However, as we said before, she continued her contacts with the sisters whom she met every day at the Fabrica chapel. I visited the chapel in April, 1964, just before it was torn down to make room for the highway that was being built from Oviedo to Mieres.

Praxedes went to this chapel, which could seat 200 people, because it was closer and easier to get to than the churches of Seana or La Rebollada. At first the liturgy was not carried out with solemnity, nor was it developed until later, as we shall see.

Things changed when in 1907 Father Luciano Fernandez was appointed chaplain. He was a great organizer and liturgist. He put life and fervor into the worship services of this temple of God that had been entrusted to his pastoral care. He now celebrated two Masses on Sundays and holy days and gave great solemnity to the Eucharistic services in the evenings on these days also. The months of October and May now became festive and devotional.

He also took advantage of the fact that the young ladies of the parish had received and were receiving a good religious training at the local parochial school run by the Dominican Sisters. On December 8, 1908 he formed the Association of the Daughters of Mary.

Praxedes enrolled herself on the same day, when she was 22 years old. The first president of the Association, Germana Gonzalez, had this to say about Praxedes: "I became acquainted

27

with Praxedes when the Daughters of Mary was formed. Up until then I only knew her by sight. She always impressed me as being very good. She had such an agreeable personality that she was liked by everyone. We had occasion of coming together many times, such as for general Communion once a month, the Triduum of Our Lady of Lourdes, for May devotions, and for the Solemn Novena of the Immaculate Conception in December. She was always faithful in observing the regulations of the Daughters of Mary. She disliked speaking ill of anyone. She had no enemies. She received only praise from everyone. She was so good and the best. She was a homebody and wasn't one to go out just for amusements.

"She showed great enthusiasm, however, in the observance of the Novena of the Immaculate Conception and even took it upon herself to decorate the altar of the Blessed Virgin Mary assigned to the Daughters of Mary."[1]

In a sworn statement Germana added, "I became a very good friend of Praxedes because her goodness attracted me greatly. She was an example to all and in everything. She was present at all the meetings and at all the religious exercises of the Association. She also frequently received Holy Communion. Her time was divided between her home and the chapel. Mundane things were of no interest to her. She was extremely prudent in giving counsel and always proved to be very sincere. Her mode of dressing and her appearance in general were a true reflection of her beautiful soul. She was very humble and if ever she was overlooked she rejoiced. She was held to be a saint."[2]

In the official book of the Association one can see where Praxedes was named the choir directress for the young women of Sueros and of Puente de la Luisa. This took place at the meeting held on March 1, 1909. At the meeting held on March 24, 1912 she was elected as first Councillor of the President of the Association of the Daughters of Mary.

Sister Pilar has also given us the following details: "I asked one of her friends, Honorina Espina, who was also a member of the Association, what they talked about in their meetings. She told me that Praxedes never tired of enhancing the Association of the Daughters of Mary, and that she enthusiastically encouraged her companions to be good and to be recruiters.

She also urged them to do their part in making the liturgies solemn and beautiful to give honor and glory to the Blessed Virgin."[3]

There are abundant testimonies of Praxedes' life during this period. Each one tells what most impressed her. Maria Folguera said, "I knew Praxedes since 1912, when we were both Daughters of Mary. She was very pious. Even when she was still very young she stood out among her companions in this regard. When there was some disagreement among us, all that had to be said to end the argument was to quote Praxedes on the subject. Her opinions were held in such high regard. She thought everything out. She was very reserved."[4]

In a later statement Maria said, "I joined the Daughters of Mary when she [Praxedes] was directress of the third choir. It was evident to me that she was far ahead of all in the practice of virtue. She went to daily Mass and Communion. She often made visits to the Blessed Sacrament, said the daily Rosary, and made the Stations of the Cross. She avoided anything that was worldly. She was very prudent and was gifted with the gift of counseling. She was filled with the holy fear of the Lord. She was loving and attentive with everyone. She was such a loving person. The sick and the poor won her affection and she made it her business to be the peacemaker between enemies. Her good reputation was her treasure."[5]

Obdulia Iglesias, referring to this period in Praxedes' life, said to her son Marcelino, "She was forever occupied with the fact that she wanted everyone to behave well, as members of the Association. She wanted everyone to imitate Mary."[6]

Maria Hevia, on her part, said, "We were both Daughters of Mary. She had the face of a saint. She always seemed to be recollected, very modest and spoke very softly. She just was different than the rest of us teen-agers. She was often in church and, again, very recollected and devout. Everyone remarked that she was so mature and adult-like. I never saw any defects in her. She was, as they say, a saint."[7]

Julia Iglesias shared her views about Praxedes in 1964 as to how she counseled the Daughters of Mary. "I was very young when Praxedes was president. She never stopped urging us to be good, to place ourselves under the protection of the Blessed Virgin. She wanted nothing more than that we be genuinely pious."[8]

Manuela Jove was impressed by Praxedes because of the following: "I became acquainted with Praxedes the last year she was a member of the Daughters of Mary. She was a daily communicant. She was a person who was completely natural and even-tempered, that is, not like the typical teen-ager. She was friendly with everyone without partiality. One could not help noticing that she was different from the rest of us. She was more religious and given to Him and His ways."[9]

As to her ability and success as directress of the third choir (which included young ladies from Sueros and Puente de la Luisa) one of the members of the choir, Julia Suarez had these concrete and interesting details: "During all the time that I was a member of the choir, Praxedes was the directress. As such, she was zealous in fulfilling her responsibility and anxious that we remain good and pious and faithful. Yet she was not the kind that preached to us. Instead, she won us over by her pleasantness and friendliness. Thus she saved us from the pitfalls of youth and instilled in us a love of fidelity to our commitment as Daughters of Mary. Some of the girls came from families that fostered anti-religious sentiments. With these, Praxedes was very careful and prudent not to irritate the parents and make them react. From the rest, she elicited the best in them.

"With her delicate and discreet sensitivity, Praxedes was a young woman with a very special personality who was very agreeable, and the possessor of the gift of persuasion. She spoke little, but always made sense when she spoke. One can say that she possessed a distinct and special gift that was natural to her and not learned from having traveled, because she never did. There were some problems among the members of the Association, problems of youth, such as not keeping the rules, loose conduct or immodesty in dress. With these Father Luciano was uncompromising. I remember the problem that we had with a young lady from Sueros whose parents owned a bar. She gave occasion for gossip when she began to befriend a married man who was well-known. In a circumstance like this there was nothing else to do but to ask her to leave the Association. Before asking her to leave, however, Praxedes, in her great concern and love, talked it over with some of us to make sure that what was said was true. She also helped us see that such conduct was not compatible with the Daughters of Mary."[10]

A cousin of Praxedes, Benigna Fernandez, who was the treasurer of the Association, added: "Praxedes, as directress of the choir of Sueros, was successful in enrolling all or mostly all of the young women of the town in the Association, but made sure that they were faithful and good ones. She had a way of persuading that was admirable. She was greatly appreciated and loved by all."[11]

But above all these testimonies and many others, the most significant one and the one that crowned them all was that given by the founder of the Association, Father Luciano Fernandez. The information was not direct, but overheard by Sister Consuelo Giner, who wrote: "Praxedes in her youth was distinguished by her humility, modesty, prudence and other virtues. Because of this she was named the President of the Association of the Daughters of Mary. She carried out this responsibility with the approval of all and especially of the founder, Father Luciano, who held her up as model for the rest."[12]

In another letter written later Sister Consuelo again brought out this point when she said, "Father Luciano spoke to the faculty on one occasion when he praised Praxedes and pointed out the fact that she truly was the model of the Association."[13] A more fitting testimony could not have been given.

Praxedes always wore and held with great veneration the blue and white ribbon worn by the members of the Daughters of Mary. Her love and veneration for the Association lasted throughout her life. One day when she was already a widow, a young girl who was a member of the Association came to her home. Praxedes learned that she was the directress of the choir, a position that she had held, and wondered how such a young person had been given such a great responsibility. In their conversation Praxedes said, "The Daughter of Mary ought to be the most exemplary of all young women."[14] This was exactly the goal that she had set for herself when she joined the Association in 1908.

Praxedes did not leave the Association until the very day of her marriage. At that time Father Luciano gave her a beautiful picture of the Immaculate Conception with an inscription commending her for her exemplary conduct as a young Christian. She hung this precious gift at the head of her bed.

Pope John XXIII once had a recommendation for the ladies of Catholic Action, namely that they not complicate the simple things in life and that they do what they could to simplify the complicated ones. Praxedes knew well how to do this in the spiritual, as well as in the material.

It took great ingenuity on Praxedes' part to plan her day to comply with the variety of tasks that had to be done around the house and still have time for her own personal religious practices. She found great consolation in the devotions that she knew helped her temperament retain the peace with which her whole being was wrapped.

She was open to and took advantage of all that would benefit her soul. This strengthened her spiritual foundation with a marvelous harmony, without being considered "churchy."

This is why, when the Passionists moved to Mieres in 1908, Praxedes took advantage of their presence. She realized the good influence that these religious could have on her spiritual life. She turned to them to help satisfy her thirst for God. The presence of these sons of St. Paul of the Cross in the mining valley was certainly a great and important step in the elevation of the spiritual climate for Praxedes. It was at that time, because of the sermons preached by the Passionists, that she developed her great love and devotion to Jesus Crucified.

On June 18, 1911, Praxedes joined the Archconfraternity of the Passion, which had been established earlier. From that time on she invariably assisted at the special services held the fourth Sunday of each month. This meant Mass and Communion at eight o'clock in the morning as well as Eucharistic devotions at four o'clock in the afternoon, which included a sermon on the sufferings of Christ. This she would not miss for anything in the world. Thus she learned to orient her thoughts on that highest of mysteries of the Redemption. She learned to love the Cross with that madness that St. Paul talks about.

Later she used this wisdom to answer the questions of her sons over this mystery. One day, her youngest, Gabriel, told her that in his opinion others had suffered more than Jesus. To that the mother answered, "Don't say that, son, there have never been, nor will there ever be sufferings greater than those that Jesus suffered for us." She then began to read the Passion from the Bible and commented and explained as she read. She did it so well that tears ran down the boy's face.[15]

Praxedes' son Enrique, when he was only five or six years old, brought a picture of St. Francis being embraced by Jesus on the Cross, to find out how Jesus could do this when He was nailed to the Cross. The saintly mother, coming down to the mentality of the child, explained that it was not so much the nails that held Jesus to the Cross, but rather love. In this way she was able to satisfy the child in a way that brought out the essential meaning of the mystery of Calvary.[16]

Praxedes got into the habit of placing the image of Jesus crucified wherever she worked. A large wooden crucifix hung in her bedroom. Toward the end of her life she wore a cord around her waist with a small crucifix hanging from it in order to be able to kiss it frequently. Finally this great devotion to the Cross drove her to practice incredible penances, even to engraving the Cross on her chest with a hot iron.

The Passionist Fathers were her favorite confessors.[17] The person who affirmed this is Rosario Calleja who said, "She often went to confession to the Passionists." Rosario had a store not far from the Passionist church, and when Praxedes went shopping she left her packages with her while she went to confession.

Some of the Fathers who heard her confession, among them Father Jacinto, have told of the high regard they had for her. Father Jacinto, who was twice provincial, had this to say: "I knew Praxedes during the years 1929-1932, when I was rector of the house in Mieres. During that time she often came to confession to me. She didn't overdo it. It was usually every two weeks and sometimes less often. She often came to our church for Mass and usually to the early Masses. Her confessions were simple and normal, but with a great fear of the Lord. There was nothing in her confessions that savored of scruples. or interior tension. At times she asked for direction in her spiritual life, but never asked me to be her spiritual director. I don't think she had one.

"One could not help but notice her great sensitivity and equilibrium, her practical sense, and the deep prudence of her spiritual life. Praxedes possessed a very simple soul, without

complications. She was sweet, humble, constant, highly virtuous and one who quietly went about living her Christian life.
She was one of the holiest persons I ever met. This is why
I am not at all surprised that her cause for beatification is being
introduced. As far as I can judge, she is in the presence of God
enjoying the Beatific Vision, and she is an excellent model for
all Christians in our day. I consider her worthy of canonization."[18]

Father Jacinto's successor was Father Constantino, who was
rector of that convent during 1932-1935. He wrote the following in a letter to Father Enrique: "I never directed your holy
mother, nor did I ever have anything to do with her; I only
heard her confession occasionally. I can truthfully say that even
without discussing her spiritual life, as often happens with people coming to confession only on passing, I was able to sense
something very special in her. She was one of those persons
that leave in the confessor a feeling of shame and embarrass-
ment upon comparing his spiritual life with a person living
in the world, as your dear mother did. She was consumed with
the desire to live a life of perfection and not be satisfied with
the ordinary 'everyday' sins. Saintly people always look at performing as perfectly as possible. Your mother was one of these
souls."[19]

Even though she was very reserved in the things that per-
tained to her interior life, Praxedes was avid in getting everyone to enjoy the blessings she experienced. This is why she
became an apostle of the Passion. She never failed to invite
others to join the Confraternity of the Passion of Mieres. The
first one to join was her father. He was received into the Confraternity on December 24, 1911. This "conquest" was another
sign of the father and daughter being of one mind and heart
in the things of God. Later on she also had her oldest brother
join the same association.

It was with an extraordinary fervor that Praxedes prayed the
Stations of the Cross. One of her friends from Mieres, Antonia
Castano, who also went to Mass at the Passionist church, has
told us that many times before Mass she and Praxedes made
the Stations of the Cross together. While Antonia said the
prayers of the Stations by heart, Praxedes wept.[20]

Mindful of all she had received from these good priests,

Praxedes always had great love and gratitude for them. Just as St. Teresa of Avila said of the Jesuits, so Praxedes could say of the Passionists: "They are my fathers, and after Jesus, Our Lord, it is to them that I owe all the good that I have and am, if any."[21]

The following incident is yet another proof of her great love and the high regard Praxedes had for the Passionists. One day in 1934 she met some of the Dominican Sisters who had taught her. One of the Sisters, Sister Maria Canal, who had two brothers who were Dominicans, exclaimed, "I love the Dominicans." Praxedes, who had a son who was studying to be a Dominican, said very earnestly, "Sister, I love the Dominicans very much too, but I also love the Passionists who have done so much for my spiritual growth."[22]

And the Passionists, for their part, can very well consider her a flower from their garden. In view of this, it is no wonder that the superior of the Passionists sent a letter to Pope John XXIII in 1959. In the letter he begged the Holy Father to "inscribe as soon as possible the Servant of God, Praxedes Fernandez, in the catalogue of Saints, for having reached while still alive the perfection of all the virtues in the highest degree and for brilliance of the miracles being reported through her intercession."[23]

Chapter 7

LOVE AT FIRST SIGHT

The daughters of Celestino, as we have seen, attracted the attention of the young men of the Neighborhood of Joy. In spite of the fact that Praxedes was reserved, the young men were not discouraged and continued to want to escort her and eventually marry her if she would consent. This is no wonder, for she was beautiful, as photographs of her at this time attest. Moreover, she was a good worker. She also belonged to a prestigious family which was socially and economically well-off. She was gifted too, with all those qualities that a man looks for in a woman who will be a good wife forever.[1]

What were Praxedes' intentions in regard to matrimony? It is difficult to guess, because she was very private about her sentiments. She was a most exemplary Daughter of Mary, of irreproachable conduct, and had a horror of appearing even in the least provocative.[2]

There is no doubt that she savored the possibility of embracing the religious life. Her contact with the Dominican Sisters at the school and the religious at the Fabrica Hospital nurtured these desires. Her desires escaped her in her conversations with her first boyfriend. She also loved to spend long hours in the company of the sisters. Olvido Estrada accompanied her to the convent one Sunday afternoon. On the way home she said to Praxedes, "I will never come to visit the sisters with you again. You stay forever!" All that Praxedes said was, "They live such a holy life and are so good!" A little later she said, opening her heart to Olvido, "If I didn't love my father so much, and he is so sick, I would become a religious."[3] This reflection shows what was in the depth of her soul and explains her indecisiveness in regard to matrimony, as well as to the religious life.

Her cousin Benigna Fernandez tells us why Praxedes abandoned the idea of going to the convent. It was the counsel of her spiritual director, Father Luciano Fernandez. "She wanted to be a religious sister, but Father Fernandez took that idea out of her head. She had no interest in marriage. She married because her family advised her to do so."[4] Be that as it may, the truth is that as long as her father lived, being as sick as he was, it never crossed her mind to leave him, neither to get married nor to enter the convent. She was very content at home and for the present did not wish to change her way of life. Her father, however, as much as he loved her, was worried about her future, for she was letting her future pass through her fingers, without making a choice of a state in life.

For this reason her father called Praxedes aside one day and in private said to her, "Look, daughter of mine, you must realize that your mother and I are not going to live forever, and if you don't get married, you will someday be alone in the world. It is necessary, therefore, that you think of getting married."[5] It was at this time that Praxedes, although very reluctantly, consented to allow her admirers, among them Jose Alvarez, to court her.

After this first love affair, ending with no results, a young handsome widower—a doctor, and quite wealthy—fell madly in love with Praxedes and wanted to marry her. "Oh, I don't want to marry a widower!" was Praxedes' comment to her sisters, and she did not.[6]

This doctor had visited Praxedes quite often, even though she did not pay much attention to him. Moreover, his father made a trip to Sueros incognito, to see who she was, and this displeased Praxedes very much when she found out. Not long after this, the doctor unexpectedly proposed to her. She was so taken aback that she refused right there. Her refusal almost ended in a tragedy.

The disenchanted suitor told her upon leaving her forever, "Look, Praxedes, I am going to the train station of Albana to leave Oviedo. I am going to walk right down the center of the railroad and if a train comes, I am not moving. Let it kill me." Frightened by this threat she ran crying to her cousin Benigna,

"If the train kills him, I will be responsible." But her cousin put her at ease by saying, "Don't worry, he won't do it. He told you that to make you suffer because he was rejected."[7]

A third suitor, who was very rich and lived alone in Mieres, also did his best to win Praxedes for his wife. But she, so used to being surrounded by her family, thought it strange that he should live alone. And so that, too, became past history.

Celestino, now more concerned than ever for the future of his beloved daughter, talked to her more firmly than before and made her see that "youth was quickly passing by, and that if she did not marry now she would have no choice but the crumbs."[8]

In order to satisfy her family Praxedes agreed to consider seriously her new admirer, a distant cousin, Jose Fernandez. He was rich, as were her other admirers, but he had a reputation of being stingy. To her, who was so generous to the poor, this would be difficult, to marry a miser! She laughed over this and jokingly said, "If I marry Jose, he won't let me have my cup of chocolate every afternoon." She said this because this was customary in her home.

Everything was going well, and this union was so desired by both sides that it seemed to be destined for a happy conclusion. But when Praxedes found out that her fiance was visiting a young woman with a tainted reputation, right in town, she broke off her relationship at once. Her delicate soul could not suffer the least suspicion of him with whom she had intended to live forever. This irrevocable decision, which neither side of the families could change, is to be chalked in her favor. Sweet and amiable, she proved that she had a strong and decisive character. Almost 35 years later, in 1944, a sister of Jose, Aurora, recounted the incident to Father Enrique, recalling the terrible frustration felt by her parents and her whole family. They had wanted so much that that union take place.

After this breakup Praxedes was courted by a handsome young man by the name of Isidoro Cosio, from Seana and superintendent of some mines. He had quite a reputation of being a ladies' man, and although Praxedes consented to go out with him she begged her sisters, "Please, never leave me alone with him." On one occasion, to tease Praxedes, her sisters left her alone with him and went to other parts of the house. Praxedes, without worrying what her suitor might think, followed them and left him alone! Surprised and disappointed, he later said to Celestina, "What is wrong with Praxedes?"[9] Some time after that, because he got a little fresh, Praxedes broke off her friendship with him, in spite of the fact that they were beginning really to love each other. Another young man from Seana, named Jesus, also tried to win Praxedes' hand. Not having any success, he married a young woman who was employed at the Fabrica.

Gabriel Fernandez Martinez was Praxedes' last suitor, and it was he who finally won her hand. He was born on March 19, 1881, in El Pedroso, Valdecuna in the same county as Mieres. His parents were Gabino Fernandez and Filomena Martinez. He was the sixth of nine children. No doubt Gabriel had seen Praxedes at one time or another in El Pedroso when she went to celebrate the feast of St. Polonia, where it was held with great solemnity. She did not go there for any other reason, as a letter from Consuelo to Celestina on February 11, 1909 clearly states. "On the feast of St. Polonia, February 9, Praxedes and I went to El Pedroso and had a good time. Prospero, Alonso's son and a good friend of Ovidio, treated us royally. He invited us for coffee and wanted us to come to his home, but we did not accept." So we see that it was not because of Gabriel that they went there, and they did not meet there either. How and where did they meet? Jose Alvarez has given us this insight.

"I am a distant relative of Gabriel's. Gabriel was always ready for a good time, as he was a happy person. All the girls were 'his girls,' but he had not yet met one that would make him a good wife. One day I suggested that he go to Sueros and meet a young lady by the name of Praxedes Fernandez. I promised that she would leave him completely satisfied and happy."[10]

Gabriel did not have to be begged, and he soon found an excuse for going to Sueros. He went with a salesman friend to the Fernandez store. While his friend did his business with Celestino, Gabriel made conversation with the beautiful young lady behind the counter. He was tall, a redhead like Praxedes, and extremely friendly and nice. He captivated her from the first moment. When he left after that short encounter they felt their hearts forever united.

It did not take long for all the girls of the town to notice the frequent visits that Gabriel paid to the Neighborhood of Joy. "Who was luckier," they asked, "Gabriel or Praxedes?"

Nevertheless, her family was not satisfied. "Considering his economic standing and social standing," said Florentina, "we told our sister that she deserved more." But she answered, "Well, he is so good and that is all that matters."[11]

On Sundays and festive days the lovers, always accompanied by one of the sisters, would go walking in the countryside. At 72, Fernando Iglesias still remembered them. "The people of Mieres were seen walking in the countryside on Sunday afternoons and we enjoyed watching Gabriel and Praxedes walking so peacefully. Many would remark, 'Look at that happy couple.' They didn't hide from anyone. He with his handsome appearance and she with her beauty and goodness captivated all."[12]

As happens to all lovers, they too had their differences. A postcard written by Gabriel on February 2, 1913, refers to a neglect on her part to which he called her attention because it hurt him very much. "Figaredo, February 2, 1913. My dear Praxedes, In spite of the fact that I was very busy with my work, I was told that you are on a trip, a thing I didn't know about. I was at your home the day before you left and you did not tell me anything about going anywhere. I think this is very strange. Good-bye and much love from him who loves you and desires to see you. Gabriel."

In April, 1964, Marcelino, Celestina's husband, told me this: "Gabriel had a heart of gold, but if anyone had the occasion of having a difference of opinion with him he did not hesitate to stand his ground. Here are some examples of this. One day he and Praxedes, accompanied by Florentina, went to Gijon to enjoy an afternoon of fun at the carnival. 'Gabriel,' says Florentina, 'mounted one of the little horses on the merry-go-round. The owner objected and tried to take him off. Gabriel refused and created much confusion. People began to gather and Praxedes began to cry. I finally succeeded in pulling him by the arm and away from the scene, telling him that if he didn't move away he would land in jail.' "[13]

Julia Suarez has told us the following incident. "Gabriel was brusque at times and it didn't take much to make him lose his temper. One day the maid said something to him that made him angry. He wanted to know how she had the nerve to say that to him! He left the house in a huff, slamming the door as he went. Praxedes ran after him, trying to calm him down, and returned to calm the maid as well."[14]

Gabriel asked Mr. Prospero Blanco to go to Praxedes' home to ask her parents officially for her hand. Mr. Blanco was the owner of the business where Gabriel worked as an electrician. When he approached the home of her parents and they realized the purpose, Celestino experienced a heartbreaking emotion that almost overtook him. Surely, he had wanted his daughter to marry, and in fact he had constantly urged her to; but now that the time had come he could not bear the thought that she would have to leave home.

Nevertheless, he overcame his emotion long enough to toast the future bride and groom. He wished them much joy and happiness in their new life and gave his full consent for the wedding, but not without a few tears finding their way into his cup of wine. From that moment on, that was all that was talked about in the Neighborhood of Joy. All hands in the Sewing Center were busily sewing the bridal dress and accessories.

As time wore on Gabriel and Praxedes became not only anxious, but happier. Gabriel's love and admiration for his beloved Praxedes grew daily with the passage of time. One day in a conversation with Marcelino Garcia, Celestina's boyfriend, Gabriel confided to him, "I wouldn't exchange Praxedes for any other woman in the world, be she queen or empress."[15]

Chapter 8

THE WEDDING AND HONEYMOON

The wedding took place on April 25, 1914. Praxedes had not as yet had her 28th birthday. Gabriel was to be 31. It was a Saturday, the vespers of the fourth Sunday of Easter. From the early hours of the morning of that memorable day, the Neighborhood of Joy resembled a beehive. There were comings and goings, preparations, congratulations, compliments and exhortations.

At ten the entourage was formed to proceed to the parish church of Seana. Upon leaving the house Praxedes fell on her knees at the threshold and asked her father for a blessing. Celestino, profoundly touched, traced the Sign of the Cross over her, saying "I bless you in the name of the Father and of the Son and of the Holy Spirit. Amen." Praxedes embraced both her parents bathed in tears.

On that spring morning the bride was more beautiful than ever. She wore, as was the custom of the day, a blue velvet gown. A magnificent white veil fell gracefully over her shoulders and was held by an Andalucian ornamented comb. As the procession was passing along the principal street of Sueros, one could see the faces against the windows and people standing in doorways, all watching the bride who looked like a queen. All that could be heard was, "How beautiful!"

As for Gabriel, upon leaving his home, he too was crying like a child. When his bride arrived at the church, he was waiting for her. He left his mother's arm to meet his bride, who was being majestically escorted up the aisle by Celestino. The altar was resplendent with flowers and candles.

In the sanctuary the bride and groom assisted at their wedding

Mass at *prie dieu*, covered with white cloths. The Pastor, Father Jose Villar, officiated at the Holy Sacrifice of the Mass. Praxedes followed the Mass with her missal, while Gabriel looked steadily at Father Jose. The bride, who possessed a deep appreciation of the liturgy, deeply savored the words directed to her after the Our Father. Here, all the virtues of the great women of the Bible were asked for her.

The rest of her life testifies to how these prayers were answered. Of all the virtues that were asked for the bride—fidelity, modesty, purity, faith, keeping the Commandments, and instruction in the mysteries of the faith—Praxedes could have said with the young man of the Gospel, "All these have I kept from my youth."[1]

Something rare happened at this moment. All those guests present in that ancient and beautiful temple got the feeling that this bride did not have an ordinary future ahead of her.

Visitacion Vasquez recalled that she experienced a strange and mysterious sensation that made her cry all during the ceremony.[2] When Mass was over, Celestino addressed a few solemn words to Gabriel, in the presence of the whole congregation: "I entrust my daughter to you as though I were giving you a precious jewel. As I treated her, so I wish her to be treated by you. And as she acted toward me, so I wish her to act toward you."[3] These were admirable and noble words from a father who seemed to have a premonition of what was in store for his beloved daughter. Visitacion also heard Celestino whisper into the ear of one of his friends, saying, "This daughter of mine is destined to an unfortunate marriage."[4]

Because of this marriage, Praxedes was leaving her family who, because of hard work and thriftiness, had become rich. Now she was the wife of a simple laborer who barely provided enough to eat. It is important that we do not lose sight of this aspect of Praxedes' social standing, as it will play an important role in her life until her death.

In the evening after the wedding banquet they left for their honeymoon, made their first stop at the shrine of Covadonga, and continued along the coast of Cantabrico toward their destination, Santander.

Covadonga, a most celebrated shrine in Spain, was the epitome of all that Praxedes loved in the area of nature and religion.

This shrine was nestled between mountains of great grandeur and shone in its spring beauty. She could contemplate from afar the European peaks that form part of the 3,000 m. Cantabrica Range. Farther down could be seen the beech trees and spruce that formed the dense forest. Below were the valleys and plains that were profuse with all kinds of wildflowers. Praxedes loved flowers, and she herself had grown them at home. In her letters home she often referred to their beauty. On June 24 she wrote, "The weather is beautiful here and the plains are so green and full of flowers. The sight of this panoramic beauty is breathtaking."

Like Francis of Assisi she was able to capture the beauties of nature and its mysterious language. Father Enrique himself told me that he remembered going to Mass with his mother as a child and passing along an embankment of daisies. His mother exclaimed, "These flowers speak to me of God." Moreover, she seemed to see in them a symbol of her own life. She once said to Sister Maria Canal, "I wish I could be like those violets hidden in the weeds, but still give off such a pleasing aroma."[5]

From Santander, where they stayed a month, Gabriel and Praxedes wrote to Celestina, "Santander, April 29, 1914. Dearest Celestina, We go from theater to theater. It is so entertaining and nice that most likely we won't be seeing each other for the whole month of May, as we might have to walk all the way. This, of course, will take us longer to get home. With love, Gabriel and Praxedes."

I myself took that trip from Oviedo to Santander in 1966. It is an uninterrupted succession of the most beautiful scenery. For quite a long stretch one can see crystal-watered rivers like the Sella, that winds its way in and out of large vegetable patches and fields. Later one comes upon the beautiful coast of Cantabrico, which one does not leave until reaching the mountainous capital, with its incomparable beaches of the Sardinero and the Magdalena Rivers. The city with its grand avenues, spacious gardens, monumental fountains and beautiful churches offers a truly magnificent treat.

This was the second time that Praxedes had gone out of Asturias. Her trips were few and far between. In her adolescence she had traveled toward the south as far as Cordoba. Then on her honeymoon she traveled to Santander. In 1928 she journeyed with her sons Arturo and Gabriel to visit her son Enrique, who was a student at the Apostolic School of Caldas of Vesaya. In 1930 she again visited him in Corias, this time without leaving Asturias. On three or four more occasions she went north to the city of Gijon to see him.

So we see that Praxedes traveled little, and when she did it was on family business. But when she did travel, she made it into a religious pilgrimage. She would find a convent where she could stay and there enjoy hours of prayer in the presence of the Blessed Sacrament, and go to confession. She had also planned to go to Salamanca to visit Father Enrique, where he was a student, but the civil war and family deaths changed her plans. She also dreamed of visiting the tomb of St. Teresa in Alba de Tormes. Now knowing of her deeply religious spirit, it is no wonder that she chose a shrine for her first stop on her honeymoon, the shrine of Our Lady of Covadonga.

Chapter 9

A WORKING-CLASS FAMILY

Upon returning from their honeymoon the newlyweds settled in Figaredo, where Gabriel already had a home. That small village, like Sueros, belonged to the municipal government of Mieres, but it had the advantage of having an established parish, with two priests. It is situated on the right side of the Caudal River. It has its own railroad station, Vasco-Asturiano, and the main highway Madrid-Gijon passes through it. It is four kilometers from Mieres and six from Sueros. In 1914 Figaredo had a population of 700. It was known as the "black country" because with rare exception, all the men worked in the coal mines belonging to the company "Hullera Turon, S.A.," the most important of its kind in Spain.

Gabriel rented a one-room apartment from a respectable woman, Dionisia Esteban, who had three children. He had rented this apartment because he worked at the electric company that belonged to Prospero Blanco, which was in Moreda, a village two stations from Figaredo. He did this because there was no transportation from El Edroso to his home. Once he was married he took his wife to this apartment, where they lived for a little over a year. Dionisia was a very good person, and she was favorably impressed with Praxedes from the first moment she met her. There was never any disagreement between them, despite the fact that they shared the kitchen.

When her cousin Consuelo came to assist Praxedes at the birth of her first baby, Consuelo did not do so well with Dionisia. Praxedes tried to pacify her by saying, "Leave her alone. What difference does it make. Let's not quarrel over such a little thing."[1]

When it came to religious matters, Gabriel's mother was the most qualified person of El Pedroso,[2] but Gabriel in this respect did not resemble his mother. He was satisfied with the minimum, and so was far from the ideals of Praxedes. At times this difference of sentiments gave way to violent episodes that if Praxedes had not been the valiant woman that she was, the marriage might have ended tragically. Her sister-in law, Isabel, has left the following testimonial about Gabriel's psychological reactions to the profoundly religious character of his wife. "Praxedes had a marvelous character. She was not a gossiper. She was so honorable and trustworthy that I had more confidence in her than in my own brother. She was so pious. I know that my brother had a violent temper, but Praxedes was so humble that she never told my mother of the treatment she received from her husband."[3]

In those last words of Isabel are implied an incident that was not the only one, for sure. But it was of such a nature that it required the intervention of the mother-in-law. It was approximately one year after their marriage, on the Good Friday of 1915, that upon returning from church services which her husband thought were too long, he—full of anger—slapped Praxedes, who had been meditating on the many blows that Jesus had received during His Passion. She accepted it with the meekness of a lamb happy to resemble her Saviour.

Through her, certainly, no one would have known what had happened. But the incident did not go unnoticed by the landlady. She immediately told Praxedes' mother-in-law, Filomena. Indignant over the report, she went at once to Praxedes to see if it were true. But her daughter-in-law pacified her by tenderly assuring her, "Gabriel is very good to me, and I have nothing to say against him." Filomena was full of admiration and said to her family, "How good and holy Praxedes is! My son is not worthy of her."[4] This was a magnificent testimony, considering the source from which it came. With meekness and sweetness, Praxedes calmed the flare-ups of her husband; and little by little she was winning him over.

Ovidio's testimony in this respect is precious. "My sister was most exact in fulfilling her obligations as a wife. At first her piety was not to the liking of her husband. Later he obliged."[5] Florentina on her part has assured us that, "When Praxedes visited us she always said that Gabriel was not opposed to her acts of piety."[6]

On the other hand, Gabriel always repented of his flare-ups and did not fail to recognize the treasure he had in Praxedes. Jose Alvarez, who had recommended Praxedes to Gabriel, asked him a year after their wedding if he was satisfied and happy in his marriage. This is what Gabriel said: "You were right in recommending her to me. I am happy to have taken her as my wife. I am entirely satisfied and live very contented with her, and to you I am indebted."[7]

This is how the days passed in Figaredo for the young couple. In the midst of the daily occupations of a laborer who earned little and knew not how to save, and of the wife who was totally committed to her life as wife and mother, they lived under the providence of God.

In the same way she had had time as an unmarried young lady, Praxedes now found time for everything. She attended to her home, took care of her husband, cared for her children and carried out her pious practices. Far from distracting her from these practices, her married state helped her comply with them even better. Praxedes had no time for visiting neighbors. She could often be seen sewing and ironing on the porch, which was all windows. She was always busy. In 1966, when I visited Figaredo, the then-assistant pastor Father Elias Valdes told me, "I can still see her sewing by machine at such a surprising speed!" And her cousin Consuelo added, "I always had the impression that Praxedes was interiorly praying as she sewed."[8] She left her home only for necessities. A neighbor, Candida Miranda, whom I visited in 1966, upon seeing her one day said to a friend who was with her, "Do you see that woman? She leaves her home only to go to church and to get water from the spigot. She never wastes time visiting or talking to anyone."[9]

As directed by the Gospel, Praxedes had left her father and mother to become one with her husband. But she never forgot them. As often as her occupations and her husband permitted, she visited them. She made the trip by train as far as Mieres, and then walked the two kilometers to Sueros. These visits were for her a joy, but at the same time it was painful for her to see how her father was progressively getting worse.

Praxedes would cry upon embracing her father and then

would open her heart to him, telling him of her family troubles, asking for advice and relief. Thus consoled she returned to her home, very comforted and peaceful.

Her love of her family did not in any way keep Praxedes from being aware of her neighbors' hardships. When she came to visit her parents she would take time to visit a neighbor who had typhoid fever. The sick woman, Valeria Alvarez, was hostile to religion and was the head of the revolutionary movement of the town. The visits left her consoled and she herself admitted, "Just seeing her coming filled my heart with joy."[10]

Celestino had no illusions of the seriousness of his condition. For his part, he was determined to carry this cross with fortitude, perfectly resigned to God's will. He alluded to this in a letter he wrote on October 20, 1914. "In spite of my sickness, I am not preoccupied with pain. It has me so submissive that I am led by the nose, but full of Christian resignation." At the beginning of December he became worse due to an imprudent act. The neighbor slaughtered the traditional pig. Celestino was an expert at slaughtering hogs, so he killed it and received a portion of it. Contrary to his better judgment he ate some of it, and had an adverse reaction. With that gracefulness with which he always reacted in all circumstances of life, Celestino commented to his family, "I killed the hog, but now it will kill me." Praxedes was notified of her father's serious condition and she hurried to his side, "never to be separated from his side for one moment."[11] To his chronic stomach condition were added colic hepatitis and peritonitis. The pains were intolerable. His only relief was sucking on ice that Praxedes constantly gave him.

When Christmas came that year, it was the saddest that Praxedes remembered since her childhood. On December 24, Father Jose Villar administered Extreme Unction, which Celestino received with the greatest fervor. He had no fear of meeting his God. He had, throughout his life, always tried to live according to God's will. When the priest finished giving him the Sacrament he asked to be left alone with him. Celestino said, "All I ask is that you look after my daughter Praxedes."[12]

Father promised to do just that, but could not imagine why this strange favor was asked of him. On October 6, 1953, when Father Enrique talked with Father Villar, Father told him that he had been left amazed. He must have had a presentiment of what was to happen to his dear daughter.

Praxedes felt that her heart would break even at the thought that the time had come for her father to leave them. In his presence she held back her tears and even managed to smile. She was concerned only with helping him and consoling him, forgetting to sleep and eat.

In this way dawned December 17. Toward 11 o'clock that night, feeling that his hour had arrived, Celestino motioned to his wife with one hand and to Praxedes with the other. Holding their hands, he quietly inclined his head and died. A nephew of Celestino, Antonio Llaneza, told Father Enrique on November 2, 1964: "I have never seen such a beautiful death." In the meantime, Praxedes, who had hardly slept or eaten, suffered a terrible attack that necessitated the call of a doctor at that late hour. By the following morning she was ready to receive the lines and lines of people that came to offer their condolences. Praxedes, on her knees at the foot of the coffin, personally directed the prayers for the soul of her dear father.

Isabel, her sister-in-law, has testified to the following scene. When Florentina arrived at the house she screamed uncontrollably. Praxedes went up to her and sweetly said, "Don't scream like that, you will only make our mother suffer even more. We all must console her at this time. We owe this to her."[13] Certainly, her pain was no less, but forgetful of self she was thinking only of her mother. It was in the midst of the realities of life that her delicate kindness shone brilliantly.

Celestino's death affected the whole municipality. The doctor who assisted him, Dr. Candido Goitan, said, "A man like this ought not to die."[14] The funeral that was celebrated on December 29 was a potent manifestation of sorrow among laborers, leaders of the town and learned men. Never had the people of Sueros seen anything like it.

After the funeral Praxedes returned to Figaredo, with her soul torn apart. Her cousin Consuelo, as well as Dionisia's daughter, Asuncion, testified that Praxedes mourned her father a great deal. All this had happened within eight days, but the effects were lasting as she saw herself deprived of that person whom, after God, she loved the most. She returned to Seana to visit her father's grave many times, where she mixed her prayers and tears.

The days of the Neighborhood of Joy were long past. One day while crossing the street in Mieres, Praxedes unexpectedly met one of the friends of her youth, Olvido Estrada. They began to recall the happiness of those days when they used to sing and dance to the music that Celestino provided with his guitar. Now he was dead and the joys of those days were gone. "Ah, I was so happy then," explained Praxedes.[15] However, she was not one of those who wasted time lamenting the past. She was now married and had children. She must take care of them. So to this end she directed all her energies, to be "the perfect mother and wife," as Father Luis de Leon had written in a book that someone gave her on her wedding day.

Chapter 10

WIFE AND MOTHER

Soon, as Celestino had augured in the poem he composed for Praxedes on her wedding day, God sent Gabriel and Praxedes their first son, fair and beautiful, a little angel. He arrived on February 11, 1915, ten months after they were married and only two months after her father's death. Perhaps for this reason, the baby was given the name of Praxedes' dear father, Celestino. But here again, we see Praxedes' sensitivity to her husband, when she added the name Gabino to Celestino, for this was Gabriel's father's name.

The Baptism was put off longer than Praxedes wanted, but it had to do with the godparents. This made her anxious, for she wanted their son to be a child of God as soon as possible. Consuelo, who assisted her during this time, has said that she often heard Praxedes exclaim, "Oh, I am so anxious to have this child baptized."[1] Finally, the ceremony took place when he was two weeks old. Forty days later, Praxedes went to the church to offer him to God as Mary had done with her firstborn, Jesus. When they arrived at the church Praxedes took the baby and solemnly walked up to the main altar, which was dedicated to Mary, the Mother of God, to offer her son to God. After a long while, Consuelo, tired of waiting for Praxedes, walked out into the entrance of the church. Finally Praxedes came out and Consuelo complained to her, "It took you so long, Praxedes!" All that Praxedes had to say was, "I was consecrating him to Mary."[2]

Praxedes was delighted with her son, and loved him with a love that transformed everything. Consuelo, however, saw him with different eyes. She has claimed that he was quite flat-nosed;

she even remarked about this once to Praxedes, who answered, "Don't say that, woman, it isn't so!"[3]

Through the windows of the apartment one could see the young mother cooing to the little baby. With the coming of little Celestino her sewing took even more of her time, as she sewed all of the clothing for her family.

In September of 1915 the young couple moved out of the apartment into a two-floored home with a yard large enough for a garden and through which ran a stream. Praxedes was soon in her glory, growing her own vegetables and flowers. In this garden, too, she spent many hours sewing and playing with the children.

Dionisia's daughter, Asencion, has said this about Praxedes at this period: "We were so happy that Praxedes was able to move to her own home, for our joy was her joy. We loved her so much. We used to take the babies so that she could work unhampered in the many household chores that a mother normally has. My mother, who found herself in economic straits at times, used to borrow money from Praxedes. To needs of this kind she always responded with such sweetness and kindness."[4]

In this new home were born Arturo on June 9, 1916; Enrique on November 5, 1917; and Gabriel on February 17, 1920. They were all offered to the Blessed Mother as was the first one.

Praxedes loved her children with such a profound love that whether in private or in the presence of others, she showered love and attention on them. It was so obvious that the neighbors could not help but exclaim, "How she loves her children!"[5] When she took them to church, she would take time to explain the meaning of each object and taught them to bless themselves, guiding their little hands.[6]

The young family lived in peace under the protection of the Holy Family, whose picture hung on the wall of the bedroom. However, even the most ideal households are not spared the trials and sorrows of life.

The following incident, which took place shortly after the birth of Arturo in 1916, once again demonstrated the truly Christian attitude that Praxedes held for everyone—even those who became her "enemies" through no fault of her own. A certain Encarnacion Dias, whose nickname was "Encarnona," lived close by in Figaredo. She considered herself Praxedes' rival because she had been Gabriel's girlfriend before his marriage.

Praxedes had been able to nurse Celestino, but now with Arturo it was different. She took him to the doctor because he was such a weak child that even his little legs were getting crooked. She was told that her milk was not sufficiently rich and that she would have to feed him with the bottle. Her rival's mother heard of this, and as she worked in the bar which Gabriel frequented, she took the opportunity to say to him, "Your wife is very beautiful; but this is only apparent for inside she is spongy, as she cannot even nurse your children."[7] Encarnacion went even further than this. She sent Gabriel a postcard with a picture of a man milking a cow, but whose milk was coming out in the form of flour. It was clearly seen that this was an insult to poor Praxedes, who was unable to nurse her children. One day she was looking for something in her husband's dresser drawer, with her neighbor Otilia Moro present. She came upon this postcard and said to her, "This is a gift from Encarnacion to my husband." She never disposed of it, as any other wife might well have done.

Moreover, the bar which Gabriel frequented was situated in such a way that Praxedes could easily see him go in. Consuelo has told us, "Praxedes did nothing but cry at such times, but in silence, and not once did she reproach him for his behavior. On the contrary, she redoubled her attentions to him, without neglecting her children or herself."[8]

So as a result of these intrigues, Gabriel's love for his wife cooled. Her cousin Consuelo testified under oath to the following: "I saw Gabriel treat her quite harshly at times, despotically and disdainfully, as though he did not appreciate her. At times like this, Praxedes, who was always sewing, without ever answering him or defending herself, would just lower her head and cry."[9] And Felicidad Fernandez, another neighbor, has declared that she heard the same from others, that "Gabriel made it hard for Praxedes, but that she never complained or said anything to anyone."[10]

Praxedes realized that this situation which was threatening her marriage was truly intolerable, and that it had become urgent that she do something about it beside lowering her head and crying. Nicanor, her paternal uncle who lived in Santullano, not far from Figaredo, was the one to whom Praxedes went for advice and to unburden herself.[11] He persuaded her to go to her mother-in-law and tell her the whole story of what had been going on. This she did as a last resort.

"Your mother went to El Pedroso when your father was at work," Carmen Vallina wrote to Father Enrique. "She made sure that she was back before he was, so that he knew nothing of her visit to his mother. Your grandmother consoled your mother, telling her that as soon as she saw him all would be taken care of. And so it happened, for in a few days your father went to visit her and she gave him a good tongue-lashing. She threatened to bring Praxedes and the children to her home, leaving him alone, if it ever happened again. Your father almost went crazy wanting to know who told his mother. But his mother told him, 'I believe every word that person told me, for that person has a great respect for God and is not capable of lying for anything in the world.' And from that day on, according to your mother, he was an exemplary husband and never again did he enter that bar. And since that time, too, he permitted no one to offend Praxedes in any way."[12] Thus peace and joy returned to the home where a marriage had been so threatened.

The difficulty now was economic. Gabriel's salary was the only income. He was earning normal wages, but he did not know how to save. He smoked; he went out to eat with friends and gallantly footed the bill. Celestina has referred to this hard time in Figaredo, saying, "They were getting along fine even though money was scarce, as Gabriel was not a saver."[13] Ismael, Praxedes' oldest brother, became aware of this precarious situation and offered a great amount of money to Praxedes to alleviate the problem. Gratefully, but sweetly, she refused the money saying, "I must do all I can to help my husband resolve this problem."[14]

In their home, the door was always open to friends and family. The assistant pastor of their parish had this to say: "Gabriel was a very good friend of mine. We were both from Valdecuna, where we were classmates. When he married Praxedes my friendship was extended to her. As I lived very close to them, they often invited me to lunch or dinner. I enjoyed those very agreeable visits, as they were both very hospitable and friendly. I never noticed anything extraordinary about Praxedes except that she was a good woman, very recollected and attentive. If I had known what was later to happen, I would have noticed her more. God willing, I hope that someday she will be raised to the honors of the altar."[15]

It is notable from this authentic testimony that mention was made of Praxedes' recollectedness in the midst of what was seen as an ordinary life. This is precisely what her classmates, Sister Pilar Vila, and her suitor Jose Alvarez could see. Everywhere and in all circumstances, even when she had invited guests at her table, she gave the impression that she lived recollected in the "cell of her heart," as St. Catherine of Siena was wont to do, without neglecting her household duties.

This interior life was sustained by the exercises of piety that constituted Praxedes' defense. Her cousin Consuelo, who spent long periods with her, has given us very reliable information on this facet of her life. "On the days when I stayed with Praxedes, which were many, she went to daily Mass and Holy Communion. After Mass she remained for a long visit to the Blessed Sacrament. Before she went to bed she prayed the Rosary and many other prayers. She went to sleep with the rosary wrapped around her hand. She prayed a lot, and even as she went about her work she moved her lips in prayer. She appeared so recollected. She urged me to pray much, so much so that I once said, 'It's too much praying!' She then patiently explained how important it is to pray. She said that we should all pray more than what we are accustomed to."[16]

The more Praxedes loved God, the more she loved her family. She was always disposed to attend to her husband's needs and looked for ways to please him in a thousand ways. "With Gabriel," Consuelo tells us, "she was very loving. When he returned from work she received him with so much joy that it surprised me. Before he arrived, she would go to the spring to get fresh water, so that he would have fresh water when he got home. She had so many delicate ways about her."[17] She was particularly careful about keeping her house immaculately clean. Those who visited her were full of admiration over this. One of her nieces, Rosario Fernandez Lopez, has declared, "I remember my mother telling me that Praxedes' home was as clean as a mirror."[18]

Teresa Viejo, the wife of one of Praxedes' cousins, Jesus Atuna, has affirmed the same: "My mother-in-law, Pilar Garcia, Praxedes' maternal aunt, praised the extraordinary cleanliness of her niece's home. One day as we were going through Figaredo, she said, 'Look, that is where my niece Praxedes lives. She keeps her home as clean as a silver cup.' If sometimes I was careless in my housekeeping I would think right away that if my mother-in-law would come she could not say what she did about Praxedes."[19]

And as charity "looks not for one's gain, but for that of others," Praxedes, who heard her husband complain of dangers connected with his work as electrician, encouraged him to look for another job, one that was more to his liking. Fortunately, in no time he found another job—and a better one—with the largest telephone company in Spain, Hulleras Turon, S.A. In this way Gabriel was now fully incorporated to the world of mining, as were all of Praxedes' family, and as two of her sons would also be in the future.

All these attentions only served to make Gabriel love his wife all the more. "One day," said Carmen Vallena, Gabriel's sister-in-law, "a neighbor insulted Praxedes because of little Celestino's mischievousness. Gabriel found out about the incident upon his return from work and, full of anger, wanted to go out and get an apology from the woman who had insulted her. But Praxedes' tears and pleadings stopped him from causing further trouble. 'Against my wife,' he said angrily, 'no one can say absolutely anything because she is a saint, a treasure.' "[20]

Florentina has left us the most precious and beautiful testimony in this respect. "When Gabriel came to visit us, I often heard him say, 'For me Praxedes is the best in the world.' "[21]

But these peaceful, happy days were soon to end...Misfortune was knocking at the door of this home.

Chapter 11

BROKEN HOME

Since Gabriel no longer worked on cables carrying such high voltage, he felt relieved from the constant fear of being electrocuted. He was at peace with his wife and three boys, and expecting a fourth child in February of 1920. It was during this period that Praxedes began to have a presentiment that her husband would soon die. Father Enrique told me in 1965 that he heard his mother say that when she went into their bedroom a strange feeling of fear would come over her from head to foot. She felt, in other words, that death was surrounding their home, knocking at the door. Unfortunately, that presentiment proved to be true.

After Praxedes had gone through the pain of her father's death, her sister Consuelo, the one she loved above all her brothers and sisters, died on January 22, 1920, following her fourth miscarriage. Shortly after that Praxedes gave birth to her fourth son, on February 17, 1920. For this reason, her mother Amalia came to be with her. She returned home after three days, taking with her the two younger boys, Arturo and Enrique. Celestino stayed at home in the care of cousin Consuelo, who cared for them all.

Gabriel accompanied his mother-in-law and the two little ones to El Puente de la Luisa. After an animated visit, as well as a joyful one with Florentina, he decided to start back home. He left to return home as soon as he heard the train approaching. Arriving at the station, he briskly jumped into the locomotive beside his engineer friend "el Charrero." In no time they were in Mieres. Here the locomotive was parked to await the passenger train that Gabriel was to take to Figaredo. While they were quietly waiting, two freight cars loaded with bricks became detached from their locomotive and rolled downward toward Mieres. The unevenness and incline is appreciable about five kilometers from Mieres. There was nothing to stop the freight cars as they gathered speed—until they hit the locomotive in which Gabriel was having a lively chat with his friend.

The impact was tremendous. The sound was like that of a bomb and could be heard all over Mieres. Everyone ran terrified to the sight of the accident. Charrero had been thrown out of the car and by a miracle was alive. Gabriel and the stoker were crushed inside the locomotive.

The news reached Figaredo, causing great consternation in the whole town. The pastor, Father Vicente Quiros, came into the rectory and said to the assistant pastor, "We have a terrible disaster in our town. The train just killed Praxedes' husband. What a sad and painful situation she is in now!" Father Elias Valdes, the assistant who was a good friend of Gabriel, wrote 38 years later, "The pastor and I were very sad and upset over Gabriel's tragic death. We had gone to school together. Even today, the tears come to my eyes in recalling that sad day."[1]

Meanwhile both families came together to decide how and what to say to Praxedes. This was considered a serious situation because she was still recuperating from the birth of her last baby. Both sides agreed to simply tell her that as Gabriel was leaving his mother-in-law's house he met a cousin of his with whom he was at odds, and during the argument he had slapped her. For this he was put in jail. Consuelo, who was present when they told her, said that upon hearing this Praxedes was overcome but said, "Of course! He has such a temper!"[2] She believed it without any trouble. At this meeting the family had also agreed to take Praxedes the next day, February 29, to her mother's home which was then in El Puente de la Luisa.

This sad event had affected the whole district, where both Gabriel and Praxedes and their families were well-known and esteemed. All that anyone could talk about in those days was of how this young couple with their four little children had now been torn apart.

As the days went by and Gabriel did not return, it was evident to Praxedes that just for a slap he could not have gotten such a long prison term. Then her family told her that his former boss, Prospero Blanco, was in Madrid and they were waiting for him to return so that he could get him out of this predicament. They also told her that in the meantime Gabriel had contracted pneumonia and it would be a matter of days before it would be known whether he would live or die.

When Praxedes heard this she was determined to go to him. "What must my husband think," she said, "being so ill and I not visiting him." It was then that her mother took her into her arms and told her, crying, "My darling, don't go, because Gabriel died the same day he left my house." Then she told her the whole story. One may wonder why this was done to Praxedes, but in a letter written later by her mother, she said that this was done at the doctor's advice because of Praxedes' precarious health condition. He had said that she should not be told for at least two weeks. Praxedes was petrified and broke down crying, saying between sobs, "He is already judged by God!"[3]

At that sad moment, when everyone was crying and not knowing what to do, her mother once again embraced her saying, "Look, Praxedes, you have always been very religious. It is very necessary that once again this give you strength and that you resign yourself to this cross that God has sent you."[4] The sad young widow took these words to heart, and taking them as coming from Heaven, exclaimed, "Yes, God has given him to me and has taken him away. I accept it. May He be blessed."[5]

To a young friend who used to come to visit her during this period of loneliness Praxedes said, "Oh, how you deceived me!"[6]

One of her relatives, upon returning from giving her sympathy, said to Praxedes' family, "I never saw such conformity to God's will as hers! What patience! I have never seen anyone like her. This woman gives me a lot to think about. There is something special about her."[7]

During this crucial time of her life Praxedes demonstrated such dignity that she edified all those around her. Sister Consuelo Giner from the school at the Fabrica has said that it was at this time that she began to realize that Praxedes was truly a saint.[8] In the midst of her complete resignation to the will of God, one thing only caused her great pain and suffering. Her husband had died without a priest and had not had time to prepare for his death. Antonia Castano had this to say: "Whenever I met her in church after her husband's death she would tell me of her concern over her husband's death—the manner in which he died. She would say, 'If I only knew if he had time to repent and that God has taken him to Himself, I would be so peaceful.' It was evident that she came to church to pray for him. At this time, her main concern was with his salvation—more, even, than having to raise her children all by herself."[9]

So now, as she went about caring for her boys' spiritual and material well-being and praying for her husband, Praxedes was very busy indeed. One day while she was still at her mother's she again took her four boys and consecrated them to our Blessed Mother in front of a statue of Mary Immaculate. This brought her much peace. To her friend Julia Suarez, who one day was lamenting her situation, she said, "As far as my boys are concerned, I have no worries. I have given them over to our Blessed Mother and I count on her help."[10] Sister Consuelo Giner wrote to Father Enrique saying, "When your father died, your two older brothers came to study in our school. She used to accompany them. She told us once that in the midst of all her sorrow she enjoyed great peace because her whole family was under the protection of the Blessed Mother, and that she knew that as a good mother she would always care for them. We could not help commenting on this beautiful example among us."[11]

The Lord wished to answer the prayers of His faithful servant whose unlimited trust and faith had been proved. He showed this with an extraordinary sign of assurance, which she confided to her son, who was a Dominican religious student, Father Enrique. Father Enrique told me this himself. "On July 16, 1929, she had a Mass offered for the repose of the soul of her husband. That night while she was in bed she began to hear footsteps that seemed to be coming up the ladder on the side of the house. At first she thought that it was Ovidio, who was staying there at the time. She soon realized, however, that those footsteps were not of the living and neither was the ladder, for like Jacob's ladder it seemed to go on indefinitely. A great fear invaded her for a moment. But when that passed, a great peace and joy filled her. She realized that those were the footsteps of her husband. This mysterious ascent lasted about 15 minutes, until the echo of the footsteps disappeared into the heavens. "That was your father," she said, full of joy, "that climbed into Heaven."

Chapter 12

WIDOW AND SERVANT

Praxedes had been the wife of a common laborer who earned only enough to sustain his family. He had no social security, no pension, no account in the bank, nor any property. He left his wife with four children, the oldest who was five and the youngest just a few days old.

Her mother, Amalia, on the other hand, was a wealthy woman. She owned 16 houses, numerous farms, and had a substantial bank account. Her brothers, all superintendents of mines, had also become very wealthy. Celestina had married a superintendent of mines; and Florentina, who lived with her mother, owned everything that she did. The only member of the family who had become poor was Praxedes. She had joined the working class, with all the privations and economic shortages that this class suffered in that era.

Florentina has told us that at the death of her husband, her sister did not have enough money to pay the rent, the light bill, nor even enough to pay the woman who had washed her clothes while she had been recuperating after the birth of her baby. Her mother paid all these bills at this time.

We know, however, from Praxedes' testimony that before dying, her father had said that all the inheritance would be retained by his wife. But in case one of their daughters became a widow, her part should be given her immediately. Becoming a widow, of course, was the case with Praxedes.

One day Justa Curieses observed this scene. Praxedes was sweeping and Florentina came up to her and said in a loud voice, "It would be better if you and your children would go, leaving mother and me in peace." Without stopping her work,

Praxedes said, "If I receive the inheritance that is coming to me according to father's dying wish, I will be happy to leave. Otherwise I have nothing to live on."[1] Celestino had died without having written down his wishes, and Praxedes had nothing. If as an unmarried woman she had never known want in the home of her parents, and as a married woman she had only the necessities of life and a roof over her head, now she could in truth repeat the words of Jesus, "The birds have nests, the foxes have their holes, but the Son of Man has nowhere to lay his head." [*Matt.* 8:20].

Her mother, who loved her so much, found a solution that was advantageous for both parties. She would have Praxedes and her four sons live in her home, and in that way she would not have to give Praxedes her inheritance. Florentina, in a very objective way, said, "All this ended by converting my sister into a servant. Moreover, she became a Cinderella. When Praxedes became a widow she came to live with Celso, our mother, and me. She came in utter poverty. She had no money and she had no savings. We had a servant at home, but she wanted to leave because she said she came to work for three—and now there were eight. In the meantime she contracted the measles, and so Praxedes and I took care of her until she had to go to the hospital. We were going to get another servant, but Praxedes was opposed to it. 'Don't get one,' she said, 'it costs too much and now I am here.'

"From then on she was busy around the house, besides doing the cooking and washing the clothes. Many times she brought mother and me our breakfast in our rooms. We always ate in the dining room, and Praxedes insisted on serving us. In our home in El Puente de la Luisa she slept in my bedroom, but later moved to the garret, where she remained until we moved to Sueros in 1926. Here too she chose the humblest room, one on the second floor where the roof was at an angle. And it was the same in Oviedo, where she chose a windowless room. My sister Celestina would say to her, 'Praxedes, you look like the Cinderella of the house.' "[2]

Remember, Amalia gave room and board to Praxedes and her sons but never any money, not one penny for anything. One of her nieces declared that she heard her mother or Praxedes say that when the children asked for candy she could not give them any.[3]

Except for food and lodging Praxedes had to meet all her other expenses, such as the education of her children, clothes, books, medicine etc. How was she to meet these responsibilities without a cent? Her total abandonment to the providence of God helped her remain tranquil and trusting. On the other hand, she had learned from her own mother how to save.

Praxedes knew how to sew and mend very well. That is why the clothing she made lasted so long. She happily wore the cast-off shoes that her mother and sister gave her. She made all the boys' clothing from the clothing left by their father. The following is a clear proof of what had been said: "Until 1922 I went to her mother's home to pay for the apartment that I rented from her. She was always working. On one occasion I saw her making clothes for her son Celestino from used clothing."[4] But she was not one of those who let themselves go to pieces because of difficulties. She often told her boys, for she was convinced of it, "God helps those who help themselves."

Praxedes came to her mother's house to replace not only one servant, but two or three that were needed to do the many chores in that big household. On the other hand she never received a salary, ate little, and worked much. She was a person of utmost integrity; so in the end, Amalia had, economically speaking, gained and not lost.

In regard to the above matters, Praxedes' son Gabriel has given us these concrete observations: "Economically, my grandmother and my aunt Florentina lived comfortably from the rents of all their houses, and from the produce from all the farms. On the other hand, even though my mother was entitled to her part of the inheritance, she never received it as it was not divided until grandmother died in 1946. My mother did all the heavy housework and even worked in the garden. She never allowed her mother to hire a permanent servant, only on occasions when company from Andalucia came. My mother was the one who always served at the table and ate after all had eaten. She was the last to retire, and never before midnight. In other words she was the servant of the house.

"In contrast, Aunt Florentina, who lived off the rents and farms, never lifted a finger to help my mother. On top of this she even dared to correct my mother and scolded her when things weren't to her liking. Mother took all this with great patience and tried to please her. This situation continued in Oviedo, even though my mother paid rent there. Nevertheless, she continued to be the servant of the house."[5]

Yes, Amalia had a "servant" who could do everything, could not say no and moreover, as Josefa Solis has testified, "She did it because she wanted to." Nevertheless, the neighbors did not like it. They did not think that Praxedes should work like a hired hand, or as if "she were a slave," being that her mother was so wealthy.

Luisa Iglesias, in a letter she wrote to Father Enrique said, "I was only a child when your mother became a widow and came to live with your grandmother in Puente de la Luisa. She took upon herself the duties of washing, cooking, cleaning etc., not because they asked her to do it but because she did it voluntarily.[6] All the neighbors criticized her for doing it, but at the same time they realized that she was a saint. My father was a good friend of Celso, your uncle, and he knew well what was going on. He used to tell us, 'There is not one of Amalia's daughters like Praxedes.' He often spoke of her as a model of goodness, humility, detachment and for being a hard worker. She always had the well-being of others in mind and never declined to give counselling and was an authentic witness at all times."[7]

Amalia truly loved Praxedes, but was naturally more attentive to Florentina as she was the youngest and always catered to. Jesus Antuna has told us, "Florentina always resented Praxedes being in her home with her four sons, as though they were eating what belonged to her."[8] She never let an opportunity pass that she did not let Praxedes know that in that house she had no rights.

Amparo Robledo, who at times used to help Praxedes when her brothers would visit from Andalucia, has told us, "Praxedes could not arrange or dispose of anything in the house. If she spent what her mother or sister thought was too much, she was reprimanded and accused of being wasteful. She gave her children the best she could, but immediately she was criticized for it. It was her sister Florentina who was so intolerant, and always finding fault with her. Amalia was a good woman, but was easily manipulated by Florentina's every whim. To all this Praxedes never remonstrated and was always loving and at their service."[9]

Florentina even kept the keys to the cupboards and controlled the food. Teresa Viejo, a relative of the family, came for a visit one day and observed the following: "I was sadly impressed that Florentina went into the kitchen three times to complain to Praxedes about some things she had bought and with which she was not satisfied. When it was time to eat Praxedes served us, but would not eat with us. After the meal I went into the kitchen and there found Praxedes drinking a glass of milk with bread. I asked her why she did not eat more. She answered that she had enough with that.

"I asked Florentina why Praxedes did not eat with us and she answered that she always ate in the kitchen. When the meal was over Florentina got some pies out of a cupboard that was locked. What we did not eat she put back into the cupboard and locked it. I was surprised that she did not offer any to Praxedes, as though she did not count."[10] This happened just one year before Praxedes died, which shows that she suffered from Florentina's overbearing conduct until she died.

The now elderly Sister Pilar Vila said in 1964, in a few words, what truly brings out the contrast between the two sisters: "Florentina was the 'lady' and Praxedes the 'servant.' Florentina was the younger of the two, jolly and more interested in a good time than in penance. She loved to sing, play the bandurria and converse. Praxedes practiced mortification, always serving others not only at home but outside as well, wherever she found need."

Obdulia Iglesias, Praxedes' cousin, amplified a few concrete details regarding her devotedness to her duties: "She used to get up very early to begin her housework. If we ever invited her to the movie or the theater she excused herself, saying 'Please excuse me, but my duties don't allow me the time.' She would even counsel me to stay home more so that I could be more attentive to my husband and children."[11]

But Praxedes loved the condition of being a servant because it made her feel closer to the "handmaid of the Lord," the Virgin of Nazareth. In the midst of all her work and service to those she found in need, she found time for her private devotions. Florentina, who is the best qualified to testify to this because Praxedes lived in her home during all her widowhood, has told us, "Praxedes loved to pray and took plenty of time for that without ever neglecting her duty. She slept very little and was up very early."[12]

This was common knowledge among her family, as well as among her neighbors. "She devoted herself admirably to her pious devotions without ever neglecting her duties which she had during the day."[13] She could do this because she had learned how to harmonize her duties with her spiritual life. One day she was encouraging her cousin, Marcelina Vasquez, to go to daily Mass. When Marcelina told her that her housework and family would not allow her, she gave her such a convincing answer that it left no doubts in her mind. Praxedes said, "That is not a good excuse. The time that it takes to assist at Mass, far from being an impediment, serves to help you do them even better."[14] This admirable answer shows us how much her spiritual life was intertwined with her everyday life.

Chapter 13

DAY BY DAY

Praxedes accepted her situation as "servant" or "slave," serving everyone who crossed her path for whatever reason. And naturally, her sons were her first priority. They had no father, so to her alone fell the duty of ensuring a successful future. She did it with much intelligence, rising above her condition with great ease. Not only did she care for their health, but she directed their education until they each chose a career.

Through a very special favor of the chaplain of the Fabrica, Praxedes' two oldest boys enrolled in the parish school run by the Dominican Sisters. The grandmother was overjoyed, for now it would be less noisy around the house. The two younger ones, Enrique and Gabriel, were still at home; and judging from a letter the grandmother wrote around that time "they cried too much."[1] Florentina did not appreciate this "music" either, and she did not hide the fact. Consuelo, a cousin, was visiting one day when in the course of the conversation Praxedes began to cry. When asked why she was crying she answered, "Because Florentina does not like my sons."[2]

Of the four boys, Celestino was the only one who did not get into mischief. The second one was "l'enfant terrible." He preferred the outdoors and horses, and did not much like school. "Arturo," said the grandmother, "handles a horse like a veteran horseman and he is only four. He fears nothing. He is a rascal."[3] This son was to be a real cross to his mother. One day Praxedes said to her friend, "I am so unhappy today because Arturo used a bad word, a very bad one."[4] The grandmother, as much as Florentina, attributed his behavior to "He takes after his father." And they let their views be known to the four winds. This reference did not please Praxedes at all. One day she voiced her opinion, "Go on, Gabriel also had his good points and virtues and you don't remember that! You should not say such things in front of him [Arturo] because he is going to think that there is no hope for his improving his weaknesses and won't try to overcome them."[5]

Come fall and winter, it never stops raining in Asturias and is the time for colds. The whole family succumbed to the illness, and Praxedes now became the nurse for everyone. "On October 17," Amalia wrote to her oldest child, "I came down with a terrible cold and fever. Arturo was sick with typhoid fever. The youngest has bronchitis. Today his glands are swollen, and he cries incessantly, for he is teething."[6]

In a letter of February, 1921 she continued in the same vein saying, "Since the 17th of January I have been down with another cold, as well as all the boys and Celso too. Enrique continues to suffer as a result of the measles. The youngest was very ill last night. These little ones, when they aren't kept in the house like little prisoners, are running outside."[7] (Not a word about Florentina.) And no wonder, for she ended by saying, "This house resembles a hospital."[8] Poor Praxedes suffered doubly as she realized how much her family's illnesses cost her mother and sister.

But the children were not only the cause for sorrow, but for joy as well. Celestino acted brilliantly in the part he took in a school play as a soldier who went to war against the wishes of his parents to defend his country in time of great peril. Every time he spoke he was applauded, for he was not quite seven yet. The next day, when Praxedes was congratulated for her son's outstanding acting, she remarked, "Yes, he defended his country—but also his religion."[9] For both ideals he was to give his life later on.

In the course of the year 1921 Praxedes received for the first time some kind of income, the 20 pesetas for the sublease of her house in Figaredo to her brother-in-law, Prospero. This is all she received until the end of 1926, when her sons received an inheritance from their paternal grandmother. They inherited a house when she died. This, however, brought in not even a peseta a day income! So we see that with that tiny amount Praxedes had to supply the boys' school needs and the considerable expenses of medicines, because they were often sick. Amalia was adamant in her original offer—room and board.

We know from the testimony of an elderly lady in an old-age home, San Jose de Gijon, who was formerly a servant of Concha Gonzalez (a wealthy lady from Mieres), that Praxedes received several large amounts of money from Concha. She always received this charity kissing her benefactor's hands.[10] And Father Enrique told me in January, 1965 that he sometimes saw the Countess of Mieres giving his mother used clothing for the children. Praxedes was authentically poor, and she was not ashamed to receive charity. She never begged for a penny. She received money from a few people, even from her brothers, who were now rich. Amalia said in a letter once, "Of Ovidio, all I know is that he makes a lot of money."[11]

In 1922 Enrique was enrolled in the Dominican school. Celestino, who had turned seven, made his first Holy Communion. He was very well prepared, not only by the sisters but by his mother as well. In September, 1966 I heard one of the parishioners in Figaredo tell how she remembered the way Praxedes always brought her three-year-old to Mass. She observed how she would point to the altar and whisper something into his ear to help him understand the things of God. She did the same with the other boys. Consuelo tells us that long before the babies could talk she taught them to cross themselves and had them kiss the crucifix and statue of the Blessed Virgin. As soon as they could talk she taught them to say the Our Father, Hail Mary and a few aspirations.

And as soon as her children could understand, Praxedes explained the Passion of Jesus and why He suffered. She also taught them about the Blessed Virgin, sin, the astuteness of the devil and the dangers of bad companions. This is the way that she was trying to plant and nourish an authentic way of Christian living in her sons.

Together with the regular sicknesses of childhood came some accidents. In 1922, when Enrique was only five, he received a kick from a horse that almost cost him his life. The family doctor had tied his horse in front of the family's house and gone in when Enrique picked up a stick to hit the horse. Instead, the horse kicked him on the head, just above the left eye. It was at first feared that he had lost his eye, but after cleaning the wound it was gladly found that his eye was intact. To this day Father Enrique carries the scars of that wound. On top of this, Enrique became temporarily blind the following year. Because his paternal grandmother and uncle were blind, everyone thought that this blindness was hereditary. Praxedes was almost devastated with sorrow. But because she had consecrated him to the Blessed Virgin, she now invoked her aid under the title of Health of the Sick, and offered the family Rosary every night for his cure. A few days later the child surprised all by opening his eyes and regaining his sight completely![12]

Later on Gabriel sat on a board and was badly stuck in the groin with a steel nail. For several years this injury gave him much pain and trouble. Then to top it all off, the two oldest boys were bitten by a dog with rabies. Praxedes had to have them undergo the painful treatment for rabies at that time. Then in 1924 Praxedes had her turn of sickness. She developed an ulcer in one of her eyes that required the doctor's attention. After this Florentina contracted typhoid fever and was so ill that the doctors gave up hope for her life.

Praxedes was not only taking care of her own, but was going to the aid of others outside her home who needed care. On one occasion she outdid herself in coming to the aid of a young man who had had his arm mangled while working in the mines. "The damage was so horrible," declared Florentina, "that no one wanted to touch him. But along came Praxedes, and with great care and tenderness and courage she bandaged the badly mangled arm."[13]

And as usual, Praxedes proved her solicitude for the poor. On one occasion when "in 1935," said Sister Josefina Martinez of Sueros, "a poor woman gave birth to twins, Praxedes went from door to door collecting clothes, diapers and two cradles for her poor friend."[14]

She consoled her cousin Benigna Fernandez, who had had several miscarriages and found herself quite weak and discouraged from the latest, by saying: "The more we suffer with patience and love in this world, the greater will our glory be in the next."[15] These words carried weight, for that is how all saw her suffer and live.

When Praxedes was a child, and even after she got married, she had not been very brave[16] in the dark and in defending herself. But when she became a mother she became fearless. "The only time I saw Praxedes really angry," said Florentina, "was the time when one of the mine guards scolded and threatened Arturo, even to the point of running after him into the house to hit him. Praxedes was very angry at him and rebuked him greatly."[17]

Amalia and Florentina lived in fear in their big home in Puente de la Luisa, isolated from all the neighbors. The continual strikes in the mines at that time and the resultant poverty caused many break-ins in the region. Celso, Amalia's youngest son, had left home; so the three women and the four small boys were left alone in the home. One night when Praxedes got up to check for possible break-ins she found that two thieves had already entered the house, but were scared away by her bravery.

Due to this incident, Amalia and Florentina decided to go away to Andalucia to be in safety with one of her sons for a time. They were away almost a year, leaving Praxedes and the four boys alone. During this year Praxedes gave hospitality to a venerable old man who had no home. She sat him at her table and served him the same as she did her children, washing and ironing his clothes as well. He was welcomed to stay as long as he wished.[18]

She even welcomed the insane to the house. Florentina has told us, "Praxedes had brought a certain Luisa Labiru, who was a little insane, to stay with us overnight. In the morning while Praxedes was at Mass, Luisa got up and went into my room and began hitting me. I had to run out and ask for help, for she could have killed me. When Praxedes returned I told her that she had to get her out."[19]

On June 1, 1926, Praxedes' mother-in-law died and left her and her four grandsons her home. Praxedes rented it for 40 pesetas a month. This added to the 20 that she was already receiving from her brother-in-law for her Figaredo house, and put her in a better economic condition. Thus it was that this poor widow, who had always trusted in Divine Providence, was now being taken care of.

The year before, on June 4, a sad incident shook all of Spain and filled Praxedes with sorrow. The Cardinal of Saragoza was shot to death while entering his residence. That was the first flare-up that announced the bloody persecution of the Spanish Church that was soon to come.

Chapter 14

THE MEETING WITH THE "BISHOP OF THE TABERNACLE"

During the first years of her widowhood, Praxedes had a singular grace in meeting the first Bishop of Malaga, Bishop Manuel Gonzalez (1877-1944). He was Bishop of Malaga in 1920-1935, and afterwards of Palencia, 1935-1944. He had a great influence on her spiritual life. He was known as the "Bishop of the Tabernacle." What impresses the visitor as he enters the Bishop's cathedral is the following epitaph that is engraved on a large square of marble in the Blessed Sacrament Chapel.

> I wish to be buried close to the tabernacle
> so that my bones, after I am dead,
> like my tongue and pen in life,
> continue to say to all who pass by:
> Jesus is here! Here He is!
> Do not abandon Him!

This tombstone covers the remains of Bishop Gonzalez, whose cause for beatification is now being studied in Rome.

It was in Mieres that Praxedes accidently met this apostle of the Tabernacle. The Count and Countess of Mieres used to spend their summers in their palace in Mieres because Andalucia was unbearably hot in the summertime. They used to invite Bishop Gonzalez to spend the month of August with them. During the week he offered the Holy Sacrifice in their private chapel and on Sundays in the Fabrica chapel for everyone. He also took time to hear confessions before and after Mass every Sunday.

In 1920, the first year of his bishopric of Malaga, Bishop

Gonzalez wrote his first pastoral letter. In it he outlined once and for all his plan of action, which had been the same when he was first ordained, then archpriest of Huelva, then auxiliary Bishop and now as Bishop of the diocese. "I do not want to be the Bishop of the learned, nor of activity, nor of the poor nor of the rich. I want to be only the Bishop of the Tabernacle." His whole letter revolved around this theme. "Jesus in the Tabernacle is the living Gospel." He signed it, "Manuel Bishop of Malaga. Fabrica of Mieres, Feast of the Assumption, 1920." This letter, so revealing of his great talent and zeal for the Blessed Sacrament, was received with great love and openness by the widow of Sueros, Praxedes Fernandez.

Praxedes not only went to confession to the Bishop during the summers in Mieres, but was often seen conversing with him outside the church after Mass.[1]

"And the children," he would say, "how they console the Heart of Jesus with their innocent and devout reception of Holy Communion! And in speaking of the devout reception of Holy Communion by the children, let me say to all the teachers of the diocese, how important a privilege it is to sow the seed of devotion and love of the Holy Eucharist in the hearts of your pupils. The more abundant this sowing will be, the more deep-rooted will their Christian learning be."

It is true that it was not the Bishop who enkindled the flame of the love of the Eucharist in Praxedes, but he was the cause of its becoming a "volcano." Since that time the Eucharist became the "sun" of her spiritual firmament.[2] The Mass and Communion became for her indispensable, so that neither snow, rain nor even sickness could keep her from going to receive the "Bread of Life," for which her hunger was never satiated. To satisfy this hunger Praxedes would rise early in the morning and walk to the celebration of the Eucharist. In the winter when it was still very dark she carried a miner's lamp to guide her steps. She almost always arrived before the door of the church was opened.[3] On Sundays and holy days she offered up three Masses, the first two in Mieres and the third in the Fabrica chapel.

Praxedes began to assist at three Masses daily, starting in 1931 until her death. One day Gabriel asked her why she went to so many Masses every day. She told him that the first one was offered in preparation for Holy Communion; in the second she received Our Lord, and the third Mass was in thanksgiving.[4] Her answer reminds one of St. John Eudes' reflection when he declared, "Three eternities are necessary to celebrate the Holy Mass: one to prepare, one to offer it and one to give thanks."[5]

Praxedes assisted at Mass and Communion with such fervor that one could not help but notice it. The first to comment on this were the sisters who also attended Mass there. Sister Maria Canal recalled vividly, "When Praxedes received Holy Communion, it was in such a manner that it is impossible to express in words. She appeared transfigured and in glory already."[6]

The chaplain of the Count and Countess of Mieres, Father Angel de la Puerta, who celebrated Mass in the public chapel on Sundays has written, "I still remember clearly how she impressed me when she received Holy Communion with such piety and recollection."[7]

There was nothing singular in her deportment. Praxedes approached to receive Holy Communion with her hands folded over her breast and returned in like manner. But there was something radiant about her appearance. Sister Asuncion Canal told us, "She was recollected and pious, but at the same time very natural and free of all affectation. Above all, she impressed me by her recollection upon her return from Holy Communion. For me it was an inspiration that stimulated my piety."[8]

Upon her return to the house, after she had cooked the porridge, Praxedes would kneel right there in the kitchen and continue her thanksgiving. One day her sister found her kneeling on the floor and said to her impatiently, "You just returned from church, and on top of this you continue to pray here!" To this Praxedes answered sweetly, "It's because God has chosen the best part for me."[9] Naturally, Florentina did not understand her answer. Was not this the very same answer Jesus gave Martha when she complained to Him of her sister sitting at His feet while she did all the work?

Praxedes' Eucharistic life was not limited to the Mass. Her visits to the Blessed Sacrament later on in the day were a continuation of that devotion. Without doubt the Bishop of the Tabernacle was responsible for her growth in awareness that there was very little or no devotion to the Blessed Sacrament. He helped her to orient her vision to reparation for the forgetfulness of men and women toward Jesus in the Blessed Sacrament. This was the thorn that he carried in his soul. He wrote, "Ah, abandoned Tabernacle, how clearly you have made me see that a priest is no more nor less than a man chosen by God to fight against the abandonment of the Tabernacle."[10]

Joyfully and with her contagious fervor, Praxedes attended all the liturgical celebrations in honor of the Holy Eucharist at the Fabrica Chapel or the parish of Seana in Mieres or in La Rebolleda. The Feast of Corpus Christi and the ceremonies of Holy Thursday were especially meaningful to her. Of this we have ample proof in her family letters.

Just as she wished to see the Blessed Sacrament honored with splendor as well as with fervor, Praxedes also trembled thinking that He could also be received unworthily. Father Enrique remembered that when the moment for Holy Communion arrived she would have him say with her, "That I may receive Jesus in the grace of God."[11] Her heart ached at the thought that anyone would receive Jesus in mortal sin. But her pain was even greater later on during the revolution when she learned of the many tabernacles which were profaned. She was especially careful to inculcate a fervent and healthy attitude toward the Blessed Sacrament in her boys. As was said before, she placed great importance on the preparation for their First Holy Communion. After that she encouraged them to receive Jesus frequently. She enrolled them in the Association of St. Tarsicius, where as members they were expected to attend Mass and receive Holy Communion on First Fridays. Later she enrolled them in the Nocturnal Adoration Association.[12]

In the 1930's the Lord, in the Blessed Sacrament, began to give Praxedes graces such as are found in the lives of the saints. Several people heard her say, "After receiving Holy Communion I feel a tremendous heat in my breast."[13]

On a visit that Father Enrique paid Father Jacinto, a Passionist, in Penafiel, on August 27, 1966, he told him, "One day, after your mother had been adoring the exposed Blessed Sacrament in the chapel in the Fabrica, your mother told me that Our Lord had appeared in the Host, surrounded with splendorous light. As I wanted to make sure it was not her imagination

I began to offer some objections such as that the lights may have been produced by some strange effect, or maybe an eyelash could have caused such an illusion. But she remained firm, saying 'It was the Lord! It was the Lord!' So when I still argued my point she became silent, with the greatest humility and modesty."

Neither is such an incident rare among the saints. St. Teresa of Avila said of herself, "Many times the Lord wished to have me see Him in the Sacred Host."[14] The Bishop of the Tabernacle, who had providentially come to Mieres, had not preached in vain when he said many times, "Jesus is here in the Host! Don't leave Him alone!" This seed yielded a hundredfold in the heart of that poor widow, hungry for God. "Someday," wrote Father Albiol, "the Church will present these two persons, signs of contemporary holiness, Praxedes and Bishop Gonzalez, surrounded by the same Eucharistic halo."[15]

Chapter 15

RETURN TO THE NEIGHBORHOOD OF JOY

The home in which Praxedes and her children had lived after her husband's death was the property of the mining company, Alta Montana, in which her brother Celso had been superintendent. In 1925 he changed companies, and consequently he and his family had to leave the home a year later. Amalia and the rest of the family returned to the Neighborhood of Joy in Sueros. This place was full of happy memories for Praxedes. She was glad the change had been made. Everywhere she turned she felt the presence of her father. Nothing had really changed except that there was no longer a grocery store, and the garden had become a wasteland.

She began at once to give life to the whole place. She planted a flower garden and soon there were roses, carnations, lilies and violets blooming all over. After a few days of the return to Sueros a dance was planned and held in the patio of their home. The women lined up on one side and the men on the other. Then came the clapping and sounding of the castanets which they rythmically moved back and forth. When Praxedes heard the music she went out and joined the dancers. Everyone clapped and marveled at how gracefully she danced.[1] Her son Enrique was there when it happened and remembers that this was the first time he had seen his mother dance. Later she said to Enrique, "To serve God and be sad, I can't imagine it."[2]

But times were bad. The atmosphere and environment of Sueros had changed since 1914, as had the political climate in all of Spain. As a result of the First World War the industry of Asturias had grown and multiplied, bringing laborers from all over the nation. Communism and anti-clericalism had taken hold of the working class. Demagogues blamed all of the ills of Spain on these oppressors of the people. Pope Pius XI called this situation "the apostasy of the masses." This was the condition Praxedes found in Sueros in 1926 when she returned. That improvised, happy dance was just an intermission, a ray of sunshine in the midst of the black clouds of dismay that were soon to turn to a bloody torrent.

The then pastor of Mieres, Father Hermogenes Lorenzo, has said that the Providence of God had sent Praxedes to this village that was so estranged from the Church. She came as a true apostle, precisely when religion was most needed in those difficult times.[3] The actual Archbishop of Burgos, Segundo Garcia, and former pastor of this mining district, wrote on September 9, 1959, "The example and witness that Praxedes gave in these most difficult times was extraordinary and splendid!"[4] And as an evangelical witness she loved, with such charity as a true follower of Christ, for the remainder of her ten years of life.

It did not take Praxedes too long to realize the strength of the anti-religious feelings that her new neighbors harbored. In 1927 began the most diabolical calumnies against all persons such as priests and religious, who were consecrated to God. One day upon getting hold of a newspaper filled with such reports, the whole neighborhood was inflamed. They all ran to Praxedes' home and insisted that she come out and listen to the account as they furiously read it. Then they all urged her with one voice to stop believing in the priests, who according to them should be abolished from the earth. For a person like Praxedes, who was so devoted to her Church and its ministers, this was most devastating. Father Enrique told me in 1965 that his mother immediately took her boys aside and tried to explain the meaning of all of this. They then got on their knees to ask God to protect His ministers.

But it was not only with words and prayers that Praxedes defended religion. The best witness was that of an authentic Christian whose life shone brightly in the midst of persecution. Her goodness and unconditional service to all had won for her the confidence and freedom to enter where the priests were no longer welcomed. Praxedes used this privilege to aid the sick and dying with such efficacy that words fail to express it. Her charity conquered all.

The Church today has reaffirmed that all Christians, by virtue of Baptism, are apostles at all times and in all places. This was the message that Praxedes gave to the world and to her world at that time. On the other hand, Providence had prepared her in such a manner as to make Praxedes be accepted with joy by those who otherwise wanted to erase all traces of religion from their hearts.

In December, 1926, Praxedes learned that Leonor Gutierrez's baby was gravely ill and was not baptized. Without fear she went to the home; the mother later said, "She came to my home with such love and concern for my baby that I allowed her to baptize him. He died four months later on January 1, 1927."[5]

On February 25 of this same year Praxedes assisted a dying woman by the name of Josefa Menendez. This time she took Enrique with her, who was eight at the time. When she saw how gravely ill this woman was she called the priest; but he was not there, so Praxedes did all she could to assist her at this most awesome moment of death. She whispered prayers and aspirations into the ear of the dying woman and every so often sprinkled the bed and room with holy water. At one point she invited all to kneel down and pray the Rosary with her. They all accepted and thus prayed for a happy death for the woman. When they got to the third mystery she expired peacefully. Praxedes then asked them all to remain on their knees to finish the Rosary for her soul.

Wishing ardently for the salvation of all her dear ones as well as for all of humankind, Praxedes placed all her confidence in prayer and especially in the Holy Sacrifice of the Mass. One day in this same year, 1927, Enrique overheard this conversation between his mother and an unbelieving neighbor who was lamenting her daughter's death. Praxedes sympathized with her and recommended that she have a Mass said for her. She answered that the priest asked for too much. "Woman, what are three pesetas? If you saw your daughter in flames would you not come to her aid? Well, with a holy Mass you can help free her from Purgatory."[6] Thus it was that she carried out her apostolate in surroundings that were so Godless, with no prayer, or any semblance of religion. Yes, filled with a spirit of sacrifice, charity, good example, a continued loving and sincere dialogue with all, she filled a need in Sueros at the right time.

Chapter 16

THE FUTURE OF THE FOUR BOYS

With a surprising ability, Praxedes outdid herself to help the priests in their pastoral ministry, which each day was becoming more and more difficult—if not impossible. She went to the side of the sick, those in want, etc., without ever for even a moment neglecting her duties as mother, housekeeper and provider for the education of her sons.

Praxedes was always the slave of her mother, of Florentina and her sons, and now she came to occupy the position of servant of all the neighbors and relatives who visited them. Celestino, who was the most sensitive to his mother's position, lamented this humiliation. He came into the house one day as Florentina was about to hit his mother, accusing her of using a chair to stand on to reach something—"a good chair that belonged to them."

Celso, Praxedes' brother, had left home to get married in Andalucia on April 28, 1928. For this Praxedes was very happy, and she and Sister Pilar could rejoice because he would be away from the temptations of the unmarried.[1]

As for Praxedes' sons, they were her first and greatest preoccupation. She worried about their material welfare as well as about their religious education. "Her fervent dream was to go to Heaven with all her sons," affirmed Antonia Castano.[2]

Gabriel has given us a detailed explanation of the formation they received from their mother. "She worked hard to bring us up. Above all, she was careful of our moral and religious formation. She sacrificed herself in every way so that we always attended a Catholic school. She was forever watchful of our conduct and found various ways of inspiring us to this end.

She explained Christian doctrine simply and clearly. She spoke to us of the power and knowledge of God. She helped us see the hand of God in all and the power of prayer to bring down the blessings of God."[3]

One day in 1928, Praxedes was seated in their midst and put this question to them. "Tell me, my sons, what do each of you want to be when you grow up?" The answers were unexpected. "I want to be an engineer." "I want to be a lawyer." "I want to be a pilot." Arturo waited until all had expressed themselves and then said triumphantly, "Well, I want to be a doctor so I can have my own horse." He often saw the doctor come on his horse, but what he really liked was to ride like the best of horsemen. His grandmother had noted this since he was four. They all laughed at the answers except Praxedes, for she appeared quite sad. She had hoped one of them would want to be a priest. She then began to expound on the dignity and beauty of the priesthood. It was a calling "superior to the calling of kings." The boys were captivated by such an exposition.

In a few days, Celestino, the oldest, who already was serving at the altar, told his mother that he wanted to be a priest. At this news she was overjoyed and immediately enrolled him at the Lyceum of Mieres. It was directed by a priest and could prepare him to enter the diocesan seminary the following year. Everything was going fine until the boys of the town found out about Celestino's plans. They began to call him the "holy one of Christ." This made him angry and so he changed his mind, which made Praxedes sad and disappointed.

"We all wished to see Celestino a priest, for he had the intelligence and good character," said Father Angel de la Puente. "It was a great disappointment to his mother."[4] She, however, was always respectful of her sons' spiritual freedom with regard to vocation, and never once did she interfere with her son in this matter.

Praxedes was very wise. She knew when to take advantage of natural occurrences to put her point across. One day she was returning home from Mass with two of her boys—the two youngest, Gabriel and Enrique—when she said, "How happy the religious priests are!" She then spoke of their life and especially of the joy it must be to have dedicated themselves to God's service. She then told them of the life of one St. Gabriel de la Dolorosa, whose virtues she had heard in the sermons in the church. He was a young saint who captivated her two sons, who listened so attentively to her.[5]

Praxedes' interior life was growing. Her charity toward the poor and sick had no limit. One could see her take breakfast to a very poor couple, Celedonio and Ceferina, day after day.[6] She also helped the Benito Lopez family with their many children.[7] She continued to welcome Joaquin of Cenera and was delighted when she could find a poor child that she could seat at the table with her children. She also had them trained so that if they ever met a child begging they were to bring the child to her. One day they brought her four at once, and she sat them at the table with her children and, with great joy, fed them all well. What greater privilege than to instill in her children the charity that burned without limit in her heart.

Chapter 17

THE SON OF HER DREAMS

During this time the Communistic propaganda was spreading more and more among the miners and the environs. Those who were fighting Communism did everything to expose its perniciousness. Florentina bought a book that related the bloody revolutions in Russia and the deportation of thousands to Siberia. They read it out loud during the long winter evenings. Praxedes was moved to compassion at hearing the vivid description of the sufferings of these poor defenseless people, and deplored the fact that the working class in Spain was becoming so enthusiastic for a cause that was so destructive and evil.

In this atmosphere of inquietude and turmoil, a ray of hope shone on the future of her sons, for which Praxedes was so deeply concerned. Enrique told her that he wanted to be a Dominican priest. His vocation was inspired by the preaching of Father P. Raimundo Castano, a Dominican preacher whose cause for beatification is being studied in Rome. Fearful that the same thing that had happened to Celestino would happen again, she immediately arranged for his enrollment in the seminary as soon as possible. The Dominican Minor Seminary was in Las Caldas de Besays, Santander.

However, Praxedes was not able to carry out her plans as smoothly as expected, for even among her family there was great opposition. Her brothers, above all, who were miners, were not immune to the anti-clericalism that was so prevalent, especially among the laborers. Religious priests, even more than diocesan, were considered not only useless but noxious to society. So in this climate, her brothers could not accept the fact that she would allow Enrique to enter the Dominican Order.

They would not have minded it so much if at least he would be diocesan, for this way he could later care for his mother. But Praxedes did not wish to discuss this aspect at all. Since he wished to be a Dominican, she was ready to do with her whole heart and soul all that she could to see to it that his wish would be fulfilled. She handled everything so quietly and competently that by October of that year, 1928, Enrique was in the seminary in Las Caldas.

As far as Praxedes was concerned, she was ready to have all her sons become priests, not only Enrique. Sister Amparo Fernandez wrote, "She was very solicitous for her sons. Her desire was that they all become diocesan or religious priests. This was her main concern."[1] For certain, she wanted them all to be good. Florentina said that she often heard Praxedes say about Enrique, "May he always be a good priest, otherwise I don't want him to be one."[2]

At the same time, Praxedes enrolled Arturo in the seminary just in case he too would want to be a missionary, for he could be fired with this desire after listening to the missionary adventures of the Dominicans in not-yet-converted countries. Maybe he would even want to be a cooperator brother.

Enrique's entrance into the seminary filled the heart of the mother with joy and was the beginning of her dream of having one of her sons become a priest. Of course, there was still a long time before this was to come about. He would not receive the Dominican habit for five years yet.

On the other hand, times were insecure. The political and economic situation grew worse every day. The Church was being threatened to its foundation. But that did not matter. With her eyes fixed on God, Praxedes always carried out her mission as mother and provider for her sons.

For the first few months all went well for the two boys in the seminary. But then Arturo began having trouble with his ears. Praxedes was notified of this by Enrique and she, full of compassion, wrote out a remedy that she had found to be very good, for she had practice in these matters. But Arturo was not able to take the discipline of the seminary and did not show the least signs of a vocation. Therefore, he returned to Sueros in May, 1929.

Praxedes, still anxious about giving her sons the best

education she could, enrolled them in the school run by the Brothers of La Salle, in Mieres. They admitted Arturo gratuitously, but he preferred to go horseback riding instead of to school. He and another friend used to go to the hills and ride horses which were grazing there, never realizing the danger they were exposing themselves to. One day a horse did throw Arturo for quite a distance, and his friend found him kissing the brown scapular that his mother had put on him and saying, "This scapular has saved me from death."[3]

It was at this time that Ovidio, who had just rented a mine in Sueros, advised his sister to let Arturo work in the mine under his supervision. He thought that the hard work would make him want to go back to school and study. This happened in October, 1929, when Arturo was almost 14 years old. Praxedes saw no other solution, so she consented. After all, it was better that he be working and kept busy, rather than walking the streets or riding horses on the hills, exposed to all sorts of moral as well as physical dangers. "His uncle Ovidio," said Marcelino Llaneza, Arturo's companion in mischief, "gave orders that he be treated no differently from the others. He hoped, with Praxedes, that this hard work would make him want to go back to study."[4]

But to the surprise of all, instead of cringing under the work, Arturo considered himself the luckiest of all mortals! Now he had become a miner by rights. After a while he was charged with helping the driver of the truck that transported the coal from the mine to the train station of Ablana, which was two kilometers away. He not only helped load and unload the trucks but helped go as well to the station to reserve the cars that were needed each day for their coal. This was at 7 a.m. each day. He did his duty to perfection and even bravely challenged someone who had tried to take the cars he had already picked.[5]

Meanwhile, Celestino was in high school in Mieres in a private school and was doing so well that he got a scholarship which paid everything, and his mother had no more expenses. He was morally irreproachable, dependable and never wasted time in diversions. But for some reason, he spoke very little with his mother and brothers. Praxedes suffered much from feeling so distant from her son who otherwise was her pride and joy.

As for Gabriel, he had no inclination to study. How his mother suffered in trying to make him study! As for the son in the seminary of Las Caldas, with all that it represented, he gave her much hope, and each day meant more and more to her.

Enrique was very happy there, and was without any other aspiration than to see his efforts finally crowned with success. For this, Praxedes was most grateful to God and doubled her prayers so that this vocation would blossom completely. Sister Angeles Mellada wrote, "I heard her say, 'I only want my son to persevere!' Of this she dreamed day and night."[6] And Mother Providencia Sole, the Superior of the hospital of the Fabrica, corroborated, saying, "I can vouch that Praxedes had only one wish, and that was that with all her heart and soul she wanted to see her son a priest."[7]

Between Las Caldas and Sueros there was maintained a spiritual stream of correspondence between mother and son, which served to augment a union with God for both. Then, besides the letters, there were the personal visits. These contacts were for the time being not fully appreciated by the young man, but would nevertheless have a profound effect on his future life.

The first time that Praxedes visited Enrique was in September, 1930. She was accompanied by her mother. Father Enrique has given me some interesting details about this unforgettable meeting. In the first place, Praxedes made such an impression on all at the seminary! One of them, Father Felix Velez, 1901-1943, to whom she went to confession once, said to one of the brothers, Martin Mateos, "Enrique's mother is a saint." For her part, Praxedes told Enrique that that priest had told her things in the confessional that, up until that time, she had never heard. She judged them all as great saints and asked Enrique if his professors ever told them, for their edification, of the great supernatural favors that they received from God. "Moreover," continued Enrique, "she asked me if in such a spiritual ambience I didn't feel extraordinary effects after receiving Holy Communion. I answered that I didn't. I then asked her why she wanted to know that. She answered as though it was not important: 'Oh, nothing. The other day after I received Holy Communion, I asked Our Lord to forgive me my sins,

and immediately I felt a great heat in my breast and I knew
I was pardoned.' " With the revelation of this secret she wished
to impress the future Dominican with the sanctifying action
of the Holy Eucharist in a prolonged thanksgiving after Communion. Or maybe, like St. Micaela of the Blessed Sacrament,
she might have thought that that was a common occurrence
with everyone.[8] Then continuing her conversation on spiritual
things, she added, "Ever since I heard a sermon about St. Zita,
that she went about her domestic duties thinking of God, I
do the same."

As can be seen, the interior life was her favorite conversation. And she knew how to do it naturally, without tiring anyone. Instead, she captivated her hearers, who listened to her
with joy. Sister Reginalda Guey has declared in this respect,
"She always spoke of God, the Blessed Virgin or of holy things.
But she spoke as if she were beholding the Lord. I was in ec-
stasy listening to her."[9]

Praxedes was very sensitive to the social situation of her country, and of the mining district in which she lived. She spoke
of it to one of the priests who had been in the rectory in Mieres.

At the end of October, 1931, Enrique was moved to Corias,
Asturias to study there during his last two years of Latin. On
the way he stopped to visit his family for three days. Once
again, but in vain, they tried to dissuade him from becoming
a Dominican.

Moreover, two apparently very strong encounters were going
to help Praxedes to intensify her union with God by means
of a more elevated kind of prayer, by a more intense and difficult apostolate, and a charity more and more heroic and universal, and of a more complete union with Jesus crucified.

Chapter 18

GENOVEVA DE BRABANTE
AND SAINT TERESA OF AVILA

Guided by the Holy Spirit and always faithful to God's will manifested in the many happenings of each day, Praxedes, like the industrious bees spoken of by St. Francis de Sales, went gathering her spiritual honey from all the flowers she came across on her way—happy events, encounters, misfortunes, etc. Thus it was that Providence put into her hands two books, *The Legends of Genoveva de Brabante* and the works of St. Teresa of Avila. These had such an impact on her, way beyond our estimation.

Genoveva de Brabante is the heroine of a legend that was spread throughout Europe. Sigfredo, the Count of Treves, had to be absent from his home to go to war. He left his wife, the daughter of the Duke of Brabante, in the care of his administrator, Golo. Golo fell madly in love with her and intended to seduce her, but his plan proved to be in vain. Out of spite he accused her of adultery, and she was condemned to death by her own husband. The executioners, filled with pity for Genoveva, abandoned her in a faraway jungle, where she gave birth to her first baby. There she ate wild roots and fruits, while the baby was fed from the milk of a servant woman who lived with them in the cave. One day she unexpectedly met her husband while he was on a hunt. He proved her innocent and Golo was executed, while she was reinstated with all honors. In thanksgiving she had a chapel built in honor of the Blessed Virgin in Frauenkirchen, the ruins of which are today an attraction for tourists.

In 1927 there happened to pass by Sueros a vendor of books,

90

and among them was the life of Genoveva de Brabante. The salesman explained that this book was just what mothers of families needed to help them educate their children. And in the prologue it said, "There is nothing more important nor effective as example in education. Therefore, I offer you, in this book, one of the most eloquent and forgotten of virtues."

Praxedes was unable to resist this attractive offer. She bought it; and every evening after the family Rosary, Florentina, who loved to read and did it magnificently, for she was a teacher, read to the family. This had been her job as far back as in the days when Celestino was still living. The whole family, who were so fond of reading, used to have her read even then. Praxedes listened attentively, and once in a while she could be seen crying. From then on everyone was calling the heroine of the story "Saint Genoveva," for the author had portrayed her as a saint. After the reading in common, Praxedes would take it and read it slowly and thoughtfully. She would also take it and read it to the sick and sorrowing and thereby console them and strengthen them by hearing about this brave woman.

There were three things that attracted Praxedes in the life of Genoveva. These were her patience in the midst of the most trying circumstances after having had such a radiant youth as a duchess; her unlimited charity for the sick and the poor, never excluding those who had contagious diseases; and her love of the beauties of God's creation.

These were the three aspects so fundamental in the spirituality that Praxedes embraced. With the reading of this book, these became even more rooted in her heart, which was so open to assimilate all that was good in her surroundings. Many were the criticisms and suggestions that she heard because she attended to those who had contagious diseases! "You are going to infect your children." And when she aided the poor, "You will be our ruination." To her this was worldly prudence, almost always inspired by self-interest. But Praxedes preferred to follow the evangelical reflections that the author of the biography put on Genoveva's lips. Her charity in benefit of whoever needed it was Praxedes' constant practice, which she exercised as the most logical and natural thing to do. The day would come when she would even practice charity toward those who were considered enemies, and in fact the persecutors of the Church, but whom she never treated as such, much less as evil.

There was another testimony of Genoveva's that had a parallel in Praxedes' life. "Whatever happens to me has been disposed by God. He allows me to suffer. If He wants others to think that I am an unfaithful wife, being innocent, if He permits that from my innocence and loss of honor, some good will result, then I should humbly submit to God's will and be resigned to God's designs. My life belongs to God, as He is my all. In the end then, He is only dealing with what is His. Lord, I am Your humble servant. Do with me what You wish. Is it required of me to suffer more? Then I will, without murmuring."

We should realize that the spirituality in this story is of the highest quality, even though simple, and that it encouraged Praxedes to imitate something that she was already practicing. Every flower, plant and stone was for Genoveva a reflection of God! She was forever praising and glorifying God for His splendor and glory and power. Now that we know Praxedes' singleness of heart and her ability to adapt herself to any situation in order to better benefit from any good that crossed her path, we can imagine the impact that this book had on her.

This was without a doubt a means used by the Holy Spirit to guide her on her journey to perfection, without much human help. This was the opinion of Bishop Barbado of Salamanca.[1] These were the means that placed Praxedes deeper on the road of holiness, for she was forever solicitous of the poor and the sick. She had admirable patience in living the everyday life of a Christian with all the vicissitudes of life, and she was constantly fascinated by the natural beauty of God's creation, wherein she found His divine perfection.

In finding the works of St. Teresa of Avila, Praxedes entered suddenly into the school of the spiritual life led by the "master" who now has been given the universal honor of Mystical Doctor of the Church. It was the discovery of a hidden treasure, the "precious jewel" that the Gospel talks about. In 1929, going through her father's books, Praxedes came across the second volume of the works of St. Teresa of Avila. It was a large edition published in Madrid in 1871. It contained the following:

1) The Carmelite Rule
2) The Constitutions of the Discalced Carmelites
3) Announcements of St. Teresa to the nuns
4) Manner of visiting the convents
5) The Way of Perfection
6) Concepts of the Love of God
7) The Castle
8) Exclamations
9) Other writings
10) Seven meditations on the Old Testament
11) Documents

And it is noteworthy that far from finding the volume hard to understand, right from the beginning Praxedes felt right at home with it, as though she had known it all her life. In the things of the soul, experience helps more than education. "Give me a person who truly loves," said St. Augustine, "and that person will know what I mean." St. Teresa herself said to the nuns, "This may appear difficult, but put it into practice and it will be understood."[2] And in another place she states, "She among you who has had some experience will know what I mean right away."[3] This was exactly the case with Praxedes. From that time on, she was never without it.[4] It was her constant companion.

Praxedes was a stranger to egoism. She never discovered nor possessed any good that she did not want to share, whether it was a spiritual or material good. Gabriel[5] has told us that on Sundays in the afternoons she would call her boys and explain some passages that were not too difficult. Of all the readings she did for them they liked the Genoveva story the best. "She even read parts of the works of St. Teresa of Avila and explained them so clearly that we were often delighted and moved,"[6] said Gabriel. In this way Praxedes was able to teach her sons the most authentic means of pleasing God and thereby becoming holy. The principle there indicated was prayer, and the indispensable condition for obtaining it, namely, humility, which disposes us to accept whatever God has ordained for us and not to desire nor feel jealousy for what others have received.

"I encourage you," said the saint, "always to take the lowest place. For that true humility is necessary, in order to be able to be a servant to the servants of God and praise Him."[7] And in another place St. Teresa said, "Imagine always being the servant of all and seeing Christ in all, and in this way to better obey and respect them."[8] Praxedes knew this, being the servant of all—to her own family, to the poor and to the sick. Moreover, God gave her the joy of feeling His presence while she served others in this manner.

Praxedes took great pleasure in reading and re-reading that delightful episode of the Samaritan woman who left her pail at the well while she ran into the city to call her neighbors. "What surprises me," she said, "is that they believed a woman."[9] This incident of the Samaritan woman had a special meaning for Praxedes, for she had had to carry water all her life; but as St. Teresa would say, "Whether carrying water or working among the pots in the kitchen, the presence of the Lord is always felt."[10] Because of this realization, Praxedes lived by the maxim, "Do everything at all times as if you were beholding His Divine Majesty. Through this road much is gained."[11] This was the secret that she revealed to Enrique when she visited him on one occasion. "In the midst of all my occupations I am always thinking of God."

St. Teresa was always encouraging all to practice the habitual presence of God. She suggested a method by which Praxedes also gained much. "Fix in your mind a picture of the Lord that you particularly like. Talk to Him often. He will teach you what to say and you will converse with Him as you do with others. Why should you be at a loss as to what to say to the Lord?"[12]

Without being a religious, Praxedes gained much from these lessons of St. Teresa. Her family as well as others noticed her great recollection. Some criticized her, while some admired her. And according to Ovidio, she increased her penances to an alarming degree.

Gabriel has made reference to his mother's condition in this phase of her life, saying that it started at the beginning of 1929 when she found the works of St. Teresa. He claims that many times he found her on her knees in her bedroom in complete recollection so profound that she was apparently oblivious to all that was going on. When she would finally hear someone calling her she would have to do violence to herself to pay attention to what was being said to her.[13]

Florentina, who always liked to talk, said that "when we used to sew, she hardly spoke, and it was easy to see that she was completely recollected interiorly with God, of which I often complained."[14]

Besides her family, it was the sisters who noticed that spirit of recollection and prayer that had completely taken hold of Praxedes. "It was her soul, invaded with a deep interior peace and prayer that one couldn't help but notice. Whether she was in the church or outside, she was always recollected. She was a person of few words, very quiet, an authentic Christian."[15] And Sister Olvido Gonzalez confirmed the same in these words: "My own impression of her after knowing her well is that she is a person of very deep spirituality and virtue. I really believe that she was in constant communication with God and in His presence. The whole community thinks the same of this pious woman. Everyone spoke of her life of prayer. Not one person could find fault with her. The whole town was in accord as to this judgment. What I concluded about Praxedes is that her spirituality is authentic."[16]

This allusion to the opinion of the laity is confirmed by a young woman of Sueros, who later entered religious life. "On one occasion I was with my mother, and we stopped to make a visit to the Blessed Sacrament—and there we saw Praxedes, intensely [praying] and so recollected. When we left she was still in the same position. 'See, there have to be many persons like Praxedes to expiate the many sins of the bad,' my mother said."[17]

Praxedes was a spiritual daughter of St. Teresa and she practiced the Carmelite rule as best she could in her state in life. Praxedes would have liked to be a sister. Father Enrique told me that when he visited her in 1931 his mother said to him, "I shouldn't have gotten married! If I were young again I would hurry to the convent." He explained that this was possible as soon as her sons did not need her anymore. "Ah," she remarked, "then I will enter a Discalced Carmelite monastery." Her choice could not have been more logical. Moreover, the great reformer, St. Teresa, was truly her mother. "She is my favorite saint, and every day I pray to her," she wrote to Father Enrique.[18]

Chapter 19

ANOTHER ENRICHING ENCOUNTER: FATHER MOISES DIAZ-CANEJA

The year Praxedes discovered the works of St. Teresa, Providence sent as pastor a young priest, Father Moises Diaz-Caneja (1904-1962). He was an intelligent man, full of zeal for the glory of God and for the salvation of souls. He was well—grounded in the spiritual life, in which he guided others. It was during this time that he received an extraordinary impetus toward holiness from Praxedes. Later it would be he who would become the decisive promoter of her cause for beatification.

The new pastor was, to say the least, upset to find that Communism had such a hold on the workers of this Asturian mining district. By August of 1930 Communism had taken such a hold that this territory of Seana where the parish was located was often called "a second Russia." Every year there was a grand parade with waving red flags enlivened by deafening detonations of dynamite. All of this was accompanied by shouts for vengeance and death. The parish was considered the worst in the whole diocese.

"In Seana," wrote Father Moises, "the person who fulfilled his Christian responsibilities was the object of hate and cruel remarks. With that kind of persecution many gave up baptizing their children and even the practice of their faith. All were victims of spying, and if it was learned that their Easter duty was complied with, help and even the greeting of the day was denied them."[1]

To solve this problem of the dechristianization of his people, the pastor set up a concrete program that he knew would touch the hearts of his faithful. "Two things touch the hearts of people in regard to the priest: his attention to children and the sick," we read in his diary. To these two projects he gave himself enthusiastically. He organized religion classes, with the help of the seminarians from Oviedo. They used all the means at their command to make these classes interesting and enjoyable.

To attract the adults he initiated devotion to the Sacred Heart by bringing good preachers from the outside. He started novenas to St. Rita and other popular saints and for the principal feasts of the year. But in spite of all his efforts, his people did not change.

One day a group of his people began to throw stones at a crucifix that had been placed on a telephone pole. Upon learning of this, Father Moises ran to the place of sacrilege, climbed the pole and took the crucifix down, kissed it with tears in his eyes and walked away sadly. This bravery left the mob open-mouthed and full of admiration.[2]

But in March, 1933 the situation became intolerable. The church itself was dynamited twice. The vestments and all the statues and other ornaments were burned and the pastor was constantly threatened. In view of all this, the Bishop was obliged to remove the priest, leaving the parish without a shepherd. So on April 11, 1933 the pastor left his flock broken-hearted, that flock to whom he had been sent as a "lamb among wolves."

But not everyone was turning away from God, for among them lived a genuine Christian, Praxedes Fernandez. The first time that Father Moises had met her was a few days after he had arrived in Seana. In June, 1933 Father Enrique described this meeting that his mother had had with Father Moises, as Father Moises had explained it to him. "After being in Seana three or four days, a woman came to me to ask for a Confirmation certificate for one of her boys. I did not know her then. I saw such greatness and dignity in that woman that I was obliged to lower my eyes because I felt the strangest sensation which I cannot explain. It was as though I were a child in the presence of a queen. A few days after that I began to hear of Praxedes and of her great kindness. I decided to find out if she was the one I had met, and it turned out that she was the one."

Later on he had occasion to talk to her in the confessional, and was surprised and pleased to find out that she spent two hours daily in mental prayer. He learned also that she was physically attacked by the devil. It was then that Father Moises was convinced that she was a saint and, moreover, a prodigy of holiness. He did not hesitate to proclaim this from the pulpit later on. The presence of such a holy and chosen soul in his parish was a great consolation to Father Moises. He told this to one of his classmates, Father Fausto Rodriguez, when he came to visit him in the spring of 1932. "In this parish where so many or all have fallen away from God, there is a lady who is my consolation because of her extraordinary virtue and holiness," he said. Father Rodriguez remarked, "That happens in all parishes. There is always one person who is extra holy and good." But Father Moises insisted, "No, my case is distinct. This woman I am talking about is a very special lady."[3]

This meeting of Father Moises with Praxedes proved to be, above all, a great torrent of spiritual benefits for him. They did not converse much because her home was very far from the parish. She attended Mass and other services in the chapel of the Fabrica. It was primarily in the confessional that he became best acquainted with this person whom all, good or bad, praised so much.

It was the perfection of this great laywoman that inspired this young priest to imitate her. He admitted in his writings that for him she was the force behind his great desire for holiness. "Praxedes," he wrote, "was a model for all. She was for the sisters as well, whom had a more conducive environment for holiness, and had not reached the heights that she had. Not only the sisters knew this, but the priests and brothers as well, whom she could put to shame as she had put me."[4]

The first thing that Father Moises did in imitation of Praxedes was to spend two hours daily in mental prayer. He did this until his death. In Oviedo, where he spent the last 14 years of his life, it was this aspect of his life that gave great edification. Wherever he was seen praying, his great recollection was notable. As spiritual director to many, he recommended this practice to many, without reservations. One of his directees, Sister Maria Cloux, said that he always gave the example of Praxedes in recommending the practice. "Take two hours of mental prayer as Praxedes does. Be holy like Praxedes, another Praxedes!"[5]

It was not only to his spiritual children that he suggested this practice, but he wished also that the Holy Father himself propose the example of this chosen laywoman to the whole Church by raising her to the honors of the altar. Father Moises himself became the promoter of her cause.

He had planned to write her biography. There is a letter among his belongings in which he asks that all the then existing documents concerning Praxedes be handed over to him so that he could write the biography. His premature death kept him from accomplishing this. Among his papers, his family found some references to Praxedes. The following are some of his observations of Praxedes during his stay in Seana: "I knew Praxedes well, for she was one of my faithful from 1930 to 1933. As far as I am concerned, she was a prodigy of holiness. This was in spite of the irreligious environment in which she lived in Mieres, which was notorious for its indifferent attitude. It was here that she was born and blossomed into a beautiful person. This was not only an indifferent environment, but it was a hostile one. She was a daughter of a miner, the spouse of a miner, the mother of miners and in each phase of her life she left a ray of light, the light of good example—but above all, she proved that one can be an authentic Christian, no matter what the circumstances. It is said today, 'It can't be done.' And sometimes it is said, 'Impossible!' Praxedes proved otherwise for she, by her life, showed that it can be done. This she proved by her hours of prayer, her penances, by her spirit of service to her neighbor and through her mystical phenomenon."

In this same interview with Father Enrique, the priest told him that when he would argue with the laborers over religion, he would quiet them by asking, "There you have Praxedes who loves God so much and the Church. What do you think of that?" Their answer was, "If all Catholics were like Praxedes, then we would believe in religion."

We can be sure that the most exquisite and profound fruit of Praxedes' apostolate was her influence on her young pastor, for through her inspiration he made great progress on the road to holiness. When Father Moises died, he died in the odor of sanctity; and as the faithful passed by his casket they touched his body with objects to preserve as relics.[6]

Likewise, we must not close this chapter without citing one last thing that this holy priest said: "The greatest grace that God has granted me after my Baptism and Holy Orders is the fact that Praxedes Fernandez came into my life."

Chapter 20

THE SON OF HER TEARS

In the school of St. Teresa, Praxedes learned that one is able to follow Jesus only by carrying His cross. The Saint wrote, "It is clear that those whom God loves, He takes through trials, and the more He loves them the greater the trials."[1]

Praxedes' family, the parish of Seana and all those others who knew Praxedes do not hesitate to say that her love of God was not based on words, but rather on the total abandonment to the mysterious ways of God.

The same tragedy that took her husband was now to take her son. Two trains cross the mining district of Mieres, the Vasco and the Renfe. The first took her husband's life and the second her son's. But Praxedes was well prepared to drink to the dregs the bitter chalice offered her.

Arturo continued to be the rascal. One day he ran into the house white as chalk screaming, "Mother, Mother, I killed a little girl!" Full of fear Praxedes asked, "My son, what are you saying?" Arturo then explained that he was running very fast through the street and that upon turning one of the corners he had run into a little girl and killed her. The little girl was the daughter of Perfecta, the "Guardeza." Praxedes ran to the site of the accident, praying all the while. Luckily, she found the child in the arms of her mother. At another time Arturo was seen playing toreador with the oncoming train. On another occasion he crossed the town standing barefoot on his galloping horse's back!

We are now in 1931. In January it was now 18 months that Arturo had been working in the mine with his uncle. He had done the work to perfection, and the important thing for him was to proclaim to the four winds that he was a miner. To be a miner was the most important thing for the men of that area, and the popular songs of the time expressed it as well.

Among Arturo's peers he was the leader of the group. He was a friend to all and was loved by all. He identified with the workers at the mine. One day when his mother corrected him for one of his many offences, he felt hurt and reacted by blaspheming, as he had often heard the men do at work. Praxedes was overcome with consternation. She would rather have died than be a witness to such an offense against God. Arturo, upon seeing his mother's tears and sorrow, repented and asked for forgiveness, and promised to go to confession that same day. She offered to help him prepare himself for this confession, which should be a serious one because of the serious offence. Florentina says that she began to read aloud from a book that dealt with the punishment of Hell.

Arturo was not a bad boy. That blasphemy was probably the only one that ever escaped his lips. One of his friends, Marcelino Llaneza, has said the following: "I was with Arturo a lot. In 1930 I worked with him in the mines. Even though he was impulsive and mischievous, he had a good heart and loved his mother. It was easy to see the formation he had received. He went with all the boys in town and he was one of the leaders. He never blasphemed as did the others. He didn't even use dirty words. The most he ever said when he got angry was one of his own concocted words, completely innocent."[2]

Along with this information from his friend, Father Jacinto, the superior of the Passionists of Mieres, had this to say: "I used to hear his mother's confession quite frequently. She often brought Arturo to confession as well....I remember hearing his confession a few days before he died."[3]

Arturo proved his sincerity by listening meekly and mildly to his mother as she read. This happened on January 15, a Thursday. She was planning on taking him to confession the following Saturday, but at the last moment he was not able to accompany her. So they let it go until the next day, which was Sunday. On Sunday Arturo woke up with such a bad cold that Praxedes was afraid to take him out on such a cold day. On Tuesday Arturo was struck and killed by a train as he was riding in one of his friends' coal trucks.

That evening Praxedes had gone to El Pedroso to collect the rent from the house she owned there. Upon her return, around nine o'clock, without anyone saying anything to her about the accident—and neither did she suspect anything by the great number of people that had gathered at her home—she came in asking with great anxiety, "Where is Arturo? Where is he?" Florentina came out and said that he had been in an accident and that he was badly hurt. But Praxedes, guessing the reality, began to weep inconsolably. She cried out, "My son has died! My son has died!"[4] Then Dolores Garcia, who had brought the bad news, told her everything. The poor mother, drowned in tears, just said, "Yes, in this world I too should suffer as Christ suffered."[5] This idea of the sufferings of Jesus was well-rooted in the soul of Praxedes. Manuela Vega has said, "She suffered all adversities with such patience, submitting herself to the will of God, assuring us that we should all sustain them because Our Lord suffered for us first."[6]

The shock of Arturo's death was especially terrible for Praxedes because her husband had died the same way. This tragedy elicited the compassion of the neighbors. But she knew how to support her heavy cross so valiantly that all who saw her were filled with admiration. Her pastor, Father Moises, has told us, "She faced all her previous misfortunes with the greatest Christian patience, and this was no exception. While we were all in consternation, she remained serene."[7]

The chaplain of the chapel of the Fabrica was also impressed with the Christian resignation that Praxedes displayed. Antonia de la Uz, a niece of the chaplain, Father Luciano Fernandez, has said, "My uncle went to the house to offer his condolences to Praxedes. When he returned he exclaimed to us, 'What patience that woman has! I have never seen anything like it.' And when I gave her my sympathy she answered sweetly, 'My son was not mine but God's, who was his only owner. He has chosen to take him back. All I have to do is be content with God's holy will.' "[8]

Even more surprising was the answer that she gave her friend Encarnacion Garcia. "May God give me more to suffer, because this is not enough for me yet."[9]

The Sisters too were very edified with the exceptional way in which she supported this loss. Sister Teresa Arguellas has written, "The death of her son was something terrible. We could not speak of it without crying. God treats her like the saint that she is. That must be the reason that God sends her such heavy crosses. We noted, too, what an example of resignation she was. We considered her a martyr for the way she supported the death of her young son, without complaining and with such patience."[10]

The accident happened like this. The young owner of the truck, with whom Arturo worked transporting the coal to the station in Albana, had invited Arturo to go with him to Mieres to buy gasoline. Upon their return, as they were crossing the road and reached the front of the tunnel of La Pereda, the train ran into them—killing Arturo and injuring the owner, Juan Antonio Magdalena, in the head.

Juan felt responsible for Arturo's death. He was anxious to go to Praxedes to excuse himself as soon as possible. This is what he himself has told us of his meeting with Praxedes: "On the day after the funeral, I went in person to Praxedes' home, to give her my sympathy and tell her how sorry I was that it was I who invited Arturo to go with me outside working hours, and without her knowing it. I was afraid that when she saw me she would begin to scream and blame me for her son's death. When I arrived, she opened the door for me. She received me with such sweetness and invited me to the living room. I did not accept. When I gave her my sympathy and excuses she said, 'God has so disposed to take him and I am resigned to His will.' She also told me that she was glad that I did not suffer worse injuries. During all that time she did not shed a tear, nor did she create a scene, as I was afraid she would. I was very surprised."[11]

This attitude of beautiful resignation was indelibly engraved in the hearts of all who knew Praxedes at the time, and the passage of the years has not been able to erase this impression of her. When in April of 1964 I visited the mining district of Mieres, I spoke to Sister Pilar, who was then in her eighties, and she had this to say of those times: "When this accident brought death to Arturo, we used to say to one another, 'Look at the peace and resignation on that mother's face, in spite of the death of her son and all her sufferings.'"

As was the case with the death of her husband, Praxedes'

greatest concern with Arturo's death now was that he might have been lost because he had died without confession and the last Sacraments. Just thinking that he might have lost his soul made her tremble. This was a great suffering for her. "Your mother," Florentina wrote to Father Enrique, "was always crying because he [Arturo] was not able to get to confession after he had uttered a blasphemy. What a desolation for her! Every day she bemoaned the fact that she did not take him to confession the same day as he had suggested he wanted to go, saying, 'Mother, I want to go to confession now'."[12]

As was natural, Praxedes shared her feelings with her confessor. He recalled, "I remember the tragic accident that took the life of her 14-year-old son. She recounted the whole story that I had already read in the paper. I could sense, however, the great resignation of the mother to the will of God. The only thing that filled her with pain was the fact that her son might not have gone to God, but at the same time she was consoled by the thought of God's mercy since Arturo was such a good boy." This was Father Jacinto's view.[13]

Leaving then, the repose of the soul of her son in the hands of God, Praxedes did all she could for him, as her love and faith demanded. She offered prayers, penances and above all, Masses for his soul. She paid the stipend for the 30 Gregorian Masses and others that she could afford for him. When Celestino gave her 30 pesetas for some flowers she said to him, "These flowers will wilt and die. It is better to use this money for Masses for his soul." She also undertook such a rigorous fast that it had her family worried for her health. It was at this time that she started to go to three Masses daily. The first two were at 5:30 and 6:00 a.m. in the Passionist church and the third was at 7:00 a.m. in the chapel of the Fabrica. To be on time she took the train that left Mieres at 6:45 each morning.[14]

Heaven could not remain deaf to these sighs, and so one day at the third Gregorian Mass that was being offered for Arturo, Praxedes saw her son in the arms of the Blessed Virgin. She had him wrapped in her scapular. Full of joy, Praxedes returned home saying, "Now I am happy, for my son has been saved."[15] This was told by Florentina.

After having allowed her to carry such a heavy cross, the Lord was now consoling Praxedes in this ineffable way. From

this moment on, she never again worried about Arturo's salvation. Instead, she blessed God for having taken him before "he
could go astray like the bad companions who were beginning
to surround him," as she herself told her sister Celestina.[16]

Praxedes' love for the Blessed Virgin increased greatly, because it was through devotion to her scapular that she attributed
Arturo's salvation. She was at a loss for a means of showing
her great gratitude for this favor.

She gave this advice to Gabriel, who also wore the scapular:
"Never take the scapular off, for it was this devotion that saved
Arturo."[17]

Chapter 21

SPAIN, A TURN FOR THE WORST

The year 1931 was one not easily forgotten by Praxedes, because this was when she lost her son—and it was the beginning of great political convulsions for Spain.

Let us recall some of the episodes that brought the Church of Spain to this phase of history. In the elections of April 12, after eight years of dictatorship, the republican and socialist coalitions were overwhelmingly victorious at the polls. On the fourteenth, a republic was proclaimed and the king abdicated. A new era in the annals of the history of Spain was initiated. No one could foresee the consequences of the step at that time.

At the completion of this change, Pope Pius XI sent his congratulations to the leaders of the new government. By this movement he wished to show that the Church was not tied to any special political system, but wanted to live in peace with all. Unfortunately, it was not long before the new government showed its strong anti-religious face. On the 11th of May the infamous burning of convents took place. "All the monasteries of Spain," said a member of the government, "are not worth the life of a republican."

After the elections for the Parliament took place, on the 28th of April, the Cortes proceeded to confirm the anti-religious actions of the newly elected government. "The plan was to suppress everything that bore a religious semblance, and to usurp all church properties and establishments of any kind."[1] On the 20th of July the Primate of Spain, Cardinal Segura, published a pastoral letter in which he protested the persecution that had been unleashed. As an answer to his protest he was expelled from Spain.

The head of the government, Manuel Azana, gave an historical speech before the Congress. "That which is called the religious problem, is, strictly speaking, the implementation of
secularism by the state with all its inevitable and rigorous consequences. Gentlemen, Spain is no longer Catholic."

On November 20, the Metropolitan Bishops of Spain issued
a pastoral letter directed to the faithful, exhorting them "to
form their consciences in respect to the Church and how their
love for her should be even greater now that she is undergoing
such attacks."[2] One month later, the Parliament approved and
passed the new constitutions which completely ignored the
concordat of 1851. It imposed annoying laws against religious
orders, obstructing the teaching of religion in their schools and
colleges. It restricted the voice of the Catholic newspapers.

The growth and vigor of this anti-religious propaganda was
especially strong among the laborers in the mining zones of
Asturias. In Mieres, for example, the very same day that the
constitutions were passed a bomb was thrown at the Passionist
church. Luckily it exploded against a tree and never got inside.
A few days later the chapel of the Fabrica was profaned. This
probably occasioned the vision Praxedes had of Christ wrapped
in splendor and whom Praxedes adored.

To relive the atmosphere of those first few months in the
Republic of Spain in which Praxedes lived, we have a few very
precious memories that were told to me by Father Enrique.
He was permitted to visit his family on his way to his new
location, Corias, Asturias, in October of 1931. When Father
Enrique arrived, his grandmother's home was filled with relatives: his grandmother, Florentina, his two brothers, Celestino
and Gabriel, and four uncles with their respective wives. During all this time he never saw anyone help his mother cook,
carry water or help her in any way.

"My uncles," Father Enrique told me in 1965 while we visited
in Burdeos, "started a campaign to try to get me to give up
my Dominican vocation. They argued that it was clear from
the direction that the persecution was taking that there was
great danger for all remaining in the priesthood and especially
, as religious. My Uncle Celso said, 'No one likes the friars any
more.' He reminded me of the burning of the convents on May
11. My mother suffered much at hearing them talk like this

Left: Amalia, the mother of Praxedes. Amalia gave birth to 12 children, of whom five died in infancy; she considered them all "blessings from God." Amalia was known as a great worker, an excellent administrator, and a person of great thrift. Yet she gave alms generously, and was often asked to be a peacemaker in others' marriage problems. Amalia was very religious.

Right: Celestino, the father of Praxedes. Celestino was an intelligent and industrious businessman who enabled his family to prosper. He was also a good Christian, and a man who gave alms generously. Celestino was respected and loved by all who knew him; he was known as a gentleman of untouchable honesty and unquestioned prudence, and was often called upon to arbitrate family arguments for others. At his death, Celestino made the attending priest promise to watch over Praxedes; he seems to have had a presentiment of the sorrows that were to befall her.

Upper: The Valley of Mieres. On the first level are the dependencies of the steel mill "The Fabrica." In the background at the left is the town of Mieres, where Praxedes lived between ages 5 and 9.

Lower: "The Neighborhood of Joy," as the neighbors named the Fernandez home in Sueros because of the innocent happiness and gaiety that reigned among the family members there. In the foreground to the right is the two-story house Praxedes lived in as a young girl. In the basement Amalia set up a delicatessen and bakery, herself tending the ovens and selling the bread. The home soon became the heart of Sueros.

Praxedes at age 12. At this time she was her mother's "right arm" in the housekeeping chores as well as in running the bakery, in gardening, pasturing the sheep and tending her little brothers and sisters. Praxedes also went to school every day and frequently attended Mass. She was known for her exemplary obedience and charity. Praxedes received her First Holy Communion near her eighth birthday; she looked forward to this event with great anticipation and after returning home on the momentous day was heard to say, "I feel so happy for I have received Holy Communion today."

Praxedes playing the guitar as a young girl; she played quite well. Praxedes also excelled at folk dancing (at home), and had the most beautiful flower garden in Asturias.

Praxedes at 25 years of age; at this time she was still unmarried. Praxedes was a devout member of the Association of the Daughters of Mary, an organization for young unmarried women. A fellow member has stated that Praxedes always urged the others to place themselves under the protection of the Blessed Virgin Mary. Praxedes was very devout, prudent, mature, and kind to the sick and poor. She also had a gift for counseling others. Even at this time she was considered by many to be a saint.

Praxedes and her husband, Gabriel Fernandez Martinez, on the day of their marriage in 1914. Praxedes was soon to be 28 and Gabriel was almost 31. Gabriel was a common laborer, and Praxedes' well-to-do family felt she should set her sights higher, but Praxedes replied, "Well, he is so good and that is all that matters." The couple's first child, Celestino, was born ten months after their marriage. Gabriel

was not a religious person like Praxedes, and his temper sometimes led to violent episodes, but Praxedes won his heart by her goodness and many attentions. He often said, "For me Praxedes is the best in the world." Gabriel was to die in a train accident in 1920, just a few days after the birth of the couple's fourth child.

Celestino, Praxedes' firstborn son. Praxedes was delighted with the baby. She was also very anxious to have him baptized as soon as possible, and she offered him, as she did each of her subsequent children, to the Blessed Virgin Mary. Regarding Praxedes the neighbors would exclaim, "How she loves her children!" Long before they could talk, Praxedes taught her children to make the Sign of the Cross and had them kiss the crucifix and the statue of the Blessed Virgin; she took them to church and explained the meaning of each object, guiding their little hands in the Sign of the Cross. As soon as they could understand, Praxedes taught her children about the Passion of Jesus and why He suffered, about the Blessed Virgin, as well as about sin, the astuteness of the devil and the dangers of bad companions. She was constantly watchful over her sons' spiritual welfare, putting their eternal salvation before all else.

Arturo, Praxedes' second son, a boy who liked the outdoors and riding horses and did not much care for school. When he was almost 14 it was decided to send him to work in the mines so that the hard work would make him want to return to study. But Arturo loved mining. Arturo was killed suddenly in a train accident at age 15. His mother accepted this with heroic submission but was extremely distressed about the possibility of his eternal damnation. After much suffering and many prayers she was shown a vision of Arturo in the arms of the Blessed Mother, wrapped in her scapular. Praxedes was immensely consoled by this vision, and immensely grateful; she never again worried about Arturo's salvation. To her son Gabriel she said, "Never take the scapular off, for it was this devotion that saved Arturo."

Gabriel, Praxedes' youngest son, and Father Enrique Fernandez, Praxedes' son who became a Dominican priest.

Gabriel accompanied the author to Asturias to gather information on Praxedes after her death. He has provided many valuable stories of his mother's life and of her great charity. Praxedes' attitude was, "Charity is not practiced with leftovers for the poor. The best quality and quantity should be served to them just as to any relative." Rather than letting the poor stand at the door, Praxedes would invite them in to be served at the family table. Gabriel said, "I saw cases like this frequently." (Gabriel is still living at the time of publication of this book.)

Enrique's vocation was very precious to Praxedes. She continually encouraged Enrique and prayed for him every step of the way, often saying, "May he always be a good priest, otherwise I don't want him to be one." Praxedes died before being able to witness Enrique's ordination and first Mass. She said, "God has asked this sacrifice of me." Praxedes, too, felt drawn to the Dominican Order; she became a member of the Dominican Laity, and was buried with the Dominican scapular. (Father Enrique is still living at the time of publication.)

Praxedes' mother, Amalia, and sister, Florentina. After being widowed, Praxedes spent the rest of her life with her mother and sister in their mother's home. There she voluntarily accepted the work and status of a servant, being treated like a servant by Florentina. Praxedes lived a life of hard work, much prayer, great penance and constant charity to the sick and poor. During the Communist revolution in Spain she suffered the many physical and spiritual evils of that time, making reparation, baptizing babies in danger of death and preparing souls for death when no priest was available, and encouraging everyone she knew to practice forgiveness of all wrongs. During the terrible days of the Revolution, Praxedes said, "All this is happening because there is no prayer life and there are no sacrifices in the lives of the people." She had offered herself to God as a victim of reparation.

The most famous picture of Praxedes Fernandez, showing her wearing a dark veil. (In Spanish her name is pronounced Prahk-SAY-dus, but in English the accent is on the first syllable.)

El Puente de la Luisa. In the background to the right is the house in which Praxedes was born; in the foreground is the house where, as a young widow, Praxedes and her four boys first lived with her mother and sister Florentina from 1920 until 1926, when the entire household moved to Sueros.

The church and convent of the Dominicans. Praxedes was a lay Dominican and she owed much of her spiritual formation to this order.

Symbolic execution of the Sacred Heart of Jesus by a Communist firing squad in Madrid, Spain, 1936. The Communists destroyed the national monument by dynamite shortly thereafter. King Alfonso XIII built a new monument and consecrated Spain to the Sacred Heart. In 1952 President Francisco Franco reconsecrated Spain to the Sacred Heart and in 1954 consecrated the nation to the Immaculate Heart of Mary.

The coadjutor Archbishop of Oviedo signing papers in the process for the beatification of Praxedes Fernandez.

and begged them to stop, saying, 'Let him follow his vocation if that is what he wants!' Later when we were alone she said, 'You know that I never push you or detain you in your vocation. The only thing I want is that God's will be done.' "

During the days of his visit Father Enrique saw and heard many disagreeable things. He saw a group of laborers throw stones at and insult a priest as he was going down one of the important streets of Mieres. No one stopped them, nor said anything to them. From all sides he heard insults against the Church and its ministers. His mother, with whom he would express his feelings, explained that unfortunately the majority of the laborers were Communists and that was why they hated religion without understanding it. But she reminded him that they were not bad people.

When Enrique was in the bus returning to the seminary in Corias, he heard many of the passengers talking against the Church and criticizing the youth from Catholic Action who had a procession in honor of Christ the King of Oviedo.

In Mieres, in Sueros, on buses and in all public places the Church was openly attacked. In the parish of Seana more than in any other place, the religious situation was very grave. Not only was assistance at Holy Mass on Sundays practically non-existent, but it was impossible for the priest to carry on his ministry in any visible way. The people spoke about the priest with complete disdain.

During the times when the doors were closed to the priests, Father Moises appealed to Praxedes to help. There was, for example, a young man, Juan Antonio Alonso, the son of parents who were deadly against the Church and priests; the son was dying of tuberculosis. Father asked Praxedes to go and ask the parents if they would welcome him and allow him to give Juan the last Sacraments. She went and got permission. However, upon the arrival of the priest at their home they slammed the door in his face.

The young man died shortly after that in the arms of Praxedes, to whom he listened with great peacefulness and love. She had visited him every day, saying the Rosary with him, talking to him about the Passion of Our Lord, His mercy and the glories of Heaven, and of the goodness of the Blessed Mother. She prepared him well for death and even accompanied his body to the grave. She returned for nine days to recite the Rosary for the repose of his soul. In the meantime Father Moises wrote in the parish book of the deceased, "Today, December 16, young Juan Antonio Alonso was buried. He was not able to receive the Sacraments of the dying because his parents refused to allow it." During that year Praxedes helped with the dying, four of whom received the Sacraments. She also baptized four babies who were in danger of death.

Untiringly she visited the sick, wherever they were. A mother of six children who was tubercular, Trinidad Gonzalez, lived in Figaredo where Praxedes went once a month to collect the rent. She always visited her on these trips. Once after Praxedes spoke to her about resignation and death, she answered quite skeptically, "It is easy to talk like that when one is well. I wish I could see you in my place!"

"Very well," answered Praxedes, "I will show you something if you promise to keep it a secret. If God so wishes, I will put myself in your place and gladly die." Moved by curiosity, the sick woman who was resisting death with the excuse that her six children needed her, promised her silence. Praxedes then rolled up her sleeve and showed her blackened arm. It was black as coal, according to the sick woman. "Do you see how this arm is? This is the way my whole body is. This is how much I care to live."[3]

Penance, and extraordinary penance at that, had always been part of Praxedes' life. She saw this to be even more necessary now because of the hapless death of Arturo and of the turbulent conditions of anti-religion and politics in Spain.

Beginning with June of that year we have some precious documents, the letters that Praxedes wrote to her son who was in the seminary. In her letters of 1931, we looked in vain for some mention of the events in Spain at that time. But she did not say a word about them. She did not complain about anyone or anything. In a letter dated June 15 she alluded to devotions to the Blessed Mother and a grand procession in honor of the Blessed Sacrament which took place in a neighboring parish called La Rebolleda. Although she did not mention why it was held, it was probably in reparation for the desecration of the Blessed Sacrament in the chapel of the Fabrica. She also told him, "Celestino was enrolled in the confraternity of the

Passionist Fathers. He goes to Communion every month."

On July 15, Enrique's birthday, Praxedes wrote joyfully that he continued firmly in his vocation. "I see that you are greatly interested in receiving the holy habit. I am very happy over this. If God so wills, you will receive it and if not, may His will be done, and not ours." It is admirable to see how she looked at everything that happened as God's will. And in view of his success and happiness at the seminary she said, "I am very happy that you have received good marks in your seminary classes. I thank God and St. Thomas Aquinas, to whom I pray every day for you and your brothers." This filled a theology professor at the seminary, Father Manuel Cuervo, with surprise and joy. He said to Enrique, "I congratulate you in having such a mother. Women are by nature more pious, but they generally don't have devotion to the Angelic Doctor!"

Thus did this marvelous woman deal with the human and the supernatural. Everything in her was admirably ordered. Instead of creating anxieties and concerns in her son by telling him of the growing irreligiousness that she came across every day, she preferred to encourage him in his studies and talk about the good side of things. She was not one of "these prophets of doom," as Pope John XXIII said of some. It was not her style or her temperament. Praxedes was always and in all circumstances—and even in the most critical—"a sower of peace and joy," to quote the words of her old boyfriend, Jose Alvarez.

Chapter 22

THE SEARCH FOR SACRIFICE

Praxedes believed that voluntary suffering, accepted and joined to the Passion of Our Lord, contributes to the salvation of the world. Suffering with Him, we atone for our sins and the sins of others. For this holy soul, it was a devotion that helped to re-establish the equilibrium of life destroyed by sin.

The question for Praxedes was what to do to compensate for the evils done by the enemies of God? Her answer was to redouble her generosity in prayer, and in sacrifices so that "the Lord will forgive the persecutors and sustain the persecuted," as is the Gospel formula. This answer had to do with God, the Church, the salvation of people and of the faith of Spain. We see Praxedes confidently seconding the voice of God from on high, which was calling her to be a victim for her country. She began to immolate herself with frightful penances that make the most robust cringe. She kissed the floor frequently. She put dry peas in her shoes. When she sewed she pricked her fingers. She gave up most of her sleep, as much as humanly possible. She was always up by 4:00 a.m. so she could go to the 5:30 Mass.

But above all she fasted and disciplined herself, following the Constitutions of the Discalced Carmelites and the example of the great saints of the Church. At first she gave herself the discipline in her room, but the sound gave her away and so she went to the chicken coop. "Why do you do that, Praxedes?" asked her sister-in-law Teresa. She answered, "To go to Heaven one must do penance."[1] One day when she was late in coming in, her mother sent Florentina to see what she was doing. "I walked very quietly so that she could not hear me

112

coming and I found her whipping herself hard with a leather strap! 'For the love of God, woman, what are you doing, killing yourself? Why do you do this?' I asked her." Praxedes answered, "Don't you see how the world is? It is necessary to do penance for the conversion of sinners."[2]

Fasting was another of Praxedes' great penances, because St. Teresa recommends it in her constitutions. Father Enrique told me that his mother confided in him that she fasted three days a week. She hardly ever ate breakfast. She almost always gave her supper to some poor person, and her lunch consisted only of one dish. On Fridays she ate only one tablespoon of chick peas, and on Saturdays she fasted on bread and water.[3] She ate candy only on Easter Sunday.[4]

Praxedes was very beautiful. Nevertheless, she never looked in the mirror, even when she combed her hair. Naturally, the ones who noticed her were the women who lived with her. Teresa Bolea said, "She never used the mirror. When we were in the sewing room, she purposely turned her back to the mirror when she combed her hair. If by chance she had a smudge on her face when she came from the kitchen, either Florentina or I would tell her."[5] Praxedes started this penance because of the Carmelite Constitutions, which read, "There should never be a mirror in your room nor other luxuries, but be indifferent in your looks."[6]

But it was not her lack of vanity that troubled Praxedes' family. It was her fasting and disciplines. This exasperated them greatly and made Ovidio say indignantly, "I curse the confessors who ask you to do this." To this Praxedes answered, very upset, "Please don't speak of God's ministers in that manner. It is not they who ask me to do it. I wish to do it."[7]

Upon my first visit to the mining district of Asturias in April, 1964, Sister Pilar Vila, by now a senior sister, told me an interesting episode that well reflects the thinking of Praxedes' family toward her penances. "It was a Sunday morning and we were returning from Mass. Amalia was walking with me, as Praxedes had gone ahead a little to cross a bridge. Her mother, pointing to her, said 'Scold her, Sister, because her mortifications are going to kill her and I am now too old to care for her children.' Praxedes heard her and turning to Sister, said, 'Sister, don't believe that it is as bad as Mother says.' "

One particular incident reveals more clearly than any other the holy interior of her spirit and the motive for all of her penances, during that dark night in the history of Spain. The Countess of Mieres and owner of the Fabrica met Praxedes, accompanied by Gabriel, who has told us of this meeting. The illustrious lady began to lament the terrible conditions across Spain. Then Praxedes, with great boldness and without fear of offending her, put her finger on the wound. She exclaimed with the bravery of the authentic daughters and sons of God, "It is important to make many sacrifices, many sacrifices."[8]

Chapter 23

A CHRISTIAN OF HER TIMES

In 1932 a grave offense was enacted against the Church. On January 23 the government decreed that the Jesuits be expelled from Spain because they added obedience to the Pope to their canonical vows. The government officials considered the Pope a dangerous foreign power.

In Rome Pope Pius XI protested before the Consistory; and in an encyclical which he issued he declared, "This injurious decree thrust against the divine authority of the Vicar of Christ has caused a grave wound in our paternal heart."

Praxedes too felt the wound in her heart, for she was a loving daughter of the Church and of the Pope. She was scandalized by the repressive measures that the government took against the religious orders' way of life, to which her son belonged.

Another law initiated by the government affected her in a very special way. The government had confiscated all the cemeteries that were Catholic, and had prohibited the placing of crosses on the graves without special permission from the civil authorities. In a letter that she wrote to her son in the seminary on January 26, Praxedes said, "Today I received permission from the civil authorities in Mieres to place the cross over Arturo's grave. I was anxious to do this."

These annoying laws against the Church darkened the religious climate of Spain. Priestly ministry was becoming more and more difficult as time went on, and especially in Seana. Father Moises had set two priorities in his pastoral ministries, the children and the sick. Some of the children still went to Mass, although the number got smaller and smaller. But the sick people no longer called him. Since he was denied entrance into their homes, he continued to rely on Praxedes to take his place. She did this with great zeal and tact, and with her went the Lord.

On January 13, Ludivina Losa died. Praxedes had visited and prayed with her daily. Finally, she stayed with her in her death—and burial as well.[1] Sixty-five-year-old Victoria Salgado died on April 15 without receiving the Sacraments. But Obdulia Iglesias has told how she was visited by Praxedes daily; Praxedes talked with her about God and prepared her for her holy death.[2]

As time passed, Praxedes baptized three babies in imminent danger of death, as well as a baby who later got well. She baptized a baby girl named Presentacion, who later died, and another child called Josefina Iglesias who died when 11 months old.[3]

Praxedes did not forget to pray for her own families in their sicknesses. Two of her cousins, Ismael Llaneza and Eloy Fernandez were both very ill. The latter was already more dead than alive, but both were cured when Praxedes prayerfully placed a medal of the Blessed Virgin on them.[4]

On June 19, a neighbor, Engracia, died. Hers was the first funeral in Sueros, where there was no priest present. Florentina has told how she went to the funeral, thinking that the priest would be there. When she saw that he was not there she immediately returned home, very angry. Praxedes stayed and went into the hall to pray the Rosary for the repose of her soul.[5]

In the month of August, upon the recommendation of her doctor, Praxedes went to Gijon to spend a few restful days with her cousin Florentina, who was the daughter of her Uncle Nicanor who loved her so much. One day she returned quite late and her cousin asked her what had delayed her. "I went into St. Joseph Church," answered Praxedes, revealing yet another secret of her spiritual life, "and when I was praying in front of the Altar of Our Lady of Mount Carmel, it seemed to me that the Blessed Virgin was talking to me and I lost track of time."[6]

During this month of August another of her heroic acts of charity was recorded. When a neighbor, Luisa Gonzalez, had a heart attack, Praxedes visited her every day and prayed the Rosary with her. At the same time, she encouraged her to carry her cross of sickness with patient endurance. "She would tell my mother that she must suffer with patience because Jesus had suffered for us too,"[7] Luisa's daughter said. When Luisa was moved to a different house higher up the mountain, Praxedes continued to visit her twice a week until she died.[8]

Her ministry to the sick and dying did not interfere in the least with fulfilling her duties as mother and homemaker. She also visited her seminarian son in Corias, accompanied by her mother. On one of these visits, after breakfast on the day after she arrived, Enrique ran to the visitors' quarters where his mother and grandmother were staying. When he did not find Praxedes right away he asked his grandmother where she was. "Where else would she be but in the church," answered Amalia. He found her there saying the Stations of the Cross. After waiting for her to finish he said, "You come to visit me and you spend the time in church." To this she answered lovingly, "My son, at home I have so much to do that I can't dedicate all the time to prayer that I would like. It is only right that here, where all I have to do is visit you, I should give Him a little more of my time."

In her conversation with her son, Praxedes spoke about things that would strengthen his vocation, as an apostle of the Word. She talked of the need for penance and for confessing the Faith without the fear of human opinion. She told him of a personal experience that proved her point. "One day on the way to Mass at the Fabrica Chapel there was a lady walking in front of me, also going to the chapel. A workman was going in the same direction and began to make fun of her and tried to make me do the same. 'How can I make fun of her when I too am going there?' " she told him.

Upon her return to Sueros, Praxedes wrote this to her son on September 19: "I was a little dizzy when I arrived. In Oviedo I went to Mass at St. Isidore's. Then at 3:00 p.m. we went to the station to take the train for Sueros, and at 5:00 I was already at the Rosary Chapel for Benediction."

From her letters one cannot sense the hostility that reigned in the mining district. She just wrote of everyday family affairs, of liturgical celebrations, and of her strivings each day to get her boys to be good Christians and good students. "I pray, my son, that you will be successful in your studies. You must apply yourself much, for God says, 'God helps those that help themselves.' "[9] On his nameday she wrote, "Pray often to your patron saint so that you will never dishonor his name with your faults, and that you will someday come to the same port to which he came, to enjoy your reward as he does."[10]

In a letter dated March 22, Praxedes' apostolic soul was once more revealed as she again wrote her son in the seminary. One can almost feel the zeal that burned in her heart for the salvation of all humanity. "I only wish that you become a great preacher; that your words will touch hearts and, like the words of the prophets, will convert many and take them to eternal life. This is your mother's wish. May God see fit to have it thus." In a letter of June 9, she gave him this rule of life: "I want very much that you apply yourself in your studies and that you be humble and obedient to the priests there and that your faith will grow more and more. Pray very much for us. These are the desires and wishes of your mother, who embraces you and loves you very much."

Among the family news in her letters there are some characteristics that show Praxedes' beautiful character and joy of life. She wrote, "Your Uncle Celso and Aunt Consuelo are here visiting us, with their two little ones. They are very sweet and smart, as well as playful. The little boy goes up and down the stairs without holding on to anything. If someone wants to help, he refuses. And he is only two and a half years old! The little girl sings and tells stories with such artistry. We are well entertained with them." When Uncle Celso and his family came it meant that Praxedes had 11 in the family to care for. For this reason her correspondence was a little slower with her son, as she fondly explained. "My reason for my not writing any sooner is that your Uncle Celso and his family are staying here. Every day I thought of writing you, but the little ones are so lively that they can't be left alone for a moment." Soon Consuelo got so sick that Praxedes had to take care of her, which meant that she had to give up going to Mass and Communion every morning, which was "the sun" of her spiritual life. In a way she envied her son, who could freely go to daily Mass and Communion. "Since you are privileged to attend Mass and Communion every day, pray for us all as I cannot go now, for Consuelo is ill."

But in all of this we can see that the obligation of charity came before her personal devotion. Her piety was such that it never kept her from wholeheartedly fulfilling her duties. No one can accuse Praxedes that her piety was troublesome to others. After all, she only "left God for God."

Remembering her apostolic charity for her family and neighbors, while never losing her sense of humor during the days of persecution, one can compare Praxedes to St. Thomas More, "the saint for all seasons." But this saying is better applied to Praxedes as "a saint for all circumstances." In any case we can give thanks to God as the Bishop of Oviedo, Javier Lauzurica, said, "for having brought forth in our hostile world souls such as this holy woman's, whose example constitutes a calling to persons striving for Christian perfection and a holy life, so that neither the obstacles nor the environment will overcome them."[11]

This is how the year 1932 passed and ended, always with the same ideals of prayer, penance, untiring work, material as well as spiritual help to the poor, the sick and the dying, and her concern for her sons' future.

Chapter 24

THE CENTENARY OF THE REDEMPTION

The year 1933 opened the Jubilee of the Redemption. It was convoked by Pope Pius XI to commemorate the 19th centenary of the Mystery of the Resurrection.

In Spain the Holy Year was truly the "hour of the powers of darkness." Systematic persecution by the government and the anti-religious furor of the masses reached an incredible climax. The civil authorities tenaciously pursued plans to exterminate the Church by suppressing the teaching of religion in the schools. They ordered the removal of crucifixes from the walls of classrooms, refused to pay the clergy and began nationalizing all Church property.

For their part, the enraged rabble freely burned convents and churches without the government taking the least trouble to prevent them. The workers of the mining districts of Asturias and Seana (the "second Russia," as they were called) were among the leaders in the acts of violence against the Church in Spain.

Praxedes lived in the heart of this hostile area, deeply united in the best way possible to the mystery of the Redemption during the Holy Year. Some words that escaped her on Good Friday of this year paint a picture to help us see the conditions of her life. We are also able to tell what was happening around her through her letters. The first letter we quote is dated February 8. In it she congratulated her seminarian son for the good marks he received for the first semester. "I congratulate you for your good marks. This fills me with joy because I see that you have applied yourself and want to be like Celestino. God willing, you will continue like this."

As was customary in the family, patron saints were assigned to each member of the family, including the absent ones, for the new year. Without mentioning any particular reason, Praxedes wrote the following phrase that leads us to believe that things were not very stable nor tranquil: "May the saints be our guides as we pass through the dangers and obstacles of this world and may they not abandon us until they leave us in Heaven." And nothing was more natural than to pray for the family. "It gives me great joy to know that you pray for me and for your brothers. It is only just that parents pray for their children, and that children pray for their parents."

Praxedes always had psychological equilibrium in her role of mother and educator. All her activities were inspired from above. One of the boys' teachers had this to say about her dealings with Praxedes: "Being her sons' teacher, I often had to speak with Praxedes regarding her boys. In 1933 I taught Gabriel, and in speaking to me about him I noticed that she was not interested only in his studies, but above all in his spiritual development.[1] She was concerned about his conduct outside the school." She communicated her concern for Gabriel's spiritual growth in a letter written about him in February. After she told how he was inscribed in the Childrens' Eucharistic Crusade of St. Tarsicius, she said, "He goes to confession and Communion every First Friday and also goes to Nocturnal Adoration."

Praxedes also had to face the hard realities of providing for her family. Her brother-in-law bought the house that she had managed in Figaredo and left her deprived of the 20 pesetas a month that she formerly received from the rent. "Now," she wrote, "it is 20 pesetas less that I receive."

Attentive to all the happenings around her, Praxedes lamented the hardships caused by the frequent strikes that lasted for long periods of time. She suffered much seeing the sufferings of the laborers and their families, to whom she had belonged since her marriage. She wrote, "The laborers of the Fabrica and of the mines are on strike again. I don't know when all this will be resolved." During these periods the laborers did not receive salaries and their families suffered hunger. Praxedes suffered as well, because she did all that she could to relieve the situation—many times going without food herself.

Her life continued full and intense. In a letter referred to before, where Praxedes told her son that she prayed that his words as a preacher would be like the Prophet's, she ended by saying that God willing, it would be thus. These words were inspired, no doubt, by her deep faith in God, for we see that Father Enrique has spent his whole life preaching the Gospel in Spain, Mexico, Cuba, Costa Rica, and especially in the United States of America. He has been preaching missions for over 20 years from California to Florida and in northern Ohio. He preaches an average of 25 week-long missions a year. This is a splendid apostolate. Father Enrique considers it miraculous through the intercession of his saintly mother, who he believes is praying incessantly for success in his work of preaching salvation for the world.

Sensitive to the least sign of attention or concern, Praxedes was overcome with emotion when her millionaire brother gave her a most generous gift. "Your Uncle Ovidio," she wrote, "gave me a thousand pesetas now that he has retired from mining. He said that he remembered how well Arturo worked there and that he wanted to do this. He really had no obligation in this because Arturo did not die at work. He is so good, and his goodness is expressed like this."

But the turbulent and social situation seemed to get worse in the country, which was such a contrast to the beautiful panorama of the fields. During the year of the Jubilee of the Redemption, the powers of darkness extinguished the religious life in the parish to which Praxedes belonged. This was something that did not happen anywhere in Oviedo, nor in all of the rest of Spain.

The anti-religious first tried to destroy the parochial church in Seana so that the few who still went to church would find themselves with no place to assemble. On the night of March 28 a bomb exploded in the back of the church, leaving a large, gaping hole and destroying many objects of devotion. On April 1, Oviedo's newspaper, *Region*, announced in giant headlines on page 13, "Efforts made to blow up the Seana church." Then after giving all the details, the reporter added, "As citizens of Mieres we strongly protest these acts of terror that so express the wretchedness of the cultural betrayal of our people."

This was when the Bishop decided to transfer Father Moises

from Seana, because his life was in grave danger. On April 4 he was sent to San Roman de Villa Parish. Nevertheless, he remained in Seana until after the Holy Week services, which were during the 9th to the 16th of April.

Praxedes wrote about this particular Holy Week without ever saying a word about the bombing, as was her way. By temperament she was inclined to see the good and beautiful, and she told her son how the occasion was celebrated with such "recollection and solemnity." Then after describing in detail the liturgical celebrations in the parish and at the chapel of the Fabrica, she ended by making reference to the Resurrection; this reveals the important place that this feast held in her interior life. "The Feast of the Resurrection is the most beautiful of all the feasts in the Church. It seems that peace comes alive in the hearts and souls of all."

Praxedes lived this Holy Week with more intensity than ever. She fasted every Friday of the year, eating only a little in the evening, and as Sister Amalia Villa[2] has testified, she fasted from Holy Thursday until Holy Saturday, without eating anything. On Good Friday her godmother, Elena Garcia, died—and Praxedes kept watch all night on Thursday until Friday, again without eating. Her maternal uncle, Manuel Fernandez, who had communistic ideas, tried to force her to eat by saying, "Praxedes, if you don't eat, I swear that I will be buried civilly." In her concern she begged him not to joke about that. But she remained firm in her rigorous fasting.[3]

After the burial Praxedes assisted at the liturgical services, which were then celebrated in the morning. Upon her return home she felt sick and had to lie down, weakened by loss of sleep and fasting. When Florentina brought her a cup of coffee she heard her say, "I wear the crown of thorns." She also noticed that there were dried chick peas in the shoes which Praxedes had worn to the burial and to church.[4]

On Easter Sunday the sickness left her. Filled with the joy of the Resurrection, she began to sing. When Florentina heard her she ran to tell her to stop, as the aunt had just died. To this Praxedes answered, radiating with joy, "It is because the Lord has risen!"[5]

In that same letter she talked about the May devotions, and about the beautiful flowers, and about the wonderful climate.

No one would ever guess, in reading this letter so full of the smells of spring, that in Sueros and in the parish of Seana such sad happenings went on. The parish now had no pastor. In the same neighborhood was the Dominican School, which the people hated as much as they hated the priests. On May 5, when the superior's feast day was being celebrated, the people gathered outside the convent at eleven o'clock at night and stoned the convent until midnight. There was not a window left. The frightened sisters expected to be killed at any moment. These were the same sisters who had chosen to come here to these laborers to teach their children! We can imagine the pain Praxedes felt at this act.

This was bad, but something worse happened on Sunday, May 15. It happened to be the eve of the beginning of solemn vespers in honor of St. Rita. In Seana this was one of the major celebrations. On this eve, the same group that had bombed the church returned, accompanied by hundreds of strangers. They bombed it again, and this time it was left unusable. A month later they returned and smashed all the images in the cemetery and also burned the remaining benches from the bombed-out church building.

When the Bishop had sent Father Moises away from Seana, he had asked Father Ramon Merediz from the neighboring Rebolleda parish to look after the spiritual needs of the people there. Every time that he tried to fulfill his duties, the people there would throw rocks at him. The Mayor of Seana himself one day gave him orders never to set foot in the confines of the parish again. "I will return," answered the priest, "if someone calls for me." The Mayor said, "Very well, then, you will suffer the consequences."

Such was the vicious climate in Praxedes' parish in Seana in 1933. As Sister Felisa Canal said, "She offered up all her sufferings for the offenses committed against the Church."[6]

Moreover, the persecution was spreading throughout Spain with renewed furor in this Jubilee Year. On the Feast of the Assumption, August 15, the bishops once again issued a joint letter denouncing the innumerable abuses against the Church. One week later the Supreme Pontiff issued an encyclical proclaiming before the whole world "the unjust situation created against the Church in Spain."

If there was anyone in total agreement with the Holy Father, it was Praxedes. She had been convinced, and had tried to convince others, that the only solution to this terrible state of affairs was prayer, atonement, forgiveness for the culpable, and obedience to the pastors of the Church. Her greatest hope and wish in these sad, hard times was the Dominican vocation of her son. One can sense this in the birthday greetings she sent him on July 15 of that year, in which she said, "God willing, may this day and all the rest of your life be passed in great joy and peace. May God shower you with special gifts and happiness. May He also give you much patience and Christian resignation for the mishaps of life."

In a letter in March Praxedes had encouraged her son's preaching through the world with the zeal of a prophet; now she wanted him to be a man of learning. "May St. Thomas Aquinas," she said, "give you much quickness in learning so that you may become an eminent scholar."

As we have seen, Praxedes always wanted to be positive in her correspondence, because as St. Paul says, charity "is not ambitious, seeketh not her own, is not provoked to anger, thinketh no evil; rejoiceth not in iniquity, but rejoiceth with the truth."[7] "What great peace and joy you must have felt on this special day. I can just see you (in my imagination), how you must look like an angel all dressed in white. What is important now, my son, is that the Blessed Virgin accompany you at every moment of your life and that Our Lord never leave you, for he who walks with God, God walks with him."

But being a mother, she could not help but shed tears because she was so far from him. In her next letter she wrote, "When I read your letter I couldn't keep my tears back, for now I realized how really 'apart' you are from me." She also spoke about a planned visit to him in Salamanca that never actually took place. What was important to her was that he continue to persevere in his calling as a Dominican. This is what she talked most about in her letter of November 6.

Now as a Dominican novice, Enrique added Joseph to his baptismal name in honor of St. Joseph, the husband of Mary. Praxedes commented, "I see that you have changed even your name. I am so happy to see that you have chosen the Holy Family to guide you in your religious life. To this same family

I always prayed that they would give me success in educating all my children well. I see they have granted me this desire. I am fully satisfied because the three of you are on the right road. There is no greater joy for a mother than to see her children well educated and with a profession. This is the main obligation that we as parents have in this world."

Celestino had just registered at the University of Oviedo to study law. Gabriel was just starting in the Mieres High School, which was under the direction of a priest when Enrique had become a Dominican novice.

Satisfaction for the present and dreams for the future. "How I had hoped to be present when you received the habit, and how happy and proud I would have been to be there! The obstacle was the great distance. But I do plan to be there for your first profession. Then when you sing your first Mass, what a great occasion for both of us! May the Holy Family accompany you at every instant and open the gates of Heaven for you." These were beautiful plans, but tragic events and circumstances impeded the fulfillment of them.

Praxedes' fundamental goal was to orient all toward God. Thus she carried out all her activities most discreetly, whatever they might be. This was seen during the November elections of that year.

The protests of the Bishops of Spain and of the Holy Father's encyclical, urging the faithful to get behind their pastors to remedy these injustices, created a deep echo in the hearts of all Catholics who had remained faithful. They united to defend their faith in the elections of November 18. This was also the first time in the history of Spain that women were allowed to vote!

Praxedes answered the Holy Father's call "for the defense of God and country." She did not understand politics, but she could see that some parties such as CEDA and Accion Nacional defended the Church openly, while the others fought it to the death. For her, as for most faithful Catholics, there was no doubt as to what party deserved her vote. She undertook discreet political activity during the campaign. To her relatives and friends she passed out fliers which had one line: "Vote for Those Who Defend Religion."[8]

Those who defended religion were overwhelmingly

triumphant. This filled Praxedes' heart with joy and gratitude. What mattered most to her was the fact that those who defended the Faith had won. Consequently an era of peace and fervor would follow, after the Church had suffered such persecution for two years.

In that atmosphere of security and joy, Praxedes celebrated Christmas with a lively jota (a Spanish folk dance). Her letter to Enrique arrived two days after Christmas because, "My intention was that you would get my letter by Christmas so that you could celebrate it with more enthusiasm, but the many things to be done got in the way and spoiled my good intentions. I hope that Christmas Eve and Christmas Day were happy and full of joy, as this is the happiest feast of the year. It was wonderful for us. We bought special holiday bread and killed some chickens and had a dance Christmas Eve with Grandma, Gabriel, Dolores, another lady and myself."

Enrique was finding the novitiate hard and rigorous and begged his mother for prayers. She told him of an infallible means to victory: devotion to our Blessed Mother.

He asked her once about comments made about his being a friar. She satisfied his curiosity by saying, "Around here some know that you are a friar and some don't. And in spite of the fact that they are not very religious, they think it isn't so bad. In another letter I will give you more details about this matter." The interesting thing is what Praxedes thought of her neighbors and how she assessed them. Remember that they were anti-Catholic and, as we have seen, they knew how to demonstrate it...nevertheless, for her they were not truly bad.

Later, in another letter, Praxedes gave news that filled her with consolation: "Gabriel is doing very well in his studies. His marks are above average and more. I thought that he didn't care about studying, but now I see that I was mistaken. You have no idea how happy I am in thinking that, please God, he will have a good profession. When we would tell him that he would have to register to go on with his studies, he would cry and couldn't sleep. I was afraid he would get sick. But now I am very much at peace and happy. Thanks be to God." She ended her letter and that Holy Year of the Redemption with this wish: "May God shower you with many gifts and favors and may He give you peace and joy of soul!"

Chapter 25

"YOU ARE THE MOTHER OF THE POOR"

The Jubilee Year of the Redemption was marked by the most ferocious "power of darkness." But we know that that hour was also the hour of the redemption.

Praxedes lived through that tragic period, until her death, more and more in union with the Redeemer and always responding to the light of the Paschal Mystery.

As a true daughter of the Church, like St. Teresa of Avila, she faithfully obeyed the directives of the bishops in their bold pastoral letter of May:

—Parents should send their children to Catholic schools only;

—Remain faithful to the Church in these dark and sad times and do not fall into the temptation of seeking revenge, for only God is competent for this;

—More than ever, perform the Works of Mercy;

—Be eager to cooperate in the apostolate;

—But above all, work, be alert and pray without ceasing.

All this Praxedes continued to do as she had done in times past. Work and prayer constituted a great part of her deep spiritual life. Her hard struggle to support her boys and her life of prayer were never an obstacle to her duties as parent. She had always enrolled her children in Catholic schools. As for vengeance, it never even crossed her mind. When Gabriel would make angry remarks against those who bombed churches his mother would always say, "No, my son, don't say that they are bad. They are good and have a good heart. What happens is that they do not know what they are doing."[1]

As for works of mercy recommended by the bishops because of the mounting misery of the working class, we have already seen what Praxedes used to do. But now during these tragic times, her charity reached unsuspected heights.

The events of those depression years multiplied the material as well as the spiritual needs of Praxedes' neighbors, and thus her compassion grew as well. Time and again she came across the miseries of the poor, and each time she overcame them with her characteristic charity and attention. The very same hatreds and rancors among which she lived seemed to foster the growth of genuine Christianity which inspired all those around her.

An interesting episode demonstrates very well how Praxedes practiced her Christian charity. Marcelina Vasquez, the wife of her cousin Eloy, had stopped in to say hello to Praxedes. Upon entering the kitchen she noticed a youth comfortably seated at the beautifully set table, eating an abundant meal. Marcelina was suprised to learn that he was not a relative, but a beggar, and she let Praxedes know that she thought it very strange. "Charity," Praxedes commented very simply, "is not practiced with leftovers for the poor. The best quality and quantity should be served to them just as to any relative."[2] And without giving it another thought, she washed the beggar's dishes after he left.

I got this information in April, 1964, from Marcelina, in the street not far from the house where Praxedes was born. It was during my first visit to Asturias. I was accompanied by Gabriel. While hearing this story, a neighbor, Amparo Robledo, came up and exclaimed, "Ah, are you looking for facts concerning Praxedes? When I was a child, my mother became a widow and so we became very poor. There were eight of us children. Every morning Praxedes brought us breakfast, shared from her own table."

Gabriel also commented, "I saw cases like this frequently. I remember a certain teen-ager who was all marked with chicken pox. Uncle Ovidio found him eating in our kitchen once and scolded my mother. He told him that he was a loafer and that he had quit his job in the mine for no reason at all."[3]

From the time she received the 8,000 pesetas for Arturo's death, Praxedes began to aid the poor, not only with food but now with money, which she had been unable to do before. She left 100 pesetas under the pillow of one of her patients, an amount which at that time was quite significant.[4]

No, Praxedes did not practice charity with leftovers. It was with her own food and later with that of some of the members of her family, which she gave to the poor. Even though her mother was charitably kind, Praxedes said that this particular practice of hers did not please her mother; but she did not feel she could be exempted from it to satisfy her. She said that on one occasion her mother scolded her for being so thin because of her concern for the hungry. Then they watched to see if she ate. They found out that she continued to share her food with the poor.[5]

This was her way, and there is a French saying that illustrates perfectly what Praxedes did for the poor: "The way a gift is given is worth more than the gift." Marcelina Vasquez has emphasized, "What impressed me was the respect she had for the poor when she aided them in any way. She never left them at the door, as was customary when charity was given. She always asked them to come in and then hospitably attended them. This made such a great impression on me that I do it now."[6]

Evidently those who received Praxedes' charity returned not only to thank her, but to receive more, because they knew they would be treated kindly. We know of a certain Joaquin de Canera, a dwarfed beggar who was retarded and who used to be welcomed in Praxedes' father's house long before she was married. He continued to be welcomed and cared for by Praxedes until he died. She would help him decide what to to with the money he got from begging. She even did his sewing for him. Although he always arrived quite untidy, he always left clean and well-dressed.[7]

When Father Enrique visited me in Burdeos in 1965 he told me about Joaquin. "I don't remember when I first saw Joaquin. It seems to me that I knew him all my life. He was part of the family. When he came to our house, which was quite frequent, my mother received him with such great joy that we, upon seeing her treat him thus, acted the same way. When he came he was always dirty and needed a bath. She would wash his clothes and boil them to make sure that they got thoroughly clean. He would sit at the table with us and stay to pray the family Rosary. He stuttered, but it never occurred to us to laugh at him. She taught us to love him, even with all his impediments. His visits were always special."

This was the treatment Joaquin received until his death. Gabriel recalled, "The last time he came he was sick and Mother put him to bed, fed him and attended him as though he were one of her sons. Seeing that he was gravely ill, she called the doctor. She filled his prescriptions and took care of him until the doctor had him transferred to the provincial hospital in Oviedo, where he died."[8]

Praxedes was especially kind to poor women. The neighbors remember Rita, the blind one, and Maria the beggar. They were always cared for by Praxedes. Gabriel recalled, "Sometimes they remained in our home as long as they wanted. Mother never asked them to leave."[9]

The caretaker of the church in Seana, Arsenio Alvarez Diaz, tells us that one day as he was passing by Praxedes' home there was a little girl begging at the door. He saw Praxedes take the little girl to buy her a pair of sandals, as she was barefoot. Then he heard her say, "Be sure to come back and I will give you a bag of clothing." Arsenio also saw her giving food to a man who had just arrived in town looking for work in the mines.[10]

Praxedes used good psychological common sense mixed with great kindness to determine what was best for each of her poor. There is the case of the 12-year-old, Jose Antonio Robledo, one of eight children of a poor widow. He gratefully made a sworn statement testifying that "every day Praxedes visited me while I was sick, bringing me meat, fish, milk, fruit and bread, until I got well. She treated me with such kindness!"[11]

What else could a sick and hungry child want? And his poor mother, who could not afford to give him even the necessities, how grateful she must have been. Praxedes herself was a widow and she knew well the worries of supplying food and medicine for the sick.

The destitute Curieses family tells us that their home was only a few steps from Praxedes' and that to avoid being seen when giving them food, she would often give it to them through the back window. She would call Justa and give her meat, bologna, eggs and other foods for her family. Unfortunately she was sometimes discovered, and Justa could hear her being scolded for her charity. She would just say in tears, "Is it a sin to do charity?"[12]

However, Praxedes did not wait for the poor to come to her. She went out looking for them to help them. Wherever there was suffering and want, there she was. "When I was sick in bed," declared Dolores Garcia, "she came to care for me and bring clothes for my children."[13] On payday all the poor of the district went out to beg at the gate where the miners came. Praxedes, who had to pass by the gate on the way to Mass, stood there too, giving alms. A witness said, "She helped us with alms and consoled us like a true mother."[14]

That often-repeated reproach of her mother, "You are going to give everything away," was exactly Praxedes' measurement of her charity. She gave herself, as well as material things, to all who had needs. She even went so far as to help even in cases where there was great physical danger of contagion. This was the case with Teresa Fernandez, "a sick woman who had little courage while suffering the dreaded sickness of tuberculosis, with running ulcers on her legs and arms."[15]

"No one wanted to go near her because of her repugnant sickness," declared Marcelino Llaneza.[16] Praxedes had begun helping her when her husband, Benito Lopez, lost his job. She visited her when she went to the public fountain early in the morning to get water. She would hide the food she took her in the pail. By visiting her at this time she would not be missed at home. While on her visit she would clean Teresa's house and her bedroom, change her bandages, wash the kitchen dishes, and give her money for her needs. While talking to Teresa, Praxedes would sit on her bed—and her cheerfulness gave the poor sick woman the courage to go on living. To get to Teresa's home Praxedes had to climb the hill that separated Sueros from Reimeses, where Teresa lived. "Why are you in such a hurry?" asked a little girl who was worried at seeing her so tired and in such a hurry. Without stopping, Praxedes answered, "My poor, sick lady is waiting for me and I must hurry."[17]

One day a neighbor came to Praxedes' home to tell her mother that Praxedes was crazy, for she was visiting Teresa who was full of tuberculosis and that soon everyone in the house would have it. The reaction of both Amalia and Florentina was alarming. They were both petrified, for to them there was nothing so terrible as to be exposed to this sickness. Immediately Amalia called Praxedes and in no uncertain terms told her, "I prohibit you from ever visiting Teresa again. You are endangering the health of everyone in this house. I do not forbid you to give her alms but don't ever go to her home again."

Without saying a word, Praxedes began to cry inconsolably. Florentina was touched by her sorrow and interceded with her mother. "Look, Mother, let her go once more to explain everything to Teresa and to tell her to send one of her children for the alms." But in the end Praxedes convinced them both that there was no danger of contagion. She knew how to take precautions. She wore a special gown when she went there and which she kept hanging behind the back door. Moreover, she washed separately and disinfected in the oven the plate and utensils she used. She also knew how to use plenty of alcohol. Finally, her mother gave in, but reluctantly. Praxedes continued to care for Teresa until 1934, when she was taken to the provincial hospital of Oviedo where she died a happy, Christian death.[18]

There was another case similar to Teresa's. A woman who was called the "leper" lived near the public fountain of Sueros. She had already lost her nose, and her face was quite deformed. For this reason the people of the town never entered her home. But Praxedes visited her, cleaned her up and encouraged her to carry her cross.[19]

"For my family," Justa Curieses has assured us, "Praxedes was truly an angel. She always gave us the best quality of food. She was like a mother to me and my six brothers and sisters. She did the same thing for other families in Sueros and other places farther away, like Reimeses and La Feidosa. I saw her many times with a basket of food to take to these places."[20]

Gabriel has told us who these "other families" were which were alluded to by Justa. They were the Huelmo, Alvarez, Losa, Arguellas, Alonso, the Leopoldo and Luisa families, the Jonas and Isidra families and the Dosinda and Jacinta Sanchez family.[21]

Aurora Fernandez, in a sworn statement of October 1, 1966, testified that she saw Praxedes take breakfast every day to Celedonio and Ceferina, his wife, who also lived near the fountain. Marcelino Llaneza also remembered the same couple when he talked to me in 1973. "Among the poor that Praxedes administered to was an elderly couple who lived near the public fountain, Celestino and Ceferina. He begged until he was no longer able to."[22] Florentina also told us of another family, the family of Leonor Gutierrez that Praxedes visited.

There was another aspect to Praxedes' charity, and that was that she would not listen to the criticism of anyone not present. Her sister once criticized the priest for being distracted. To her Praxedes said, "Please don't talk about a minister of the Lord."[23] And to Gabriel, who insisted on convincing her that those people who stoned the convent and burned churches must be very evil, she said, "No, my son, don't talk like that. They are good people, but they don't know their religion and don't realize what they are doing."[24]

A notorious opportunity to criticize and gossip was when women would gather to sew. Maria Alonso liked to join Praxedes and Florentina for sewing. She testified, "She never gossiped. If anyone was criticized she always had an excuse for it. If the conversation deviated to gossip she would say, 'That shouldn't be said. One may not talk ill of anyone.' "[25]

The reputation that Praxedes never allowed anyone to be maligned in her presence was well-known in her town, and it soon spread throughout the region. Father Jacinto, the superior of the Passionist Fathers of Mieres, has told us that once he was visiting with Ramona Canga in her home when Praxedes passed by. Upon seeing her she exclaimed, "Look, Father, there goes Praxedes, who never allows anyone to talk evil of anyone in her presence." And Father Jacinto added, "She told me this with such spontaneity that her fame must have been well established."[26]

In the process of the canonization of St. Martin de Porres, one of the witnesses affirmed that "Brother Martin was the father of the poor, the only remedy and consolation of them all."[27] The same was said in regard to Praxedes. Marcelina Vasquez gave this sworn statement: "A beggar in front of me declared to Praxedes one day, 'You are the mother of the poor.' "[28] This is the title that best describes Praxedes.

Chapter 26

THE CHARITY OF CHRIST IMPELS US

With her simple and luminous Christian vision, Praxedes understood that charity for souls far superseded that of charity for bodies, no matter what self-denial was involved. She knew very well, as St. Louis reminded Joinville, that it is preferable to have leprosy in the body than sin in the soul. Moreover, she knew how to work for the salvation of souls through ministration to the body, just as the great saints of Christian charity did.[1] Those were Praxedes' tactics.

One day Praxedes was leaving the house with a delicious pudding that she had just made. Upon seeing what she was taking to her sick patient, her mother scolded her for making such a costly dessert. She, however, calmed her mother by telling her that she did it not only to help her patient's health but also to win her over so that she would consent to receive the Sacrament of Extreme Unction before dying.[2]

She acted the same when she gave alms to the poor who came so frequently and in such great numbers to her home. She took these opportunities to talk to them of their religious duties.[3] But let us look at some concrete cases.

Leonor Gutierrez was a neighbor who, like the majority in Sueros, had no religion. Her health was very poor, and she was in bed often. Praxedes visited her and took care of her and did all she could to convert her. In fact, Praxedes baptized one of her babies who was very sick and died shortly after that.[4]

Maximina Fernandez had a cancerous growth on the left side of her face. At times the pain was so great that she screamed. Praxedes visited her over a period of four or five years. She encouraged her to sustain her pain with courage and accept it as a cross. One of Maxima's daughters heard Praxedes say to her mother, "Suffer with patience, for we must be resigned to the cross the Lord sends us."[5]

Let us recall too the case of Trinidad Gonzalez, who refused to accept death. Praxedes, realizing the will of God, told her she offered her life instead if it were God's will.

During the last visit she paid her son in the seminary in August, 1933, Praxedes told him that she was finding much resistance among the sick to receiving the Sacraments. She told him that she found that telling them about the peace that those who did receive them experienced helped them want to receive them.

But Praxedes' apostolate was not limited to the sick and dying. Whoever needed help got it, be they rich or poor, Christian or atheist, educated or ignorant. Wherever there was anything wrong in Sueros, there she was to remedy it. When she learned that there was a couple not married in the Church, she did not rest until, after 50 years, they had their civil marriage rectified.[6]

A messenger of reconciliation, Praxedes took peace to all in turmoil. "When the neighbors quarreled among themselves she knew how to bring peace to them," said Sara Alvarez.[7] But above all she was successful in bringing peace to the households of the brusque miners. One day Praxedes heard the screams of a teenage girl who was being punished by her father because he had heard that she had returned alone from Mieres. He had given orders that she was never to do this. Praxedes intervened because she had such high regard for the girl, Justa. Since the father, Victoriano, esteemed Praxedes highly, he stopped as soon as she appeared on the scene. They proceeded to look into the matter and found that Sara had in fact returned with the neighbors. Peace and calm returned to that household in no time.[8] Praxedes was indeed held in high regard among the laborers.

But more frequent were the occasions when the laborers went looking for Praxedes to settle their family problems. This filled her brother Ovidio with peace, because he had been worried for some time that Praxedes would be in danger since the people were so irreligious. "The neighbors," affirmed Ovidio, "sought her out for advice and to look for solutions to their family problems. My sister took advantage of all the opportunities that came her way to instruct and sanctify the people of the town."[9]

Since they were without a priest in their parish, it was to Praxedes that the faithful turned. She did her utmost to represent the priest in the most effective and dignified way. She baptized babies that were in danger of death, helped the agonizing to die in a holy manner, and urged those who had not completely lost their faith to fulfill their Easter duty. She was also present at all the wakes, accompanying the bereaved and praying and speaking to the people about the mercy and love of God and the promise of eternal life.

All this created some friction in her home. Ovidio, who passed long periods of time with them, argued that Praxedes was interfering in things that belonged strictly to a priest. He was afraid the people would one day turn against her as they had against the clergy.[10] In the face of this criticism, Praxedes resolutely took St. Teresa's words and made them her own. "May God be praised and understood a little more, and may the whole world shout it out."[11]

Moreover, Ovidio's fears were totally ungrounded. The neighbors received Praxedes with open arms, and not one case has been found in which anyone rejected her. This respect and attention given her by everyone without exception is truly wonderful, considering the times of irreligiosity that then prevailed in Sueros. Ovidio himself later said in a sworn statement, "I believe that my sister was never disliked by anyone, and if anyone ever did have something against her it was not said, for fear of her prestige among the people."[12] But the love and estimation of the people in these anti-religious surroundings did not make Praxedes' apostolate any easier.

And real dangers proved to be more than words, as can be seen from the following incident, which could have ended in tragedy. Praxedes was on her way to the chapel in the Fabrica, and when she crossed a bridge she noticed that she was being followed by two men who were saying to each other, "Shall we throw her into the river, shall we?" A neighbor of hers, Valeria Alvarez, overheard them and went to Praxedes, begging her not to continue going to the chapel, as she was exposing herself to danger. But Praxedes smilingly said, "Let them throw me in if they want to, I shall continue to practice my faith."[13]

Those were indeed heroic words and actions.[14]

Far from being intimidated, Praxedes took the situations of life in hand and became stronger and stronger in the confession of her religious convictions.[15] She did not live her faith solely for herself, but she touched all those with whom she came in contact. One of the clergy review publications had an article on her entitled "Apostle of the Unbelieving Laborers."[16] Through Praxedes, the love of Christ was made a reality among the workers. And even though on many occasions she was not able to see any results from her labors, her apostolate bore fruit.

These laborers not only respected Praxedes, but also loved her. When Father Moises argued with them, he would invariably shut them up by merely saying: "There you have Praxedes, who is so Catholic. What do you have to say against her?" They would in turn answer, "If all Christians were like Praxedes, we would believe in religion."[17] It was the bravery of her Gospel living that they saw and experienced that obliged them to respect and love her, even though religion was for them "the opium of the people."

What Praxedes sowed among tears and sufferings would in due time blossom and bear fruit. The following anecdote supports this. In 1965 the Capuchins of Gijon published a beautiful calendar of Praxedes with a colored picture of her on the cover. Some of these were being sold at the parish church in Seana. A certain Maria Rigo, a Mierian neighbor of Praxedes, bought one, saying, "My husband is from Sueros and he knew Praxedes very well. As soon as he heard that these were being sold he sent me to buy one before they ran out, saying, 'I don't believe in the saints, but if they had lived like my neighbor Praxedes, then I would believe in them.' "[18] This man was a miner.

This is one flower of a beautiful bouquet opening 30 years after the sowing.

Chapter 27

A FALSE CALM

The overwhelming victory of the Christian parties of the right in the elections of November 19, 1933 created an illusion that the religious problems had been resolved once and for all. Praxedes was one who shared the mistaken belief. It was in this expectation of peace that the year 1934 began.

The year started out with Praxedes attending the wedding of her niece by marriage, Primitiva Fernandez. Primitiva had often visited her, not only to make her payment for the house rented in Figaredo, but also to receive counsel. They both enjoyed these periodic meetings. Primitiva would usually come in the early evening when Praxedes was washing the supper dishes. Praxedes would fix her a snack and Primitiva would proceed to bare her heart to her dear aunt.

Praxedes had engraved in her heart the words of St. Paul: to think on "whatsoever things are true, whatsoever modest, whatsoever just, whatsoever holy, whatsoever lovely, whatsoever of good fame," and his charge that "if there be any virtue, if any praise of discipline, think on these things."[1] She lived these words with enthusiasm and dedication. She found the good in things and persons and instinctively rejected all that was negative. She was a woman who "never talked about anyone," as Father Jacinto overheard a woman describing her to a neighbor in Mieres.[2]

Everyday joys and sorrows, preoccupations and hopes were all a part of Praxedes' life. On the 17th of February she wrote her first letter of that year to Father Enrique. In it she told him all that was happening. Celestino was very sick with a cold and was having trouble with his weak lungs. This worried her. It had been a raw winter. But the family news also had its funny side. Amalia was now 75. Every so often, especially during this period of peace, she relived the days of the Neighborhood of Joy, and she would sing and dance. She loved to repeat the fable of "The Milkmaid." "She gives us much joy and happiness," wrote Praxedes, "especially when she is like a band of street musicians. When we see her so happy, we ask her to do it again."

And on and on went the news of one or the other: a visit from Uncle Ovidio, who had brought Gabriel a pair of boots; letters from Ismael and Celso; a box of fine candy came from relatives in Andalucia, and so on. Everyone in the far-flung family, as we can see, was interested in one another, and the children of their widowed sister were not forgotten.

In between the family news there was a remark which shows us that the social conditions in the country were, if not worse, just as bad as before the famous elections. "It is two months that the factory has not paid its workers. They say it is broke. The workers work now and will be paid later. We'll see how this goes. May God help us so that all will turn out well for the workers." In telling the condition, the sad news, Praxedes showed how well attuned she was to the workers' problems. Her only hope was her trust in God, and she continued her acts of charity without ceasing.

In the meantime the defeated leftist parties looked for a comeback through subversion. The daily paper of Madrid, *The Socialist*, ran this giant headline on February 4, 1933: "The Revolution Is Inevitable." It was alluding to a Russian-style revolution. It went on: "War of the classes! Hatred and Death to the Bourgeois Criminals! Concordat? Yes, But Only Proletariat Ideas That Want to Save Spain from Mockery. Happen What Will Happen, Attention to the Red Disc!"

And in the month of April the Communist leader Largo Caballero announced, "There are going to be events of such a nature that it is important that the laboring class act together to bring about their success. Without a doubt, at a given moment the proletariat will rise violently against its enemies. Let it not be said that we are uncivilized savages."

In that same month, the family insisted that Praxedes be checked by a doctor because she had been going regularly to help Teresa, the tubercular patient. Florentina, a cousin of hers, went with her and told us of an extraordinary discovery when the doctor examined Praxedes. "We went to the medical center to Dr. Jose Dominguez of Mieres. As he was examining her he discovered that she had a cross and on each side the letters J and M, the initials for Jesus and Mary, carved on her chest. The letters were two inches high and the cross a little higher. The doctor was stupefied and asked, 'What did you use to engrave these on your chest?' Praxedes answered, 'With a hot hook.' The doctor then looked at me and put his forefinger to his temple indicating that she was crazy. Upon leaving the office Praxedes never said a word about the incident, not even a comment."[3]

There was no trace of tuberculosis, but what the doctor did not know was that St. Jane de Chantal, who surely was not crazy, had done the same thing on her chest. Did Praxedes know this? What we do know is that a saint of the Dominican Order, Bl. Henry Suso, had also engraved the name of Jesus on his chest with an awl, and a picture of this saint in the act of doing it was found in Praxedes' prayerbook. After all, are there not those who have the names of their loves tattooed indelibly on their bodies? The love of Christ, accompanied by the love of neighbor, can reach this "madness" as well.

On the 30th of April Praxedes again wrote to Enrique and told him all the family news and anything else that she knew would interest him. "Aunt Florentina is still very well-preserved and the years seem to pass her by! Grandma is very heavy, but she loves to eat. We bought a radio and she sits by it all the time listening to music, theater and an infinity of things. She enjoys it very much."

Enrique had told her of the death of one of the Fathers, the first one he had seen die. His mother, always disposed to capture the spiritual, commented, "I am always impressed by the tranquility with which the priests and sisters die! To live more tranquilly in this world it is better to take whatever happens, good or bad, joyfully and resigned to the will of God." This was the program of her life, no more and no less.

"If God would give us teachers directly from His hand, how we would obey them! But in reality all the events of life are our infallible teachers which He has sent us." This maxim, written by Pascal after meditating on the mystery of Jesus, can be said to be Praxedes' norm of life. All the events of life, good or bad, no matter from whence, express the Divine will, as St. Paul says, "to the good of those who love Him."

Holy Week, the Great Week for Praxedes, with its incomparable crowning event of the Resurrection, had now passed. She never failed to tell Enrique how she spent this week. This year, with the attempts of sacrilege in the parish church, there were no services in the parish. She had not previously told this to Enrique, but now it was necessary to break the silence and tell why.

"We missed the Holy Week services in the parish of Seana. It is about eight months [in reality it was ten] since they threw a bomb into the church that destroyed the pulpit. About a month after that they burned all the statues in the cemetery and all the priest's vestments. I did not tell you before so that you would not suffer, but it is necessary for you to know so that you can pray for them." Praxedes did not tell all, intentionally, for they had bombed the church a second time and it was left useless.

In May the Feast of St. Rita was celebrated. It was the major feast of Seana and attracted hundreds of visitors. Praxedes could not help but voice her concern at not being able to celebrate it this year, and she felt that she had to tell the reason. "The Feast of the Ascension is approaching, and also the Feast of St. Rita. At this time the wounds of what they have done will be renewed. We are hoping that we will be able to get a statue as nice as the one we had and that the church will once again be full. May St. Rita, the Saint of the Impossible, pray that those who have caused all this suffering and damage will have true sorrow for their sins, and may she lead them on the right road!"

Alluding to the Feast of the Resurrection, Praxedes said enthusiastically, "This is the greatest feast, and full of graces for those of faith."

Then came the letter of June 20. Gabriel had now finished his first year of high school. Uncle Ovidio and his wife had visited, as had Enrique's godmother. Also, Antonio and Maria's son Jose had died. May he rest in peace. Praxedes did not say that she visited him during his sickness and that she had helped him with money. We know this because Maria declared in a sworn statement, "My son died of meningitis, assisted by Praxedes. She visited him every day while he was sick and prayed with him. She placed a medal at the head of his bed, and when he died she waked him and assisted at the burial. On two occasions she left 50 pesetas under his pillow."[4]

Jose, who was only 16 years old, died without the Sacraments. This happened not because he or his family wanted it that way, but because of the situation in Sueros. There was no priest available. Praxedes saw to it, however, that he was well prepared to die. One of his brothers gave the details. "Since my brother was not getting any better, Praxedes prepared him to receive the Sacraments. We tried to get the priest to come from La Rebolleda, as we were without a priest in Seana. Father Ramon Merediz did not come, perhaps because he was threatened. They told him that if he tried to cross the River Caudal they would throw him in. It was then that Praxedes stayed with Jose during his agony and until he died. We were not even able to have a Christian burial. After that my grandfather Jose Llaneza died, but before he died we tried to get a priest. My uncle, who was a socialist, accompanied me and we got Father Ramon Merediz. As we passed near the Fabrica someone spoke up and told Father that he had no business in our parish, and the leaders harshly reprimanded my uncle for this action."[5]

Jose died a holy death on June 7, 1934. Because there were no priests for his funeral, the Communists used the occasion to put on a demonstration. They covered the coffin with a red flag and accompanied the body to the cemetery. However, the Church had been represented in the person of Praxedes.

In her letter of July 13, after wishing Enrique a happy birthday, she spoke of interesting future plans. "We are thinking of moving to Oviedo to live there." Several months went by, however, before this came to pass.

On the 5th of August, Sister Felisa Canal came to visit her sister, Sister Maria, who was teaching in the school at the Fabrica. Praxedes went to visit them and the three talked happily. Sister Felisa remembered the conversation well: "I remember that we spoke of the hard times that Spain was experiencing because of anti-clericalism, and especially in the district of Asturias. Praxedes said, 'There is nothing to fear. The only thing that should preoccupy us now is the many souls that are being lost. We have to pray that these poor people will be converted.' My sister then told me, 'This woman is very penitential.' To this Praxedes answered, 'I have offended God so very much that the little I can do to make satisfaction for my sins is not much, for I am a great sinner.' And referring to her son who was now a Dominican novice, I said, 'You must be a happy mother, very happy.' To this she answered, 'Indeed, I am very happy. I only long for the day on which I will see him a priest. But if the Lord will not give me this joy, His will be done. All that I do I offer to God so that my son will be what I so much want for him.' "[6]

In her letter of August 9, Praxedes told Enrique of the fervor and enthusiasm with which she celebrated the Feast of St. Dominic. "I went to Mass and assisted with special devotion. In the afternoon we went to the Rosary and Benediction. Your grandmother and I went. We were remembering how we spent the day with you in Corias last year."

More and more Praxedes felt a closeness to the Dominican family, especially now that her son was a member of it. Even though she had told the sisters at the school that she did not feel worthy of being a Dominican,[7] she ended by entering the Third Order of St. Dominic for the laity, now known as Dominican Laity. She entered on August 16 and took the name of Catalina, in honor of the great Doctor of the Church, St. Catherine of Siena. At this time Sister Maria Canal loaned her a copy of *The Dialogue* by St. Catherine of Siena. "Now I am a Dominican," Praxedes exclaimed, radiant with joy and wiping away joyful tears.

In the school of St. Catherine of Siena, besides learning about prayer as she had from St. Teresa of Avila, Praxedes was inflamed by a passionate love of the Church and "for the sweet Christ of this world," the Pope. Her understanding of the seriousness of sin compared to the light of the sanctity of God was deepened by the writings of St. Catherine of Siena, for in these writings she has written of the call to generous souls to make reparation for the offenses done to Divine Love through deliberate indifference, by neglect and hatred. She urged all children of God to plead for the conversion of sinners.

In her September 26 letter, without giving any reason, Praxedes told Fray Enrique that Celestino was not going to board at the residence run by Father Jose Villanueva. "Pray to God that he will find a good home to board at, that he stay away from bad companions and occasions of sin, and that he continue to study well. I am truly sorry that he will not be at the residence because he went to daily Mass and Rosary. This certainly did him much good."

The local feasts outside of Seana were celebrated with great joy and fervor. In her letter she mentioned the Feast of Sts. Cosmas and Damien in the parish of Valdecuna to which she, her aged mother and Gabriel went. ·

As Fray Enrique had told her mother of all that they did to honor our Blessed Mother, she responded admiringly, "I am so excited about the way you honor our Blessed Mother. You do it with such enthusiasm! Let it be from the heart, for as you honor her on earth she will see to it that we will be rewarded in Heaven. Pray much for your brothers and for the rest of us so that she will always help us in our necessities." It would not be long, however, when all this would soon be changed, for day by day plans were being woven to bring all this to an end.

"Attention to the Red Record!" once again the newspaper, *The Socialist*, in its September 27 edition, repeated. "Next month may well be *our* October. Hard, trying days await us. We have our army mobilized, our international politics, and our plans for socialization."

During 1934 the attacks against the churches and ecclesiastical persons had multiplied throughout the mining district. The newspaper *Region* had boldly announced on page 13, "For the second time the church, La Rebolleda, was the object of an attempt at burning." The same newspaper said on March 31, "The Socialists intend to assault the church in Mieres." On May 22 it gave an account that really touched Praxedes: the church of Figaredo, the church where all her children had been baptized, had been burned. Then after reporting that the main altar had been totally ruined, the paper added, "We are confident that this incident will go unpunished, as were all the others of the same nature."

Without doubt the newspapers did not tell everything. There were other sad occurrences that Praxedes knew about that were not told in the papers. In September of the same year a group of Passionist students were leaving their grounds to go on an outing when they were attacked with stones. One of the students was hit on the head and injured seriously. He remained in the hospital for 25 days. Father Segundo wrote in 1935, "The threats became so bad that it was necessary to place guards on top of the walls surrounding the monastery every night, for it was at night that they became more violent. Undoubtedly, our monastery was not set on fire solely because they were afraid of the guards on the walls. In the face of this wave of hatred and violence, one wonders why they hate so much."[8]

Praxedes lived in the midst of all this hatred and violence, always reaching out in love and kindness.

Chapter 28

"LIKE IN RUSSIA"

The revolution finally arrived, like an unexpected earthquake. The organizers had planned it for the early hours of the 4th and 5th of October. We have read in a folder put out by the government in Madrid,[1] "The Marxist revolution enters its active and catastrophic phase, bursting with violence and potentiality as had never been seen before. Its offensive power was enormous and its means extraordinary."

False notices were received from different parts of Spain, cleverly distributed by the revolutionaries. They said that the Civil Guard had been completely destroyed by fire and the bombings of the rebels. Communication with Asturias was completely cut off. The revolution had arrived at its height.

In Madrid, at 8:30 in the evening of that Saturday, a shot was heard in the Carreteras Street, and the strike was on. It was then that the voice of the President of the government, Mr. Lerroux, spoke to the people by radio. "In face of the present situation, the government is now proclaiming a state of war in all the country, and will apply martial law without weakness or cruelty. All Spaniards must now be shamed by the madness of a few."

The forces of order soon dominated the situation in Madrid and in all the provinces except Asturias, where the revolutionaries triumphantly put up their red flags. The historian Carlos Seco Serrano, professor at the University of Barcelona, has written, "The revolution of October was fundamentally the revolution of Asturias, where the revolt resulted in terrible consequences."[2]

The following plan for the revolution in the principality was described by Arturo Vasquez, the leader of the Asturian syndicate. "The revolution was to be at 3:00 a.m. on October 5 in Asturias. The signal was a blackout caused by cutting off the electricity, so that the darkness would make it a more complete success. The first act will be the assault and complete destruction of the forts of the Civil Guards. The red terror will be established and a special revolutionary tribunal will be created for the purpose. When all the resistance in the small towns is overcome, then we will take Oviedo. The attack will begin on the morning of the 5th of October."[3]

The struggle began at this early hour. From Sueros the miners' shots could be heard against the civil guards who were stationed in the old school at Cano, which had once belonged to the Dominican Sisters, and where Praxedes had received her education. By the morning of the 5th the mining district was completely in the hands of the militants. With the coming of daylight, the pillage began with the burning of the archives of the municipal government and with killings and detentions of the enemies of the revolution. Mieres was the center of a social earthquake that threatened to destroy everything. "Mieres," wrote Joaquin Arraras,[4] "was converted into the capital of the Asturian revolution. Here came all the miners to confirm the revolution, seeing that the tide had turned in their favor, the success of the revolution." The municipality had 42,000 inhabitants; and of those, 7,000 were miners and another 1,000 worked in the Fabrica.

Bewildered by the explosions, the Passionists decided to abandon their monastery. At 10:00 in the morning the exodus began. Two of them, one 17 and the other 23, were brutally assassinated. Two others decided to escape by following the tracks leading to Oviedo. Shortly some women and children saw them and began shouting, "There go some friars! Let's go get them!" Hearing the shouting, Praxedes fell on her knees and begged God to protect them. As they left the railroad tracks two men chased them, and as they were turning a corner they took out their revolvers to shoot them—but the guns jammed and would not fire. Thus the friars' lives were saved. They themselves were able to tell their own story.[5]

On that same day the pastor of Valdecuna was killed at the door of his rectory. This was the parish to which Praxedes' husband had belonged. That evening 16 bodies of priests and civil guards were piled up in the cemetery.

That night at 10:30 the most horrendous explosion was heard. It shook all the homes all around. A witness said, "It was the most terrible explosion ever heard in Mieres, and made the homes close by shake and those farther away vibrate."[6] At once everyone knew that it was the bombing of the Passionist Church. There was not a stone left upon a stone, and all that which was inside flew up into the air, leaving only a few walls standing. After the explosion "all was profaned. The women dressed in the priests' vestments and proceeded up and down the streets. With the sacred chalices and other ornaments, they celebrated their banquets and orgies. The rest was stolen, destroyed and profaned."[7]

Praxedes' family, naturally, was not on the side of the revolutionaries. A few months before this someone had tried to set their house on fire, but with the help of the neighbors it was put out and saved. Someone was overheard saying, "We should have let the house burn and all those in it." No one would speak to them nor even greet them. The local revolutionary committee had given orders that they were not to be given milk, which was so necessary at that time. This measure made Praxedes cry for her children, who hardly had anything to eat. Before long, however, Enrique Lleneza, her cousin, defied the orders and brought them milk himself.

The only ones that went out were Gabriel, at that time an adolescent of 14 who was curious to know what was going on, and Praxedes. Because she continued to be respected by everyone, she was able to get water for the household needs and to look wherever she could for food for the family.

Those were bitter days, above all for Amalia and Florentina. Florentina told me in 1964 that during those days they kept the doors and windows closed and locked. They watched the goings on through the cracks. They did not dare sleep in the house at night; so, accompanied by their revolutionary cousins, they went to sleep in Aunt Maria's home.

The neighbors from Sueros went to search and loot the Dominican school and convent. The sisters had fled to a private home. In Mieres the militants sacked homes, banks and stores, taking whatever they wanted.

On the sixth day the march toward Oviedo began. A witness related the event in the newspaper *Estampa* of Madrid. "I saw the revolutionary miners and I declare that it was a frightening sight. They were carrying baskets, pails and bombs and were yelling 'Onward comrades!' As they walked they kept throwing sticks of dynamite that they lit with their cigarettes. The noise was terrible." The march was mobilized at Mieres with buses and trains. They were carrying black and red flags. Florentina walked out onto the balcony and pretended to be on their side by saluting them with a fist in the air, but in reality she was trembling from head to foot.

Gabriel saw her and laughingly told his mother, but Florentina tried to justify herself saying, "If I found myself in danger of death for being a Catholic, I would do what they say one of our queens did during the Moorish captivity. In words she did not say she was not a Catholic, but in her heart she confessed her faith." Then looking at Praxedes she asked her, "And you, what would you do?" Praxedes answered, "As for me, even if they killed me, I would confess that I am a Catholic." These family scenes were told by Gabriel and Florentina in 1964, while we stood there looking at the railroad on which the militants rode that day.

Arrests, killings, stealings, all these were the order of the day. Sixteen priests were killed that day in the municipality of Mieres, as well as several of the laity. The churches were used as prisons, while the prisoners from the jails were set free to proclaim the triumph of the revolution.

In Oviedo the miners destroyed the Holy Chamber of the cathedral and burned both the Church of St. Dominic and the convent. They also bombed the university, the Institute, the barracks of San Pelayo and the theater Campoamor and innumerable private and public buildings. They continued mercilessly to shoot seminarians, priests and religious.

They confiscated all the food in the stores and forced the merchants to give out the food gratis, requiring only ID cards. Praxedes took advantage of this and went to Puente Luisa, where her cousin Eloy had a delicatessen store; but as she took the food, she recorded it so that she could pay him later.

On the 10th of October Father Luciano Fernandez, chaplain of the Fabrica, was assassinated after being forced to dig his own grave. Praxedes passed the days weeping in prayer and doing great penances. She even walked to Mieres with dried chick peas in her shoes. She hardly ate and repeatedly said, "All this is happening because there is no prayer life and there are no sacrifices in the lives of the people."[8]

The militants tried to make Celestino join the red army. He resisted and they said to his mother, "He better not cause us any trouble. It could cost him dearly." Praxedes was afraid that they would kill him, and she began a novena to St. Monica for his safety. Her eyes were red with crying and her feet were swollen by her penances.

In the meantime the government attacked the miners from different directions with army units and even dropped bombs on Mieres from planes, causing several casualties. The battles lasted for two weeks before the miners were overcome and Oviedo taken.

Upon the government's victory, in Praxedes' home they hugged and wept with joy. Celestino was overjoyed, and Gabriel ran to Mieres to see the triumphant parade. Praxedes, however, fell on her knees to give thanks to God for the longed-for peace. The revolution was over in Asturias, leaving great destruction and many deaths. There were 1,034 deaths, among them 34 priests and seminarians; 2,071 gravely injured; 58 churches bombed; 60 bridges blown up; 26 factories destroyed; 63 public buildings razed and 730 homes destroyed.[9]

Praxedes lived all this minute by minute. With her were her mother and sister, almost scared to death; and her sons, Celestino the anti-revolutionary, and Gabriel, the curious adolescent who always went out and listened to what was going on so he could bring the news home.

Luckily we have a curious document in Praxedes' own handwriting in which she tells all that they had lived through. It is a letter that she sent to Enrique, seven days after the catastrophe. "Sueros, October 26, 1934. My very dear son, Fray Enrique, At last I am writing you to let you know that we have passed through a flash of great sufferings on account of the revolution. It began at 5:00 a.m. I got up immediately upon hearing shots. They were shooting at the civil guards. In just a matter of time Mieres was in the hands of the revolutionaries. For 14 days we lived as if in Russia. We could not even

mention the name of God. Celestino would not venture out.
One day on my way to get something to eat, one of the guards
told the woman I was walking with that he had orders to shoot
anyone who would mention the name of God. On another day
they came to get Celestino to register in the revolutionary army.
He refused to register. They then told him to watch out and
he had better not cause any trouble, or they would imprison
him. I was afraid that for this they would shoot him. He didn't
pay any attention to them. He said that he would rather die
than go with them. On the night before the liberation they
again came to get him. He had to go. They ordered him to
be on guard duty. But thanks be to God he didn't have to hold
a gun. I made a novena to St. Monica that he would not com-
mit a sin where he was going. You can imagine the joy we
experienced when we heard the news that we had been liberated by the national troops. Grandma cried for joy.

"Here we have as martyrs the priest of Turon, the pastor of
Olloniego and another priest from a place close to Oviedo. Three
students from the Passionist Monastery of Mieres, the Reverend Luciano Fernandez, the chaplain of the Fabrica and the
pastor of Rebollada, Father Innocencio, the Passionist who had
gone to hear the confessions of the Brothers of La Salle, were
killed with him. Here in Mieres 12 died; in Turon 14 and in
Sama 50. In all about a thousand died. All they are doing now
is arresting people. Love from your mother, Praxedes."

This is a complete report, succinct and objective. She did
not accuse anyone of anything. She made no comments in regard to the shooting of the priests. "May he rest in peace," she
said when she told him about Father Luciano's death. He had
been her director when she was a Daughter of Mary.

Father Luciano had died in atrocious circumstances. He was
chaplain of the Fabrica and pastor of La Rebolleda. The whole
region was upset over his death. He had esteemed Praxedes
ever since she had become a Daughter of Mary. The chaplain
of the Count and Countess, Father Angel, wrote the following
in regard to this spiritual relationship: "The one who truly appreciated Praxedes' virtue was Father Luciano, who no doubt
knew her best. He often said, 'This Praxedes is a saint.' In that
phrase is contained all his admiration for her."[10]

Praxedes went to Father Luciano's mother to give her her

condolences after the revolution was over. Antonia de la Uz, a niece of Father Luciano, has told us of this meeting. "When my uncle was killed, Praxedes came to give her sympathy to his mother, Esperanza Martinez. Praxedes wept with her and told her that she too had lost a son, Arturo. My aunt's answer to that was, 'The death of my son is different because he was killed by other people and your son by a train. I cannot forgive them for that!' "[11] Praxedes tried to calm her, doing what she could to help her see that we must place our eyes on God, who disposes all for our greater good.

In the midst of such horrors Praxedes had another concern, and that was that she could not receive the Holy Eucharist for two weeks. She was so used to this heavenly food! Sister Angeles Mellada has told us, "During the revolution in October, during which time she was not able to receive Holy Communion, Praxedes told me that those days without the Holy Eucharist were like days without the sun."[12]

Chapter 29

FROM HERE TO HEAVEN

Praxedes was enjoying the period of calm after the revolution, after "that flash of great suffering."[1] There was no more fighting, no more blood spilled—no more of those terrible and monstrous deeds, the fruit of the brutal impulse of hatred,"[2] as a newspaper had described the events of the revolution. This meant a lot to her.

In the intimacy of her family during the revolution, all Praxedes did was cry, pray and do penance without discussing her sufferings with anyone, especially over the killings of the priests and religious. "Her eyes," said Gabriel, "were red from crying."[3] When it was all over she confided in the sisters, "When I found out about the killings of the priests and sisters, my heart wanted to jump out of my breast."[4]

But charity was now even brighter than ever. If her heart wanted to jump out of her breast, it was nevertheless full of pardon for the culprits. It is precisely in this that we see Praxedes' great charity. She said, "Sister, I never feared death nor the tortures they could have imposed on me. The only thing that filled me with horror was the outrages they could have done to me."[5]

The following testimonies that we have attest to this. Obdulia Iglesias said, "During the October revolution I saw that she forgave the militants."[6] Sister Pilar Vila testified, "I know that she prayed for the persecutors of religion. She excused them and she was always kind to them."[7] Milagros Fernandez stated, full of admiration in December of 1964 to Praxedes' two living sons, "A little after the revolution I went to visit your grandmother. In my conversation I began to deplore the atrocities of the revolutionaries with the priests and the religious, and how they destroyed the churches. I thought that your mother, being so religious, would agree with me, but to my surprise not a word escaped her lips as she came in and out of the kitchen as she was serving us lunch."[8] The sister portress at the hospital at the Fabrica, Sister Pilar Sanza, said, "She possessed charity in a high degree. Whatever happened at that terrible 'red' period she always covered with the mantle of charity. She never said anything bad of anyone or anything."[9]

If Praxedes suffered much during the revolutionary period, her heart was now bleeding for the reprisals that the miners were now suffering. In 1964, the now old Sister Pilar Vila said, "When they began to imprison those miners who had taken part in the revolution, she suffered much and did all she could to help the families of those who went to jail until they got out. Once she and I went to the chapel at the Fabrica and there we saw a member of the civil guard mistreating one of the miners who had taken part in the revolution. Praxedes did not hide her feelings toward the unfortunate man who was being mistreated thus."

In any case, the atmosphere was tense in the mining district, above all for Florentina and Amalia, who had lived in such fear all during the revolution. Praxedes told us that her mother was unhappy in Sueros, as there was no parish there.[10] Before the revolution they had thought of moving to Oviedo, but because of the events then they did not; but now they knew they had to go. They did not doubt it for one moment. They moved to Oviedo and found an apartment on the second floor of House No. 18 on the street that carried the name of the Bishop that had confirmed Praxedes, Ramon Martinez Vigil.

When everything was ready for moving, the good-byes began. Everyone was sad because Praxedes was leaving. And more than anyone else, the sisters would miss her. The superior of the Dominicans, Sister Pia, exclaimed in front of Florentina, "Sisters, Praxedes puts us to shame with her virtues, for without being a sister, she lives such a perfect life."[11] Sister Amalia Villa said, "When she moved to Oviedo the people said that the best of the region had gone with her."[12] And Marcelino Llanez added, "She was much appreciated in the village. Even the most anti-religious didn't have a thing to say against her. When she left, the whole town went out to say good-bye, and she was missed very much."[13]

Before seeing Praxedes leave Sueros, we should reveal a mysterious confidence that the events of the time have made prophetic. In November, 1934, the time between the revolution and the moving to Oviedo, Praxedes was visiting Sister Maria Canal at the Fabrica school. Sister said that due to the horrible sufferings of the revolution it was a relief knowing that never again would anything like this happen. But Praxedes exclaimed, "Sister, soon there will be another war." After a few moments of silence and with her eyes fixed on the floor she said, "Yes, there will be another war; and Our Lord wants victims of reparation, and I have offered myself as one of them." She concluded in the same tone of voice, saying, "Another war will come but the Blessed Virgin will not abandon us, and the Sacred Heart will triumph."

The leaving of Sueros took place on December 7, 1934. On the 4th of the same month Praxedes wrote to Fray Enrique, joyfully telling him the good news. "At last the much-desired day has arrived. It is eight days since we got here to Oviedo. We find ourselves admirably well, giving thanks to God for having come here." Further on in her letter she said something that revealed her sadness at leaving Sueros. "Valeria and the neighbors cried for days before we moved, but I told them that we weren't moving too far. I couldn't cry because there we had no parish and that alone made me happy we were leaving. I pray for her and hope for her conversion."

Then she told him that the parish of Santa Maria de la Corte was very close to the house, and that the house was very comfortable and the sun filled it with warmth. Grandma then said, "From here to Heaven." She then repeated how comfortable they were.

Whatever the future, Praxedes left it all in the hands of God; but the fact is that she was the happiest woman in the world in Oviedo. There she found at last what she had always wanted—churches close by, many learned and holy confessors, good preaching. All this was for her spiritual well-being. She had much to choose from, and this pleased her. With St. Therese of Lisieux, Praxedes did not choose, "but took everything." She visited all the churches and the cathedral and spent much of her time in the church where they had perpetual adoration. What more could she desire after having passed all her life far from churches, and at the end, in a parish where there was no pastor?

"Living in Oviedo," confided Florentina, in 1964, "did a lot of good for Praxedes. It was a pleasure to see her so healthy now. Moreover, this city is much more pleasant than Sueros." It was not hard to believe, for in Sueros the streets were muddy. Florentina spoke more for herself than for her sister, to be sure.

In this frame opened the new year. Praxedes wrote to Fray Enrique to ask how he had celebrated Christmas in the convent. She told him how she celebrated it. But the memories of the past revolution lingered in her consciousness. "Many blessings in the new year to you, and please God, this year will be better than the last one. Let us hope that in our lifetime there will never be another revolution like the last one, or different, either."

Visits from the family, agreeable climate, numberless churches—all this made Praxedes happy. The inspiring liturgies were always the topic of conversation in her letters to Fray Enrique.

In her letter of March 17, Praxedes talked of some general missions that were preached in Oviedo, and which she was not able to attend because it was the hour for supper to be cooked. Gabriel and Celestino attended, though.

In the same letter she told him how everyone had suffered from severe colds, and even she had had to go to bed. She did not miss Mass nor Communion, though, just for this reason. Maria Alonso, who was visiting at the time, told how she found the bed empty when she went to visit Praxedes in her room.[14]

In Praxedes' letter of May 31, we have a beautiful testimony of her motherly love. "It is such a satisfaction when I pick up my pen to write to you. I should write to you every day."

Praxedes lived intensely the mystery of Christ in the liturgy. And of all the feasts, she loved the Feast of the Resurrection the best. "I feel a great satisfaction on the Feast of the Resurrection. I want to save all the best things to eat on that day. Since Our Lord suffered so much for us, it is only right that we celebrate His glorious Resurrection."

In that communion with Christ Praxedes found the energy to continue to serve her family as though she were a servant. Celestino came home from classes one day and found his mother on her knees scrubbing the stairs, and Florentina not even lifting a finger to help. He became furious for letting her do all the housework.[15]

On June 23 Praxedes assisted the first Mass that Father Antonio Solis celebrated in the Church of St. Dominic. He was a student in Salamanca with Fray Enrique. This event moved her very much, especially because she thought of the time that her son Enrique would be ordained and would say his first Mass here, too. She described her experience very beautifully. "I liked the first Mass that Father Antonio offered, and more so because I was thinking of the day when you will offer your first Mass. For me it was moving for this reason. May God shower you with blessings, my son, so that your wishes and mine will be fulfilled. How wonderful it will be when I see you enter the sanctuary and go up to the altar as a priest, to celebrate Mass. May God help you persevere in your studies and make you strong in your vocation." But her wishes were not to be realized. The interesting thing was that she already knew it. Conversing one day with Sister Maria Canal she told her plainly, "I will not see my son celebrate his first Mass, because God has asked this sacrifice of me."

This particular year Praxedes forgot to write to Fray Enrique on his birthday, and in her letter of July 29 she lamented it bitterly. "I looked at the calendar and noticed that your birthday had passed. This had never happened to me in the six years that you are away. All day long I regretted it. You must have felt it too. Right?" Praxedes' world continued the same in her new surroundings of Oviedo. Her mother continued to share her home with her and her sons; Florentina was there, too, and all the nieces and nephews were constantly coming and going, as well as the sick and the poor. Everything was being blessed with her union with God.

Edelmira Fernandez, who came from Seana to visit her sister-in-law who was in the Provincial Hospital in Oviedo, dying of tuberculosis, found Praxedes consoling the sick woman there.[16]

Walking one day with Florentina, just a few days after coming to Oviedo, Praxedes stopped to point out to her a certain house. "There lives a woman paralytic. I must go and visit her." Her sister could not contain herself and said, "You are really something. We just moved here and you already know where the sick live!"[17]

Chapter 30

ATTENTIVE TO THE "SACRAMENT OF THE PRESENT MOMENT"

Whatever her dreams for the future, or her preoccupations of the moment—whether she was walking on the muddy roads of Sueros or on the paved avenues of Oviedo, in the midst of the horrors of the revolution—Praxedes lived God's will today, the "sacrament of the present moment," according to the evangelical precept, "Be not therefore solicitous for tomorrow; for the morrow will be solicitous for itself."[1]

Praxedes always gave herself completely to the present moment, leaving all in the hands of God. Her mother was now on in years and needed special care, which Praxedes never denied her. Florentina continued in her easy life, going to the movies and theater. Praxedes wrote, "Grandma and I go out every evening to St. Francis Park. There we find a bench to sit on and enjoy the peace of the evening. It is just like being in Gijon for vacation. Florentina and Gabriel usually go to the movies, and Celestino goes out with his friends."

In this agreeable environment Praxedes' spiritual life blossomed. She enrolled in the Apostolate of Prayer in her parish. She soon realized that what Oviedo had was what Sueros had lost. A neighbor, Paz de la Vega, remembered her well. "Praxedes dressed like an older person, without a trace of vanity. When she went out one could tell that her thoughts were on God, as if nothing else in this world mattered. She walked with her eyes downcast and never stopped to chat with anyone. She went about her business without distraction."[2]

If this observation of Praxedes seems to describe a person who was not present to the realities of life, another neighbor,

Dolores Alvera, expressed herself more gently and perceptively. Dolores said this in the same house where Praxedes had lived: "On the one hand Praxedes was so natural, so sincere and ordinary, and on the other hand so supernatural in every way. She was so full of God that one could not help thinking that if we were like that, we would be saints."

This testimony is like the one given by several persons who went to school with Praxedes and knew her well. That special "something" that emanated from her was so well combined with her naturalness. "She was simple," said Sister Pilar Soro, "and had such a tender and docile nature. There was something admirable about her."[3] "In her way of being," said Sister Pilar Sansa, "one could see something supernatural."[4]

But one who has been able to appreciate Praxedes is a servant girl, Teresa Menendez. She said, "I had the privilege of going to the same church that Praxedes went to. I loved to see that face so full of peace and holiness that she had when she prayed. Her inner holiness shone through. She didn't seem to be aware of it at all."[5]

But above all, Praxedes' charity here in Oviedo—as everywhere else—was the greatest toward the sick and the poor. The following are two cases that demonstrate this. A young teenager of 15, Valentin Injerto, belonging to a Communist family in Sueros, had to come to Oviedo to get a two-week treatment for tuberculosis. His mother, Leonor Gutierrez, could not afford to pay for his stay in the city, so she appealed to Praxedes for help. Praxedes immediately welcomed him into her home and cared for him like a mother. When his mother came to visit him he would cry in gratitude for Praxedes' care. He would say, "Praxedes is very good to me and treats me so well."[6] Florentina, who was fearful of getting tuberculosis, had the windows and doors opened so as to avoid getting the sickness.[7]

The following case is even more indicative of Praxedes' charity without reserve. It was now five months since the revolution. Those days that followed were difficult for the militants. Many of them landed in prison, among them one of the leaders from Sueros. He got an infection while in prison. His sister from Sueros came to Oviedo to care for her brother and, as can be expected, Praxedes offered her hospitality. She never considered the Communists her enemies. The sister stayed two months. Let us not forget that Praxedes paid half of the rent for this home, so she felt that she could welcome her friends, as well as her mother hers. This friend, full of gratitude, had this to say of Praxedes: "Praxedes was kind to all the poor. I saw her take alms and food to the poor. I never heard anyone say anything against her. She was venerated and respected by all. She was so kind and never spoke ill of anyone and always had an excuse for the faults of others. Her temperament was so sweet and tranquil. I stayed with her for two months."[8]

In Oviedo it was impossible to know whom Praxedes helped. (In Sueros, because it was so small, everyone knew what everyone else did.) Praxedes would leave in the morning for Mass and would go from there to the market to distribute food to the poor and the sick. No one knew whom or how many were served. The neighbor who lived on the top floor said, "Praxedes aided the poor and the sick without limit. I myself saw her."[9]

We have seen that the neighbors in Sueros said that Praxedes gave herself completely to her housework. In Oviedo it was the same. Dolores Alvera said, "It was she who did all the work around the house. She wasn't one of those women who lost time talking with her neighbors. My sister-in-law who lived on the floor above her said to Praxedes one day, 'You work so much. You are always working!' "[10]

In the midst of all this, the thought of her son who was a religious never left Praxedes. He wrote to her that he had made a pilgrimage to the tomb of St. Teresa of Avila. She answered him joyfully on November 5, 1935: "You can't imagine how happy I am that you saw the incorrupt body of St. Teresa. God willing, I plan to go visit you next year and then I too will go to visit the tomb of St. Teresa. I have a great devotion to her."

In his letter Fray Enrique reminded his mother that he had just celebrated the first year of his profession, October 7, the feast of the Rosary. He recalled that a year ago the revolution was at its height. His mother answered, "How well I remember that last year I mistakenly went to Mass and Communion for you on the Sunday *before* the feast of the Rosary. It was fortunate that I did, for right on the feast the revolution broke out and I was not able to go to Mass and Communion on that day. Please God we will never see another revolution in our lifetime."

She loved her family, and all that happened to them—be it joyous or sad—affected her greatly. In this same letter she told Fray Enrique about the death of her brother Celso. He died on October 20, a month after he had spent his vacation in Oviedo with his mother and family. "Pray much for him. Offer your Masses and Holy Communions for him so that he will soon be out of Purgatory. The consolation that we have is that he went to confession and Communion the day before he died. Your Uncle Celso was very good. He had a kind word for everyone. The people at his funeral testified to this. The laborers didn't work on that day. His wife's brothers wept for him, lamenting the death of such a good man."

The sickness and death of her "good brother," told by her with so much detail, gave Praxedes an opportunity to reveal her profound love for her brother. She no doubt had not forgotten the help he gave her upon the death of her husband. "Celso," said Florentina, "was 'father' to her four sons many times, being that they did not have a father." She was grateful for all that was done and said about her brother, including the many flowers he received; but as she said about flowers given to Arturo, "The flowers die. It is better to pray, offer Masses and Communions for his soul. This is the best to offer for the dead."[11]

Thus ended that blessed year of 1935, with only the death of Praxedes' brother to mar it. Perhaps this was one of the happiest in her life. The year 1936 was destined to be her last, according to the plan of God. She had wished her son, in her letter of December 4, 1935, "a happy coming and going of the New Year." Little did she think that in this coming year she would take her flight to eternity.

The national elections were held in Spain on February 27, 1936. The extreme leftists returned to power. With this power the persecution of the Church began once again. From February to July 411 churches were destroyed. Strikes were in order.

The first letter that Fray Enrique received from his mother in the new year was dated March 19, 1936. She wrote one in January, but it was lost. He had asked her if she were able to go to daily Mass. She answered, "Yes, thanks be to God." He had also asked her if they were still saying the family Rosary every day. She answered sadly that Celestino was so busy in his career that he refused to accompany her any more. "He says that he says his morning and night prayers and that that is enough. Pray much for him so that he will be more obedient and have more faith."

In the midst of the persecution of the Church and other atrocities, Praxedes begged her son in the seminary, "Now that we are in Lent let us ask God to convert sinners and the persecutors, for peace and for the strengthening of our faith."

In her letter of May 8, she had special news for Fray Enrique. The religious crisis in Celestino's life had been resolved favorably. "Now, thanks be to God, Celestino joins me in praying the Rosary once again. He even leads it once in a while. This is good because when he has a family someday, he will be able to teach it and pray with his family. This devotion is very pleasing to Our Lady."

Praxedes' maternal heart was at peace and happy at the outcome of her three sons. Her dreams in their behalf were being fulfilled little by little. Gabriel was very affectionate with her. Celestino, dry by nature, was always hurt at seeing her a servant to everyone. But he was very studious and irreproachable. As to Fray Enrique, the son of her dreams, she wanted so much to see him become a great preacher and a true prophet who would go throughout the world saving souls.

Ovidio gave some practical advice concerning Gabriel. He proposed that Praxedes help him find a job in some factory so that with that experience he would appreciate his education that much more. She commented, "May St. Joseph, our guide, help us in all these matters!"

Praxedes also asked Fray Enrique if he was applying himself in his studies. "Have you passed your latest examinations? I hope so and very well, at that. Let's see if you can imitate Father Gafo or someone like him. Your order is known for its great scholars and you must study hard. May the Blessed Virgin help you always, my son."

Father Gafo (1881-1936) was a great apostle of the laborers. In Spain he was the founder of the so called "Free Labor Syndicates." One of his great apostolic triumphs in the social arena was the conversion of the then head of the Communist Party, Oscar Perez Solis. Because Praxedes had such a great love of laborers, she held him up as a model for Fray Enrique.

Praxedes wanted to visit Fray Enrique that summer, but she could not find anyone to take her place in the house. "I will come to visit you, but I don't know when exactly," she wrote to him.

The year before, she had forgotten to wish her absent son a happy birthday. This year she wrote on the same day, on the then Feast of St. Henry, Emperor, "Congratulations on this happy occasion of your name day. May this day be full of joy and happiness. And not only on this day but for the rest of your life. May St. Henry help you accomplish God's will, and become a great preacher. On this day I will offer my Holy Communion for you so that the Lord will bless you in all your undertakings and be happy in His service, which is what really counts."

The joy that had illuminated Praxedes' face since her youth— even in the midst of sorrow and the most trying events—she left as her testimony to her son, whom she had not seen for three years and would not see on this earth again. This was her last letter.

Chapter 31

"ANOTHER WAR WILL COME"

"Another war will come," Praxedes had said to one of the sisters a short time before moving to Oviedo. And it came, on July 19, 1936, with all its horrors, covering the land with ruin and blood.

Under a religious aspect, this leftist triumph marked the signal of anti-clericalism unequaled in its violence and hatred.

In the Parliament, the opposition to the regime by Calvo Sotelo soon cost him his life. He was opposed to the dictatorship of the Popular Front, which soon enough was dominated by Marxist anarchist tendencies.

Praxedes lived in this turmoil for three months, during which time she mounted on the wings of faith to be able to read the "signs of the times," His will. "There aren't enough sacrifices being done, nor is prayer alive. God wants victims and I have offered myself as one." This is precisely the divine plan which converges in Christ crucified, the only Saviour of the world. As the world continues to offend God, so more souls must offer themselves as victims—for as St. Paul says, "I now rejoice in my sufferings for you, and fill up those things that are wanting of the sufferings of Christ, in my flesh, for his body, which is the church."[1]

This generosity was accepted by God. Praxedes' intentions, those she expressed in her letter of March 19 to Fray Enrique, were well-defined: "The conversion of heretics, sinners, peace in the Church and a growth of the faith of the children of the Church." For those of God's children who had strayed from Him she happily immolated herself and became anathema for her brothers and sisters.[2]

Moreover, because of the situation in the environment and because of her oldest son, Celestino, Praxedes got involved in the politics of the day. Celestino was an ardent patriot, and he had given his name to the phalanx. This was very much against his mother's wishes, because of their vengeful ways.

On March 6, 1936 in Oviedo the Communists assassinated Doctor Alfredo Martinez, the former labor minister, as he was entering his home. Practically the whole city turned out for his funeral. The Bishop himself officiated at the funeral. As soon as the interment was over a demonstration took place to protest such a cowardly act. Then from the far end of San Francisco Park, some laborers had climbed the buildings and were throwing rocks at the peaceful demonstrators. Immediately a riot began to take place. Celestino, who was among them, picked up a camp chair and hit one of the laborers on the head and knocked him out. Thinking that he had killed him, he fled to Mieres for a few days, until the anger had subsided.

Praxedes suffered over this at seeing that her own son had been the cause of bloodshed. This assassination and all that happened because of it reflects the climate of Oviedo in 1936.

When I visited Oviedo in 1965, I was able to get some first-hand reports from one of Praxedes' neighbors, Carmen Martinez, of the months just before the civil war. "The atmosphere was very hostile. One could feel that something was in the air and that soon the revolution would break loose again. When they saw us go into church they would call out, 'You will pay for this.' The children would come and tell us what they heard in the streets, and it wasn't pleasant, for they were pitting one against the other. And still Praxedes had nothing to say against anyone."

On July 19, 1936 the civil war broke out, and it lasted until April 1, 1939. The miners then armed themselves and invaded the streets of Oviedo and easily took over the city. Then someone, and nobody knows who, gave orders that all miners were to take off to Madrid, as the government needed much help there. They took off noisily to the train station Renfe and boarded to go to Castilla. This tragedy took place on the morning of July 19, 1936. That same day in the evening, the 2,000 men who formed the military garrison of Oviedo and the soldiers from Simancas in Gijon rose against the government in Madrid and joined General Franco. The miners had been deceived.

Among the volunteers to fight for their country against Communism was Celestino, who had disappeared from the house. At first the family thought that he was in Mieres with his uncles. But one day Florentina was passing in front of the Santa Clara barracks, and to her surprise there was Celestino, guarding. She ran to greet him and scold him for not saying anything to his mother about his whereabouts. "You know very well how mother is," he replied; "she would never have given me permission to take up arms."

Upon her return home, Florentina asked Praxedes, "Where would you rather have Celestino now, in Mieres with his uncles or here defending his country?" She did not hesitate to answer, "As long as he doesn't kill, I would like to have him here in Oviedo." "Well, you have him here in Oviedo," said Florentina, "and moreover, without killing anyone, for he is not out in the trenches but here serving as a guard."[3]

Praxedes was not satisfied. She did not want her son to use a gun. During the October revolution she had written, "Thanks be to God that he didn't use a gun once." Now it was different. She was opposed to violence. Its source did not matter. But she was helpless in this case, except to intensify her penances and prayers. She did this as a victim for peace among brothers of the same country.

Later Celestino was sent to the most dangerous spot in the front lines, La Loma del Canto, situated in Naranco, where they were face to face with the enemy. While Celestino was in the trenches, Gabriel said one day in Praxedes' presence, "I bet Celestino is shooting down plenty of Reds." Full of horror Praxedes said, "Please, don't tell me that a son of mine is killing anyone, because not even in jest can I listen to that! He can defend his country but without killing or hurting anyone."[4]

During the siege Praxedes continued to take care of everything and everyone. With Celestino away fighting, she cared for her mother, who was getting older and more dependent. Florentina, scared to death, and Gabriel (who was by now 17) were lovingly cared for by her as well. Those peaceful and agreeable walks in the park were no more. They had left the mining district of Mieres looking for quiet and peace, but they had fallen into the same mouth of the wolf. We can imagine the job Praxedes had at hand.

The household tasks became very difficult for lack of water. The sources of water were now in the hands of the enemy. The women, whose job it was to carry the water, had to endanger their lives by going to other sources of water with guns and cannons going off in all directions. Praxedes first went to the fountain called "Urraca." Later she had to go quite far outside the city, to San Julian de los Prados, in Santullano de Oviedo. She went there in the early hours of the morning, to avoid the shooting. She was careful to invite her neighbors, three women from the same apartment house, so as not to go alone. They had to make several trips.

The three remembered these goings and comings, and the amazing strength that Praxedes had for work. Lucrecia Garcia has told us, "Between the trips for water my sisters and I would sit and rest, but Praxedes would sit at her machine and sew, for we could hear the machine going. This filled us with admiration of her extraordinary love of work."[5]

The house where Praxedes and her family lived was large and well-constructed. It had three floors and a full basement. During the day it was filled with people seeking protection from the constant bombing. Gabriel, his grandmother and Florentina went up to the living quarters only to eat and sleep. This situation existed since the beginning of September. Praxedes went down to the basement only once. She was busy all day with the household tasks. When the family wanted to know why she didn't go down to the basement for safety she answered, "Because the noise and commotion is too much and I can't pray."[6] But there was another reason for her not going down which was more fundamental. Praxedes knew, we do not know how, that as long as she remained on the main floor nothing would happen—no bombs would fall. She categorically assured Gabriel a thousand times that nothing would happen and would say, "You can stay here with me if you want to, nothing will happen. I know what I am saying."[7] She would say this with all tranquility.

Gabriel attested that every time the bombers went over the

city, and there were days when a count of them was 600, his mother immediately fell on her knees to pray with arms outstretched.[8]

Praxedes contrived all kinds of ways so as not to miss her three daily Masses, a practice she had started when Arturo died in 1931. She prayed and sacrificed herself for Celestino so that he would come back alive, and so that he would not be the cause of death of anyone. She also prayed and did penance for Enrique, of whom no one knew anything since the military uprising.

Praxedes, therefore, led a very solitary life up on the second floor, dedicated to prayer and mortification. From the beginning of the war she intensified her fasting in an alarming way, eating only once a day, and that only the leftovers. She did this for two reasons—in the first place out of love, so that her dear ones would have more to eat since food was scarce. Her sister-in-law, who knew her well, has written, "When the war came there was a scarcity of food immediately. I knew that Praxedes would not fare so well as she had an elderly mother, a scared sister and two sons to buy food for. There just wasn't enough food to buy. I was sure that she would solve the problem by not eating. And she did the buying and cooking; no one was any wiser about it."[9] This also gave Praxedes another opportunity for mortification.

Florentina, in order to force Praxedes to eat, asked Gabriel to pretend that he was going on a hunger strike until she stopped her rigorous fasting. "My son," she pleaded, "you need to eat. You are growing. I have to do penance. Can't you see the constant danger that Celestino is in? And I also have Enrique to pray for. We don't know a thing about him. I have to do something for them."[10] But it was evident that she was praying and sacrificing herself for the whole nation, her people, as well.

Her disciplines were also unbelievably multiplied. To whip and scourge herself, she used hooks and even the iron. "I believe," said Gabriel, "that her waist must have been raw, for that is where she used her instruments of penance."[11] Her prayer life had never been so assiduous. It was not just two hours of meditation and other prayers, now it was the whole day.

While Oviedo was in the hands of the army, the rest of Asturias, united to the Madrid government, was dominated by

terror. From the beginning of the war the churches were profaned, including the famous shrine of Covadonga, and the clergy
were mercilessly persecuted. Among the assassinated were 117
diocesan priests, 31 religious priests and 10 seminarians, not
counting the thousands from all walks of life, including laborers,
that died.

Chapter 32

"LIKE CHRIST ON THE CROSS"

The situation of the capital of Asturias, incessantly bombarded, was becoming critical. The government in Madrid expected that it would give in at any moment. A reporter from the United Press in London had this to say on September 8, 1936, which gives us a picture of the situation in the city: "Today I have been looking at Oviedo, the city of death, and I get the impression that it is almost completely abandoned. One sees there a handful of desperate men, rebels under the command of the former Colonel Aranda, who against all hope thinks that columns from Galicia will come to their aid. Only at night do the inhabitants dare come out of their homes. Even then it is dangerous, for the rebels go around at night destroying the sources of water and food. The military doctors do their best to stem the spread of epidemics and care for the sick and wounded as best that they can."[1]

Oviedo soon succumbed to an epidemic of typhoid and intestinal infections, as all the sources of water were contaminated. This was worse than all the bombs. Praxedes was to be one of the victims.

It was in the middle of September that Praxedes began to feel sickly. At first it was dysentery and vomiting that began to undermine this woman of iron. She had never stayed in bed sick, except for two or three days on two other occasions. As sick as she was, she continued her usual way of living. Florentina, fearful of the bombs, did not leave the basement, and Amalia—old and sick—stayed there with her. Gabriel, who was young and able, refused to help his mother because it was beneath a man to do the house chores. He himself has told

171

in tears of how his mother begged him to go get the water but he roundly refused, and so she had to force herself to continue bringing it. She never uttered a word of complaint.[2] Florentina has told us that when her sister returned from Mass she would lie down for a little while and then continue doing her chores.[3]

The intestinal infection was undermining her health day by day and could be noted in her pale, drawn face. To make it worse, Amalia also took sick at that time. After much searching, Florentina found a doctor for her. He felt obliged, as he, too, was from Mieres. In those days the authorities had rationed milk, reserving it exclusively for the sick. In fact, they could get it only with a prescription. Florentina begged Praxedes to ask the doctor for a prescription for milk, as the only food they had, lentils and garbanzos, would not stay in her stomach. But upon seeing her up and around and in her work clothes, the doctor refused her. She accepted the refusal with no complaints and continued to carry her cross without another thought about it.

Florentina knew very well that if Praxedes had to be in bed, she would have to take over the household tasks; nonetheless, she begged her to get into bed the next time the doctor came to see their mother. Praxedes obeyed, for she sensed that she needed rest. When the doctor came to her bedroom to examine her, he found her so sick that he gave her up as hopeless. He even prohibited her to talk. She had appendicitis and her state was so grave that in his judgment she could not even withstand an operation, which was the only thing that could save her. He also said that in Oviedo it was now impossible to operate. Florentina said that when she told the doctor that up to that day Praxedes had done the housework, he could not believe it. He kept repeating, "Impossible, impossible."

The patient, who that day before the doctor's visit had assisted at her three Masses, got up the next day and went to Mass and Communion, leaving her bed stuffed in such a way that one looking in would think that she was in bed. Her absence was discovered when a neighbor came to visit and Florentina invited her into the bedroom. They found no Praxedes! Florentina was furious. When Praxedes returned, Florentina scolded her and said, "From now on I am going to hide the house key so that you will not be able to go out any more." But she forgot, and the next day Praxedes again left the house for Mass, for she could not live without Holy Communion. When Dr. Jolin returned the next day, Florentina told him what Praxedes had been doing. Then the doctor told her in the most clearcut way, not without admiration at the patient's spirit, "From now on you are to remain quietly in bed, as Christ did on the Cross."[4] Praxedes did not get up again. Florentina has told us that her sister remained in bed with arms outstretched in the form of a cross.[5]

Praxedes' last Communion took place on September 27. She had had to go to bed on the 24th of September. On September 28 peritonitis set in, with terrible pains which she suffered without ever letting out a groan. Not once did she receive a painkiller. She was the victim that sacrificed herself on the altar of sacrifice. Celestino wrote in a letter about "the strangeness of the family for not being able to get the right food, nor doctor, nor medicine for my mother."[6]

There seems to be a mysterious coincidence between Praxedes' worsening condition and the state of the besieged city. The miners had sworn to capture it on the anniversary of the October revolution. They were preparing for a heavy assault. The attack on Oviedo was intense and furious, but its defenders not only held on to the disputed places—they even got some of the most modern equipment from the Marxists.

While all this was happening in the city, in a house battered on all sides, Praxedes was languishing on her bed of pain without any fear whatever, and consoling those around her. On one of these days Florentina was bringing her some milk when suddenly the sound of shots was heard and a cartridge was buried in the bedroom wall. The improvised nurse shook and lost control of herself while Praxedes told her with great calm, "Go to the basement and take care of yourself, for you are so afraid. You can leave me alone. I am not afraid." Florentina, finding it impossible to take care of both patients, her mother and Praxedes, and being afraid to go to the second floor, asked the tenants on the floor below to be kind enough to take Praxedes in. They agreed with joy. But always concerned about causing any inconvenience, Praxedes begged Florentina not to take her from her bedroom. "Don't take me from here, please, as I am very comfortable here in my own bedroom."[7] She had never been a bother to anyone. On the contrary, she had always taken on the obligations of others to relieve them. She preferred to be alone with God.

Three persons who were able to be interviewed had visited Praxedes during those days of her sickness. Josefa Garcia has told us, "Praxedes went to bed three days before my daughter got typhoid fever and died on October 4, after only eight days of sickness. I visited her during the first days. Conversing with her during those days she said, 'Let it be as God wills!' I noticed that she didn't think her sickness was of importance, and that she didn't fear death. I always found her totally resigned. Referring to the war, she said that that was not for Christians to do, and that it was very sad that brothers were fighting against brothers. But she never once criticized either side. I noticed also that she was as though transported into the beyond. She said something about this, but now I just can't express it. It was as though God was revealing great secrets about Heaven to her. She had a large crucifix hanging at the head of her bed. When I visited her, I was able to see, without her knowing it, the engraving she made on her chest with a hook."[8]

Carman Martinez communicated the following to me in 1964. "Praxedes was gravely ill when I visited her two or three days before she died. It was already getting dark, and her bedroom had no window to the outside, so we lit a candle to come in. I could see that she was getting worse. I asked her how she felt. She answered, 'I am alright. This is nothing!' I told her that I was sorry that I could not do more for her, but that the condition of the city was impossible. She then said, 'I don't lack anything. Celestino brings me the ice and milk that the doctor has prescribed. I don't lack anything, really.' Then in regard to the war she said, 'How sad it is that they are killing each other when they should love each other as brothers!' Then she thanked me for the visit with much love and gratitude, and we ended the visit."[9]

Here are the impressions of a third visitor, Maximina Suarez, who lived on the third floor. "During Praxedes' illness I visited her every day. It was a short visit, which consisted of finding out how she was and if there was anything I could do for her. I could tell that she was very resigned and suffered her pains with great patience and without concern for her privations. Every time that I visited her I noticed that she had the rosary in her hand. She also had, on her night stand, some pictures of saints. She always thanked me so sweetly for my visit."[10]

As to the last days of his mother's sickness, Celestino has told us what he best remembered about her. We note only those that pertain to her life of prayer shaped by the family Rosary. "When the doctor examined her he found her so sick that he forbade her even to talk. Florentina decided, in view of this, not to go into her bedroom any more to recite the Rosary, as had been customary. She, however, called us to come into her room to pray it and promised not to pray it out loud. But we didn't pay attention to her, and this caused her great pain. Again she resigned herself to God's will."

Gabriel noted also that his mother was very bloated and in constant pain. He slept in the adjoining bedroom so that he could hear her if she called for anything. He offered continually to help her. "My mother never permitted me to get up during the night, and would say, 'No, my son, don't bother. This is nothing.' But one night around 12:00 I heard a groan, but not very loud. I asked her if she wanted anything and she asked me to give her the ice bag. I thought to myself, 'My mother has to be very sick if she is asking for help and allowing me to get up at night.' That, in fact, was her last night on earth."[11]

The incident about the Rosary during these last days of Praxedes' life shows her great love of the family Rosary. This prayer had been her mainstay throughout her life. Like St. John Berchmans she also could say, "With this weapon I have fought all my life and with it I shall triumph in the hour of my death."[12]

The sixth of October was the very last day of Praxedes' life, and one of the hardest days of the siege. Seeing the gravity of her condition, Celestino got permission to be with her. That day he was able to get only a half liter of milk. Every other day he had been able to bring her a liter. This was the only food she could take. Now she did not need it any more. Her stomach could hold absolutely nothing.

When the doctor told Florentina that death was imminent and that they should get a priest and a notary, she heard Celestino coming up, and she said to the doctor, "There comes her oldest son, tell him." But neither he nor Florentina had the courage to tell Praxedes, as though she would have been frightened, when in reality the reception of the Sacraments would have been the greatest consolation for her. Everyone knew, however, that she was well-prepared, for it was only ten days since she had received Holy Communion. Her cousin Consuelo, who used to help her when she lived in Figaredo, had advised her that "It is important to be always ready to die, for we know not the day nor the hour."[13]

As to the material aspect it was not necessary to have a notary, for Praxedes had nothing to leave in inheritance. The 12,000 pesetas that were in the bank belonged to her children, as did the house in El Pedroso.

Florentina has told us that Celestino sat at the feet of his mother's bed all day. What consolation it was for her to see her son so attentive now—he who had caused her many heartaches. In fact, during those last days Praxedes had remarked joyfully, "I am so happy to have a son serving God, another serving his country and one close to me."[14]

Praxedes, without knowing the dictum of the doctor, was nevertheless aware of the gravity of her condition. Feeling that her end was near, she took great consolation that she had to the best of her ability carried out her responsibility as a mother. She knew, however, that she was able to do it only with the help of God, the Blessed Virgin and her favorite saints. Among these favorite saints was St. Monica, the patron saint of Christian mothers. In 1920 she had enrolled in the Association of Christian Mothers.[15] How she prayed to St. Monica for Celestino during those tragic days of the revolution in 1934!

The moment arrived for Praxedes to take her flight to her "native home," as she once wrote in a letter.[16] It was 6:30 in the evening. Celestino, who was sitting at the foot of his mother's bed, was not aware that his mother was dying. Florentina approached the patient and began to give her milk with a spoon. Praxedes immediately vomited. Celestino left the room as his mother exclaimed, "Oh, my sons!" Then she said to Florentina, "I have many things to say, but I can't remember now." These were her last words. Just before that she had said to her sons, "You must be good."[17] A few moments later, with her arms in the form of a cross and the rosary in her hand, she closed her eyes. She then opened them and looked up to Heaven, closed them again, and remained as if in a peaceful sleep. That was the sleep of death.

Florentina, suspecting the worst, began to call her, "Praxedes, Praxedes!" She then called to Celestino, "Come here. I don't know what has happened to your mother." Without hesitating he ran out to look for a priest. Two of them arrived, Father Joaquin and Father Jose Cabal. Father Jose administered the Sacrament of Extreme Unction and absolved her. Praxedes looked beautiful in death, with a faint smile on her face, which was a little flushed. Because of this the priests could not believe that she was dead. They kept saying to each other, "She has to be alive!"[18]

Without the death rattle, without the cold perspiration of death, without tears, without any of those things that usually accompany the death agony, Praxedes had passed from this world into the bosom of God, with a smile and an expression that was, in the words of Florentina, "more beautiful than ever."[19]

Celestino went out again, this time to look for two women who would prepare his mother's body for burial. Two women offered to do it, Felisa Alonso and Paz Ruiz. This last one has written in a letter from Argentina, "I cannot say how I happened to be in Praxedes' home. Was it by chance? Was it providential? Probably it was, because I lived nearby and when someone told me she had died I went in to see if I could be of any help. I remember clearly that she was in a small room. I found that there was the usual confusion when someone dies. Two of her sons were there, I remember. I saw that no one took the initiative to take care of the body so I said, 'I will help you.' Then with all due respect we took care of her. Her abdomen was very swollen. This I remember very well, as it impressed me very much. After we finished we put her in the front room and said the Rosary for the repose of her soul. I also remember someone saying that she was a saint."[20]

Florentina knew the desire which her sister had expressed a thousand times, that she wanted to be buried in the Carmelite habit. She sent someone to get one but was unable to do so. They were able to get a Franciscan habit, so that is what Praxedes was buried in. Over the habit of the Poor Man of

Assisi was placed the white scapular of St. Dominic. Thus in her death, Praxedes was embraced by the two great patriarchs, Dominic and Francis.

As we said, Praxedes died at 6:30 in the evening, the hour of the Angelus, when the Universal Church had begun the celebration of the Feast of the Holy Rosary. In this devotion Praxedes had found, since her childhood, the living font of her contact with Christ and the Gospel.

At that very hour, after two days of the worst carnage and furious fighting, tranquility and silence returned to the city. The newspaper of the day said, "As the day dawned the situation was re-established and the calm was complete."[21]

In the midst of all this pain and sorrow, as well as the calm that had now overtaken the city, could be heard Amalia's broken voice as she repeatedly said, "This daughter of mine was a saint."

In the calm that pervaded the room where Praxedes' body reposed, Gabriel found himself to be attuned to that peace. He described his feelings this way: "After my mother died I wanted to stay close to her. I remained there contemplating her and kissing her forehead without that fear that one has so often in the presence of a corpse, even if it's one of a dear one, as happened to me at the death of my grandmother. On the contrary, in the presence of my mother's corpse, I sensed something different, something heavenly."[22]

EPILOGUE

The burial took place at dusk on October 7, as it was prescribed because of the war. Celestino had asked one of the neighbors to buy the coffin. In a letter from this man we know some of the circumstances. "I went to buy a coffin as Celestino had asked me to do. That was a difficult thing to do in those days, as they were scarce. Most had to bury their dead without a coffin. To my surprise I found one, the only one left and of a high quality."[1]

Gatherings of any kind were rigorously forbidden then, and it was not even permitted to verify nor count the number of dead. One of Celestino's friends, Canga, rode in the truck that carried Praxedes' coffin with all the rest of those being buried that day. Unfortunately, Canga died some time later in a battle in Asturias; and in a few months Celestino also died in the Bilbao front. With them disappeared all information as to where Praxedes' grave was.

All the investigations to find her grave that were made later by her two surviving sons, Gabriel and Father Enrique, were unsuccessful. In was only at the time of the Diocesan Process of Beatification in 1957 that the man in charge of burials on that day was found. Using the burial plans and maps, he was able to locate the place of the burials for that day. Praxedes was buried in the part of the city where the diocesan seminary of Oviedo proudly stands today, crowned with a statue of the Ascension.

This place was called the "Old Cemetery." It was located outside the city and had not been used for many years before the war. Because of the siege, it was put into use again precisely on October 7. Unfortunately, this was not found out until it was too late, and all those buried there had been transferred to a common grave in the modern cemetery of San Esteban de la Cruces. Here again, even in death, Praxedes continues to serve the Church through her hidden and humble stance as a "servant of the house." We may never be able to venerate her remains, because even these have been sacrificed and anonymously returned to dust. But the witness of her life in Christ has been converted into a sap which has mysteriously fertilized the place so tormented by civil war. From there has sprung up the seeds of priestly vocations, which was her lifelong dream. Yes, she prayed and sacrificed so that many sons would consecrate themselves in service to the people of God. For Praxedes it seems there would be no more fitting tomb than beneath the Diocesan Seminary which was built over the site of her first grave in 1945.

After Praxedes' death, the struggle for the defense of Oviedo continued desperately. On the 15th of October, Colonal Aranda saw that his provisions and ammunition were giving out. He sent the following message to General Mola, commander of the army in the North: "There is nothing left for us to do but to die, but die we shall, as Spaniards know how."

Oviedo was liberated 11 days after the death of Praxedes on October 17, 1936, by the Marruecos regulares. The siege had lasted 90 days.

At the funeral rites for Praxedes held in his former parish in Seana, Father Moises Diaz-Caneja affirmed in prayer that the liberation of Oviedo was due not only to the bravery of its defenders but also to Praxedes' holocaust. She had offered herself as victim to God for the salvation of the city.

God had accepted her sacrifice, which was willingly offered over the atrocious pyre of the war itself. Gunshots had not destroyed Praxedes, but at age 50 and with a constitution strong as iron, she succumbed because of the deprivations and unsanitary conditions of the war. Concern for the future of her three sons and for her "countrymen who were killing each other instead of loving each other as brothers" possessed her during her dying hours.

Praxedes decided to offer up her life in order to combat the hatred, division and war among her beloved people. This was the only thing she could do. Yes, this was a fitting death for one who had continuously and slowly transformed herself and those she touched throughout her life of Christian witness and service, which ended in Oviedo. Praxedes had put on Christ with all the "weapons" she had in her hands, the hands of a "plain woman of her town": giving testimony to a limitless love for all in need. She discriminated only in favor of the needs of beggars and the homeless.

Praxedes' message is that the Gospel must be applied to the needs of the times and lived with our special charisms in the Church. She was a woman of her times living in the "today of God." She was a living incarnation of the New Commandment, a messenger of love without limits, and because of this, a witness of peace and reconciliation as well.

Lourdes
Feast of the Apparitions of Our Lady
February 11, 1977

NOTES

CHAPTER 1—*In the Heart of the Mining Valley*

1. Rafael Fuentes Arias, Asturias Industrial. Gijon, 1900, pp. 301ss.

CHAPTER 2—*Familiar Surroundings*

1. Sworn statement of Florentina Fernandez Garcia, September 9, 1972.
2. Sworn statement of Celestina, September 20, 1972.
3. Sworn statement of Feliciano Suarez, November 11, 1967.
4. Sworn statement of Florentina, September 22, 1972.
5. Sworn statement of Celestina, September 20, 1972.
6. Sworn statement of Julia Suarez Alonso, September 25, 1973.

CHAPTER 3—*Birth and First Years*

1. E. Albiol, C.M., *A Mother Walks from the Altar*, Bogota, 1962, pp. 149-150.
2. Ovidio's letter of June 7, 1948.
3. Ismael's letter of December 27, 1953.
4. Ovidio's letter of June 7, 1948.
5. Sworn statement by Benigna Fernandez Garcia, December 27, 1972.
6. Celestina's letter of January 10, 1961, and February 22, 1961. In another sworn statement of November 13, 1957 she added, "She [Praxedes] was the most pious of all the children since she was a child."
7. Celestina's letter of February 22, 1961.
8. Ovidio's letter of June 8, 1948. And in a sworn statement on November 8, 1957 he added, "She complied with exactness with all her duties of her state in life since she was a child."
9. Sworn statement of Josefa Solis on December 26, 1965.
10. Sworn statement of Josefa Solis on December 26, 1965.
11. Jose Ramiro Garcia Suarez, Praxedes' maternal uncle's letter from Carathas, Cuba, dated February 18, 1894. In another letter of June 6, 1894, he wrote, "Educate my nephews without that infamous religion of the perverse and foolish."
12. Ovidio's letter of June 7, 1948.

13. Sworn statement of Celestina on September 20, 1972.
14. Sworn statement of Father Jacinto of St. Paul of the Cross on September 22, 1972.
15. Ovidio's letter of June 7, 1948.
16. Ovidio's letter of June 7, 1948.
17. Sworn statement of Ovidio on November 8, 1957.

CHAPTER 4—*In the Dominican School*

1. Sister Pilar Vila's sworn statement on September 20, 1972, completed with another one on August 23, 1957.
2. Sister Covadonga Espina's letter to the Vice-postulator D. Leocadio Alonso dated in her monastery of Cintruenigo, Navarra, December 15, 1957.
3. Benigna Fernandez Garcia's sworn statement on September 23, 1973.
4. Sworn statement of Maria Paton on December 20, 1957.
5. Sworn statement of Maria Paton on December 28, 1966.
6. Sworn statement of Maria Hevia on December 27, 1957.
7. Sworn statement of Adela Hernandez on December 27, 1957.
8. Sworn statement of Adela Fernandez on December 28, 1966.
9. Sworn statement of Ismael Fernandez on November 8, 1957.
10. Celestina's letter of February 22, 1951.
11. Celestina's letter of February 22, 1951.
12. Sworn statement of Maria Iglesias on December 10, 1967.
13. Wherever Praxedes went, she left a trail of admiration. Her brother Ismael wrote in a letter dated October 30, 1946, "After four or five years after Praxedes had been with my father in Andalucia, I met Engineer Eduardo Guillon y Daban, who was directing the work in that locality at that time. He inquired with great interest about my father and my sister, whom he admired greatly for her spirit of abnegation and great piety."

CHAPTER 5—*In the Neighborhood of Joy*

1. Celestina's letter of October 10, 1961.
2. Sworn statement of Ovidio Fernandez on November 8, 1957.
3. Sworn statement of Celestina Fernandez on September 20, 1972.
4. Sworn statement of Olvido Estrada on December 27, 1967.
5. Sworn statement of Aurelia Gutierrez on September 23, 1967.
6. Sworn statement of Ovidio on November 8, 1957.
7. Sworn statement of Teresa Alvarez on December 22, 1966.
8. Ismael's letter of October 30, 1946.
9. Sworn statement of Celestina on September 20, 1972.
10. Sworn statement of Benigna Fernandez on September 24, 1973.
11. Sworn statement of Encarnacion Garcia on December 27, 1966.

12. Sworn statement of Olvido Estrada on September 25, 1973.
13. Sworn statement of Aurelia Gutierrez on September 23, 1967.
14. Sworn statement of Paulina Mahojo on November 2, 1964.
15. Sworn statement of Benigna Fernandez on February 17, 1966.
16. Sworn statement of Olvido Estrada on September 30, 1973.
17. Maria Cloux's letter of January 31, 1968.
18. Sworn statement of Jose Alvarez on August 23, 1957 and from one of his letters of November 28, 1959.

CHAPTER 6—*Devout Youth*

1. Written by Germana Gonzalez on July 8, 1953.
2. Sworn statement of Germana Gonzalez on December 20, 1957.
3. A letter written by Sister Pilar Vila on December 4, 1951 in which she gave other data from a sworn statement on September 20, 1972.
4. Sworn statement of Pilar Folguera on June 8, 1953.
5. Sworn statement of Pilar Folguera on January 24, 1958.
6. Sworn statement of Marcelino Llaneza, son of Obdulia Iglesias, on September 25, 1973.
7. Sworn statement of Maria Hevia on June 8, 1953.
8. Sworn statement of Julia Iglesias on June 11, 1964.
9. Written by Manuela Jove on July 6, 1953.
10. Sworn statement of Julia Suarez on September 25, 1973.
11. Sworn statement of Benigna Fernandez on September 24, 1973.
12. Written by Sister Consuelo Giner on March 2, 1946.
13. Letter by Sister Consuelo Giner on January 20, 1952.
14. Sworn statement of Sister Josefina Martinez on September 20, 1972.
15. Sworn statement of Gabriel Fernandez on December 22, 1966.
16. Sworn statement of Father Enrique Fernandez on December 28, 1976.
17. Sworn statement of Rorario Calleja on December 22, 1957.
18. Sworn statement of Father Jacinto of St. Paul on December 22, 1972.
19. Letter by Father Constantino of St. Thomas on December 27, 1953.
20. Sworn statement of Antonia Castano on September 25, 1973.
21. A letter of St. Teresa to Cristobal R. de Moya, on June 28, 1568.
22. Sworn statement of Sister Maria Canal on September 20, 1972.
23. A letter of petition by the Superior General of the Passionists, the Most Reverend Malcom La Velle, which copy is kept by the Postulator General of the Dominican Order, Father Inocencio Venchi.

CHAPTER 7—*Love at First Sight*

1. A friend of her youth, Julia Suarez, confirmed this by saying, "Praxedes had many suitors who came to see her at the store or sewing

room. She conversed with them but never with foolishness, nor flirted with them. She kept right on quietly working while they followed her around. I never saw her go out alone with any young man, as did her sisters." (Sworn statement on September 25, 1973.)

Her cousin Benigna Fernandez said, "Praxedes was very attractive. She had beautiful skin, long, white hands, and reddish hair, and blue eyes. She carried herself with elegance. It is no wonder that so many young men wanted her for a girlfriend." (Sworn statement on February 17, 1966.)

2. Her sister Consuelo made dresses for Praxedes and her friend Olvido Estrada. It was a low-necked style. Both wore them for the same occasion. The difference was that Praxedes made a large bow to cover her neck. She never wore it again until Consuelo fixed it. (Sworn statement of Olvido Estrada on December 27, 1966.)

A young man by the name of Feliciano Suarez had this to say of Praxedes' beauty: "I don't know why, but her beauty moved one to good thoughts and not the contrary." (Sworn statement of November 11, 1967.)

3. Sworn statement of Olvido Estrada on December 27, 1966.

4. Sworn statement of Obdulia Iglesias on January 7, 1967. Her brother Ismael confirmed the same. "I know that my sister desired to be a religious sister. She married, nevertheless, because the family convinced her that God could be served in any state of life." (Sworn statement on November 9, 1957.)

5. Sworn statement of Florentina on March 3, 1966.

6. Praxedes' sister, Celestina, related this.

7. Benigna Fernandez's sworn statement on February 17, 1966.

8. Sworn statement of Florentina on March 3, 1966.

9. Sworn statement of Celestina on September 20, 1972.

10. Sworn statement of Jose Alvarez on March 28, 1965.

11. Sworn statement of Florentina on September 27, 1972.

12. Sworn statement of Fernando Iglesias on December 15, 1966.

13. Sworn statement of Florentina on September 27, 1972, completed with other details of another sworn statement she made on March 3, 1966.

14. Sworn statement of Julia Suarez on September 25, 1973.

15. Sworn statement of Marcelino Garcia on September 16, 1966. His wife, Celestina, in a letter that she wrote Father Enrique on January 10, 1961 said, "It was to my husband, Marcelino, to whom your father said that he would not exchange his girl for any other in the world."

CHAPTER 8—*The Wedding and Honeymoon*

1. *Matt.* 19:20.
2. Sworn statement of Visitacion Vasquez on December 17, 1966.
3. Sworn statement of Celestina Fernandez on February 6, 1966.
4. Sworn statement of Visitacion Vasquez on December 17, 1966.
5. Sworn statement of Sister Maria Canal on September 20, 1972.

CHAPTER 9—*A Working-Class Family*

1. Sworn statement of Consuelo Fernandez on January 7, 1967.
2. Teresa Alvarez said to Father Enrique on November 25, 1965, "I heard a very trustworthy person who lived in Pedroso say the following: 'The only persons with whom one can discuss anything with her are Filomena and the national teacher.' "
3. Sworn statement of Isabel Fernandez on December 27, 1957.
4. Father Enrique Fernandez, O.P., in "A Mother, Model of Our Times" (Ediciones Paulinas: Mexico, 1952, chapter 3, p. 33).
5. Sworn statement of Ovidio Fernandez on November 8, 1957.
6. Sworn statement of Florentina Fernandez on October 22, 1967.
7. Sworn statement of Jose Alvarez on March 23, 1965.
8. Sworn statement of Consuelo Fernandez on January 7, 1967.
9. Father Enrique in "A Model Mother, Wife of a Proletariat, Road to the Altar" (Mexico, 1956, chapter 4, p. 45).
10. Sworn statement of Encarnacion Garcia on December 27, 1966.
11. Florentina Fernandez's letter dated February 12, 1952, in which she also told Father Enrique, "Your mother cared for our father until he died. The first thing she did was to recommend his soul to God in tears, and on her knees."
12. Father Enrique Fernandez, O.P., in "A Holy Mother of Our Times" (Editorial files, Salamanca, 1954, chapter 5, p. 71).
13. Father Enrique in "A Model Mother, Wife of a Proletariat, on the Road to the Altar" (Mexico, 1956, chapter 5, p. 49).
14. Sworn statement of Florentina Fernandez on September 27, 1972.
15. Sworn statement of Olvido Estrada on December 27, 1966.

CHAPTER 10—*Wife and Mother*

1. Sworn statement of Consuelo Fernandez on January 7, 1967.
2. Sworn statement of Consuelo F. Fernandez on January 7, 1967.
3. Sworn statement of Consuelo F. Fernandez on January 7, 1967.
4. Sworn statement of Ascension Guijarro Esteban on September 25, 1973.
5. Sworn statement of Florentina F. Fernandez on January 8, 1967.
6. Statement of Felicidad Fernandez to Father Enrique on August 31, 1964.

7. Sworn statement of Florentina Fernandez Garcia on March 3, 1966.
8. Sworn statement of Consuelo F. Fernandez on January 7, 1967.
9. Sworn statement of Consuelo F. Fernandez on January 7, 1967.
10. Statement of Felicidad Fernandez to Father Enrique on August 31, 1973.
11. Florentina F. Fernandez, a cousin of Praxedes and sister of Consuelo, in a declaration sworn on September 25, 1973, testified, "I know that Praxedes suffered much on this account (referring to Encarnacion's intrigues), and she used to come to my father, Nicanor, for consolation and advice. He was like a father to her after her own father died. She would tell him all her troubles and left very happy and satisfied after his attention." Consuelo added in another declaration on September 25, 1973, "My father Nicanor loved and appreciated her very much. When we spoke about her he would day, 'That woman is a saint!' "
12. Letter of Carmen Vallina, a sister-in-law of Gabriel, to Father Enrique on February 11, 1954.
13. Sworn statement of Celestina Fernandez on September 20, 1972.
14. Sworn statement of Ismael Fernandez on November 9, 1957.
15. Elias Valdes's letter of August 6, 1953.
16. Sworn statement of Consuelo F. Fernandez on September 25, 1973, completed with another sworn declaration on July 7, 1975.
17. Sworn statement of Consuelo F. Fernandez on September 25, 1973.
18. Sworn statement of Rosario Fernandez Lopez on March 10, 1978.
19. Sworn statement of Maria Teresa Viejo on October 7, 1977.
20. Sworn statement of Carmel Vallina on February 16, 1966.
21. Sworn statement of Florentina Fernandez on October 22, 1967.

CHAPTER 11—*Broken Home*

1. The Reverend Elias Valdes's letter of August 6, 1953.
2. Sworn statement of Consuelo F. Fernandez on January 7, 1967.
3. Sworn statement of Encarnacion Garcia to whom Amalia spoke on September 25, 1973.
4. Sworn statement of Florentina Fernandez on March 3, 1966.
5. Sworn statement of Antonia Dastano on December 27, 1967. The last phrase "God be blessed for everything" is a testimony of Sister Consuelo Giner on March 2, 1946.
6. Declaration of Otilia Moro to Father Enrique on December 22, 1967.
7. Sworn statement of Edelmira Fernandez, Praxedes' second cousin.
8. Sworn statement of Sister Consuelo Giner on August 20, 1966.
9. Sworn statement of Antonia Castano on September 25, 1973.
10. Sworn statement of Julia Suarez on September 25, 1973.
11. Sister Consuelo Giner's letter to Father Enrique on January 20, 1952.

CHAPTER 12—*Widow and Servant*

1. Sworn statement of Justa Curieses on September 25, 1973.
2. Sworn statement of Florentina Fernandez on September 27, 1972.
3. Sworn statement of Primitiva Fernandez on September 25, 1973.
4. Sworn statement of Julia Suarez on September 25, 1973.
5. Sworn statement of Gabriel Fernandez on July 23, 1973.
6. Cfr. E. Albiol, *A Diamond in the Mining Valley* (Madrid, 1960, p. 193).
7. Sworn statement of Sister Pilar Vila, on September 20, 1952.
8. Sworn statement of Jesus Antuna on September 24, 1973.
9. Sworn statement of Amparo Robledo on September 25, 1973.
10. Sworn statement of Maria Teresa Viejo on July 29, 1973. There are many testimonies concerning Florentina's attitude toward Praxedes. In a sworn statement on September 25, 1973 Justa Curieses said, "Florentina was forever interfering with Praxedes' affairs. She reproached her for any little thing. To all this Praxedes never showed impatience, nor was she unkind with her sister. On the contrary, she was always kind and sweet toward her and waited on her at every opportunity." A sworn statement of Maria Alonso on September 25, 1973, stated, "Her sister Florentina made her suffer greatly. Praxedes at times went to another part of the house to avoid arguments of any kind. In a sworn statement of Sister Maria Canal on November 13, 1948, Sister said, "Praxedes suffered much on account of Florentina, whom God had chosen as the instrument of mortification for her. This sister of hers insulted her, called her names such as 'holy one,' and others like it. Florentina didn't hesitate to bring up matters right to her face, so much so that she would have her in tears often. Without doubt, she is the one who made her suffer the most."
11. Sworn statement of Obdulia Iglesias on January 14, 1958.
12. Florentina's letter to Father Enrique on March 22, 1974. And in another one, of October 3, 1949, she insisted, "I tell you that even if your mother prayed much, she never neglected her duties." In regard to her rising and going to bed, this is taken from a sworn statement of Florentina on November 11, 1957.
13. Sworn statement of Manuel Vega on March 16, 1959.
14. Sworn statement of Marcelina Vasquez on December 27, 1965.

CHAPTER 13—*Day by Day*

1. Amalia Garcia's letter of May 24, 1920.
2. Sworn statement of Consuelo F. Fernandez on January 7, 1967.
3. Amalia's letter to Ismael on May 24, 1920.
4. Sworn statement of Asuncion Cueto on December 12, 1967.

5. Sworn statement of Julia Suarez on September 25, 1973.
6. Amalia's letter to Ismael on October 17, 1920.
7. Amalia's letter on February 14, 1921.
8. Amalia's letter to Ismael on December 8, 1920.
9. Sworn statement of Sister Dolores Robinat on September 3, 1966.
10. This resident related this incident personally to Father Enrique at Christmastime, 1965.
11. Amalia's letter to Ismael.
12. Florentina's letter to Father Enrique on August 11, 1946 in which she said, "When you became blind, I would see your mother crying many times. How I prayed to the Blessed Virgin so that you would regain your sight. We prayed the Rosary daily for that intention."
13. Sworn statement of Florentina on September 27, 1972.
14. Sworn statement of Sister Maria Josefina Martinez on July 23, 1973.
15. Sworn statement of Benigna Fernandez on January 14, 1958.
16. Her sister Celestina referred to these episodes concerning Praxedes' fears. She recalled that one night when they were still at home and unmarried, they heard noises for the greater part of the night. They were petrified, for they could not tell what it was. In the morning they discovered that it was the donkey which slept in the basement. Celestina also recalled the time she visited her after she was married. "My sister Consuelo and I visited her in Figaredo. She never told us of her troubles in her marriage, but I do remember that she told us of some scares she got. At times she would even make Gabriel get up to see what the noises were all about. Once he almost used his gun." (Sworn statement of Celestina on September 20, 1972.)
17. Sworn statement of Florentina Fernandez on September 27, 1972. Father Enrique is also a witness of this. The guard ran after Arturo, entering his home—which was against the law, trespassing or housebreaking. This is what displeased Praxedes.
18. All these details have been given to me personally by Father Enrique, in January, 1965. We met several times in the Dominican convent of Burdeos.
19. Sworn statement of Florentina on September 27, 1972.

CHAPTER 14—*The Meeting with the "Bishop of the Tabernacle"*

1. Sister Amparo Fernandez said, "One morning upon leaving the church after Mass, one of the sisters asked for Praxedes and someone answered, 'She is in the confessional going to confession to the Bishop.'" (Declaration written by this sister on May 12, 1955.) Sister Josefina Martinez, then a teenager and a native of Sueros, said in a sworn statement in July 23, 1973, "I saw Praxedes go

to confession to the Bishop of Malaga several times. I also saw her conversing with the Bishop several times outside the church. And it wasn't just a mere greeting either, but a real, serious conversation."

2. Sister Maria Canal has declared in a sworn statement on September 20, 1972 that "Her devotion to the Mass and Communion was very great. She once said to me, 'The day on which I cannot go to Mass and receive Holy Communion, that is a day without sun for me.' " The same is affirmed by Sister Rosa Gonzalez in another sworn statement on July 23, 1973, and Sister Angeles Mallada in another declaration on January 7, 1958.

3. Sister Pilar Sanza, from the hospital at the Fabrica, testified in a declaration on September 27, 1958: "Many times Praxedes arrived before the doors of the chapel were opened. She had to wait by the door." And the Passionist, Father Segundo de San Gabriel, in a letter he wrote to Father Enrique and signed in Habana on January 24, 1969, stated, "Every day when the porter opened the door of the church Praxedes was there waiting."

4. Sworn testimony by Gabriel on December 22, 1966.

5. Cfr. Rafael Garcia Herreros, *S. Juan Eudes*, Bogota, 1943, p. 65.

6. Sworn statement of Sister Maria Canal on March 1, 1965 and of Sister Concepcion Arias on September 25, 1973. "One could not help but notice her great recollection when she prayed in the presence of the Blessed Sacrament. She revealed an extraordinary spirit of devotion and faith that was out of the ordinary. I especially noticed her great respect and devotion when she returned from Holy Communion. Just looking at her made me fervent."

   Sister Pilar Soro on January 2, 1968 said, "I saw her often at our chapel at the Fabrica. She never lost her recollection in the chapel by looking around or noticing people coming in or going out. She gave all her attention to God. This gave me great edification. When she visited us on Sunday evenings she would always end her visit by going to our chapel to make a long visit to the Blessed Sacrament."

7. Letter of Rev. D. Angel de la Puente Careaga on August 26, 1954.

8. Sworn statement of Sister Ascension Canal on July 23, 1973.

9. Sworn statement of Florentina Fernandez on September 27, 1972.

10. Cfr. Enrique Fernandez, Le Acompana D. Manuel. Editorial OPE, 1967, pp. 14-16.

11. Gabriel in a sworn declaration on December 22, 1966, declared that his mother had him make this supplication as each person approached Holy Communion.

12. Praxedes' letter of July 15, 1931.

13. We have three witnesses of having heard her say this: Father Enrique, Gabriel and Carmen Vallina.
14. Cfr. St. Teresa of Jesus, *Life*, chapter 38, number 19.
15. Cfr. E. Albiol, *A Diamond in the Mining Valley*, (Madrid, 1960, p. 88).

CHAPTER 15—*Return to the Neighborhood of Joy*

1. In 1966 Amparo Robledo recalled, "as if I were seeing it right now," according to her own words.
2. This phrase was repeated many times by Praxedes throughout her life.
3. Father Enrique relates the complete story of Fr. Hermogenes in his work, *A Holy Mother for Our Times*. Salamanca, 1954, chapter 20, p. 271.
4. Letter of His Excellency Bishop D. Segundo Garcia dated September 9, 1959.
5. Sworn statement of Leonor Gonzalez on May 22, 1966.
6. Sworn statement of Antonia Castano on September 25, 1973.

CHAPTER 16—*The Future of the Four Sons*

1. Sworn statement of Sister Pilar Vila on July 23, 1973.
2. Sworn statement of Antonia Castano on September 25, 1973.
3. Sworn statement of Gabriel on September 26, 1973, and completed with another declaration sworn on November 14, 1957.
4. Letter of Rev. Angel de la Puente on August 26, 1954.
5. Father Enrique told me that he was one of those who accompanied her. The other was Gabriel.
6. Sworn statement of Aurora Fernandez on October 1, 1966, where she affirmed, "I noticed that for a whole year she took her breakfast to a woman by the name of Ceferina who lived next to the public fountain."
7. Sworn statement of Marcelino Llaneza on September 25, 1973.
8. Sworn statement of Gabriel Fernandez on December 22, 1966. Father Enrique himself told me that he saw this himself.

CHAPTER 17—*The Son of Her Dreams*

1. Written by Sister Amparo Fernandez on May 12, 1965.
2. Sworn statement of Florentina on September 27, 1972.
3. Statement of Marcelino Llaneza on November 2, 1964.
4. Sworn statement of Marcelino Llaneza on September 25, 1973.
5. The following was told me by Florentina in a sworn statement in April, 1964. "Arturo, having reserved a truck, and some of the other miners wanted to take it said, 'Let's see if you dare come to take it!' "

6. From a letter by Sister Angeles Mellada on October 4, 1953.
7. Sworn statement by Mother Providencia Sole on September 26, 1958.
8. Saint Maria Micaela wrote, "The Lord gave me such a great consolation every time I received Holy Communion for so many years that I took it for granted that everyone had the same experience." (Autobiography, Part II, p. 192.)
9. Declaration by Sister Reginalda Guey on May 12, 1955.

CHAPTER 18—*Genoveva de Brabante and Saint Teresa of Avila*

1. *Genoveva de Brabante, Historical Legend* by Antonio Contreras, Madrid. Manuel Castro editor. T.I., p. 625.
2. *Way of Perfection*, Chapter 31, No. 4, St. Teresa of Avila.
3. Ibid. See also *The Life*, chapter 10, No. 9.
4. Sworn statement of Gabriel on July 26, 1973.
5. Sworn statement of Gabriel on July 26, 1973.
6. Sworn statement of Gabriel on July 26, 1973.
7. *Way of Perfection*, chapter 27, No. 1.
8. *Advices*, No. 25.
9. *Concepts of the Love of God*, chapter 7, No. 6.
10. *Foundations*, chapter 5, No. 8.
11. *Advices*, No. 21.
12. *Way of Perfection*, chapter 4, No. 2.
13. Sworn statement of Gabriel on December 22, 1966.
14. Sworn statement of Florentina on March 3, 1966.
15. Sister Asuncion Cuetara's letter of August 26, 1953.
16. Sworn statement of Olvido Gonzalez on July 23, 1973.
17. Sister Josefina's letter of July 7, 1955.
18. Praxedes' letter of November 5, 1935.

CHAPTER 19—*Another Enriching Encounter: Father Moises*

1. A paper written by D. Moises that is preserved in the archives of the Secretariat of Praxedes.
2. Sworn by Edelmira Fernandez, a neighbor in Seana, on October 18, 1966.
3. Sworn statement of Father Fausto Rodriguez on April 20, 1966.
4. Writing by D. Moises that is preserved in the Praxedes' Secretariate.
5. Declaration of a Sister of the Secular Institute, Sister Maria Cloux on January 10, 1968.
6. The biography of Father D. Moises was published in the section "Exemplaries" of *The Supernatural Life*, a magazine dedicated to mystical theology put out by the Spanish Dominicans. It also appeared in a work called *Those Who Practice the Faith*, Editorial

OPE, 1970, pp. 231-245, and in *The Christs of the Earth*, Ediciones Paulinas, S.A., Mexico, 1975, pp. 143-163.

7. This affirmation was made by Father Moises to Father Enrique in an interview on June 7, 1953 in the convent of St. Dominic in Oviedo.

CHAPTER 20—*The Son of Her Tears*

1. Works of St. Teresa of Avila, *Way of Perfection*, chapter 18, No. 1.
2. Sworn statement of Marcelino Llaneza on September 25, 1973.
3. Declaration of Father Jacinto de S. Pablo on August 27, 1966.
4. Sworn statement of Florentina on March 3, 1966.
5. Sworn statement of Dolores Garcia on January 2, 1968.
6. Sworn statement of Manuela Vega on January 16, 1968.
7. Sworn statement of D. Moises Diaz-Caneja on January 16, 1966.
8. Sworn statement of Antonia de la Uz on December 26, 1966.
9. Sworn statement of Encarnacion Garcia on October 7, 1966.
10. Sworn statement of Sister Teresa Arguelles on December 29, 1966.
11. Sworn statement of Juan Antonio Magdalena on October 18, 1966.
12. Florentina's letter of January 20, 1948.
13. Father Jacinto's letter of June 10, 1953.
14. Father Segundo, a Passionist, wrote a letter dated January 24, 1969 from Havana, Cuba: "Every day when the brother opened the door of the church at 5:30 a.m., there was Praxedes waiting for it to be opened. One has to realize the sacrifice that this must have entailed. It was early, very early, for it was still dark. There were also the dangers of walking on the roads of the North and the Vasco. We walked these roads and found out for ourselves how dangerous it could be." Sister Maria Canal also testified that she arrived in Mieres after these Masses for the 7:00 a.m. Mass at the Fabrica. She took the train to arrive on time.
15. Florentina's letter of January 20, 1948. In another sworn statement on March 3, 1966, she stated that when Praxedes was told that this vision must be a figment of the imagination all she said was, "I have seen it, I have seen it!"
16. Celestina's letter of February 22, 1951, where she said that Praxedes told her this.
17. Sworn statement of Gabriel on December 22, 1966.

CHAPTER 21—*Spain, a Turn for the Worst*

1. Cfr. Daniel Rops, *History of the Church*, Illustrated Edition, Vol. 13: "The Great Battles of Pius XI." Red Triangle, pp. 106-110.
2. Letter published in all the Spanish diocesan bulletins by the Spanish Metropolitans.

3. Sworn statement of Carmen Vallina, to whom Trinidad Gonzalez told this immediately, on February 16, 1963. Trinidad died a happy death on August 23 of the same year. In regard to her six children Praxedes had said to her, "You can help your children better from Heaven."

CHAPTER 22—*The Search for Sacrifice*

1. Sworn statement of Sara Alvarez on January 14, 1958.
2. Sworn statement of Florentina Fernandez on March 3, 1966.
3. Sworn statement of Sister Angeles Mellada on January 7, 1958.
4. Sworn statement of Isabel Fernandez to Father Enrique on October 6, 1953.
5. Letter of her sister-in-law Teresa Bolea on June 7, 1947. Florentina also confirmed this in another sworn statement on March 3, 1966.
6. Constitutions of the Discalced Carmelite Sisters, chapter 4, No. 4.
7. Declaration of Isabel Fernandez on October 6, 1953 to Father Enrique.
8. Sworn statement of Gabriel on December 22, 1966.

CHAPTER 23—*A Christian of Her Times*

1. Sworn statement of Obdulia Iglesias on January 10, 1967.
2. Sworn statement of Obdulia Iglesias on January 10, 1967.
3. Sara Alvarez's letter of April 7, 1968. Also a sworn statement of Dolores Garcia on January 2, 1968.
4. Ismael Llaneza, after being seriously ill with typhus for over a month and with no hope of recuperation, was cured after Praxedes placed the Miraculous Medal on him. Eloy's case was also despaired of. When Praxedes arrived to visit him she asked his wife how he was. She answered, "There is no hope for him." Praxedes' comment was, "I have the remedy right here." She gave him the Miraculous Medal and assured him that he would get well. On the eighth day after this incident the doctor came to visit him and to his amazement he found him sitting at the table eating with his family. He had had a serious case of angina. Both he and Ismael died many years later, advanced in age, in 1966.
5. Teresa Bolea in a sworn statement on July 26, 1973, declared, "Around 1932 one of my neighbors died. Because of the pressures of the times her family was not able to have a Christian burial for her. Praxedes and I went to her home to pray the Rosary while her body was still there. The house was full of men waiting the time of burial. No one said or did anything."
6. Sworn statement of Florentina Fernandez, Praxedes' cousin, on September 25, 1973.

7. Sworn statement of Manuela Vega, daughter of Luisa Gonzalez, on January 16, 1958.
8. Praxedes herself referred to this in her letter to her son in the seminary on July 15, 1932.
9. Praxedes' letter of July 15, 1932.
10. Praxedes' letter of July 15, 1932.
11. From an article written by the Bishop of Oviedo, Bishop Francisco Javier Lauzurica, published in the book *A Holy Mother For Our Times*. Salamanca, 1954, p. 5.

CHAPTER 24—*The Centenary of the Redemption*

1. Sworn statement of Pedro Martinez on November 30, 1964.
2. Sworn statement of Sister Amalia Villa on December 28, 1957.
3. Sworn statement of Ma. Dolores Garcia on December 24, 1965.
4. Sworn statement of Florentina on March 3, 1966.
5. Sworn statement of Florentina on September 27, 1972.
6. Sworn statement of Sister Felisa Canal on July 23, 1973.
7. Cf. *1 Cor.* 13:5-6.
8. Sworn statement of Marcelina Vasquez on January 10, 1967, who has assured us that Praxedes gave the fliers to "whom she knew would heed them."

CHAPTER 25—*"You are the Mother of the Poor"*

1. Sworn statement of Gabriel on December 22, 1966.
2. Sworn statement of Marcelina Vasquez on September 25, 1973, in which she added, "Praxedes helped all the poor, especially the very poor, which at that time were many in the neighborhood. She visited those sick that had infectious diseases and the most repugnant, those that were the most neglected of all."
3. Sworn statement of Gabriel on September 26, 1973.
4. Obdulia Iglesias, in a sworn statement on January 10, 1967, in which she testified that her son who suffered from meningitis for 15 days had died. Praxedes left 50 pesetas under his pillow on two different times when she visited him.
5. Teresa Bolea's letter of June 7, 1948.
6. Marcelina Vasquez in a sworn statement on September 25, 1973.
7. Julia Suarez in a sworn statement on September 20, 1973. Gabriel, in another sworn statement on September 26, 1973, in which he added, "Joaquin was like a little child. When he was approaching our house he began to call my mother in a loud voice so that she would come out to meet him when he arrived. He would stay several days and be well taken care of. He left when he was ready."
8. Gabriel in a sworn statement on September 26, 1973.

9. The names of these women are found in sworn statements by Justa Curieses on September 25, 1973 and of Gabriel on September 26, 1973. Justa Curiesis in this statement added, "She aided with much concern all the beggars that came from all over asking for alms or board to pass the night in. When they came to her door she invited them in." Maria Alonso, in another sworn statement on September 24, 1973 said, "She always gave a bed to all who asked."

10. Arsenio Alvarez in a sworn statement on November 25, 1965.

11. Jose Antonio Robledo in a sworn statement on December 29, 1965.

12. Justa Curieses in a sworn statement on September 25, 1973.

13. Dolores Garcia in a sworn statement on January 2, 1968.

14. Pedro Martinez in a sworn statement on November 30, 1964 and on September 25, 1973, in which he added, "I was able to observe her untiring charity, especially on pay days in the factory in Mieres. One could see her there giving alms and consoling the poor as they begged from all the men that had received their checks. She was a true mother of the poor."

15. Marcelino Llaneza in a sworn statement on September 25, 1973.

16. *Ibid.*

17. Olvido Garcia in a sworn statement on December 27, 1966.

18. Sworn statement of Florentina on March 3, 1966. Gabriel also testified to this in a sworn statement on December 22, 1966 saying, "I myself saw my mother wash her own dish separately to as to avoid infecting the family. After washing it she put it in the oven and thus killed any germs that might have been there. It was an old battered dish." Marcelina Vasquez said that she saw the dish and even asked Praxedes why she ate out of such a dish. As an answer, Praxedes just smiled. Florentina in a sworn statement on March 3 added, "She visited all the sick in town and also assisted at all their funerals. As many of the sick had contagious diseases, she wore a special gown when she visited these. Upon her return she hung it behind the door in the entrance. She used alcohol and ate from a special plate, which she washed separately and always put in the oven to disinfect it."

Felipa Lopez, in a sworn statement on September 25, 1973, testified, "I know of the great charity that Praxedes had with my stepmother, Teresa Fernandez. She also aided my father, Benito Lopez, when he was without work and very sick. After my father died she was left in abject poverty with two children. She couldn't even pay the rent and remained in the house out of pure charity of Mr. Reimeses, the owner. The two children begged when they were not in school in Sueros. A few days before the revolution my stepmother was taken to the hospital in Oviedo, where she died in

1934. Praxedes helped this family for many years." In another sworn statement in May 24, 1966 she said, "I saw her give her some money to buy whatever she needed."

Aurora Fernandez in a letter of January 29, 1975 wrote that, "I remember seeing Praxedes washing Teresa's ulcers and changing the bandages. Olvido Garcia saw Praxedes washing Teresa's utensils in the river that flowed by Reimeses. One day she offered to help her but she answered her saying, 'I have the pleasure of doing it.'" This is a sworn statement of Olvido Garcia on December 27, 1966. Another daughter of the sick woman, Rosario, was in tears one day telling Sister Pilar and others of all that Praxedes had done for her mother. And in another sworn statement on January 24, 1958, she testified, "Praxedes was so charitable with all the sick and the poor! When my mother became tubercular she cared for her even then, and brought her her own food."

19. Sworn statement of Gabriel on December 22, 1966.
20. Sworn statement of Justa Curieses on September 25, 1973.
21. Sworn statement of Gabriel on December 22, 1966.
22. Sworn statement of Marcelino Llaneza on September 25, 1973.
23. Sworn statement of Father Enrique on September 17, 1981.
24. Sworn statement of Gabriel on December 22, 1966.
25. Sworn statement of Maria Alonso on September 24, 1973. Antonia Castano who often met Praxedes at the door of the church of the Passionists in Mieres, before it was opened, wrote in a letter on August 4, 1947, "In my conversations with Praxedes she always gave me advice as to the necessity of being good so as to go to Heaven and do much good for our neighbor. I never heard her speak ill of anyone and if she heard any of us doing so she would kindly reprimand us."
26. Sworn statement of Father Jacinto, a Passionist priest, on the 23rd of July, 1973.
27. San Martin de Porres. Process of beatification. Palencia 1960, p. 368.
28. Sworn statement of Marcelina Vasquez on September 25, 1973.

CHAPTER 26—*The Charity of Christ Impels Us*

1. Pope Pius XI wrote, "Convert those that have been seduced by the doctrine of Marxism in the way that you show your faith by performing the works of charity inspired by the love of Christ."
2. Sworn statement of Isabel Fernandez on December 27, 1957.
3. Hortensia Quiron's letter in which she said, "I don't know how to explain the charity that Praxedes had for everyone. She visited and consoled all the sick with such love. She also assisted many in their last agony. She gave alms to all the poor as well as her

food and counseled them to go to Mass and receive the patience that they needed to live their daily lives."

4. Sworn statement of Florentina on September 27, 1972, where she said, "She also visited Leonor Gutierrez, whose family was Communist. She was sick many times and Praxedes assisted her, always trying to convert her. They all admired my sister and, in spite of their irreligiosity, they said my sister was a saint."

5. Sworn statement of a daughter of Maximina, Encarnacion Garcia, on October 7, 1966: "Praxedes was continually performing acts of kindness. She thought of nothing else. When my mother Maximina contracted cancer, and died of it later, Praxedes visited her, and upon seeing her suffer such pains she would advise her to suffer with patience." And in another sworn statement on September 23, 1973 she added, "When my mother got cancer of the face, and which ate the left side of her face, Praxedes came often to console her and urged her to suffer patiently for the love of God."

6. Sworn statement of Sister Maria Canal on September 10, 1972, in which she affirmed, "Praxedes never told me of all the charity that she did, but I knew about it through other persons. A woman who used to come to the school to beg told me that she and her husband had just had their marriage blessed by the Church after 50 years of living together, and all because of Praxedes. She was then 70 years old."

7. Sworn statement of Sara Alvarez on January 14, 1958.

8. Sworn statement of Justa Curieses on September 25, 1973, in which she said, "As everyone knew that she was so good and was very capable of giving such good advice, she was able to bring harmony and peace to many families."

9. Sworn statement of Ovidio on November 8, 1957. Ismael, the oldest brother, in another declaration on November 9, 1957 said, "I know that my sister was outstanding in her works of mercy for all the needy and sick. She was also a consolation to the lonely. She instructed those who needed religious instructions. She brought peace to many families. She never seemed to feel anger, and when she knew someone needed prayers she interceded for them. Many spoke of the admirable gift she had of counseling." Benigna, in a sworn statement on January 31, 1958 said, "She supported me and counseled me in my distress at having several miscarriages. The more you suffer patiently in this world the less you have to suffer in the next. She treated everyone the same, with such consideration. She never was angry with anyone."

Sara Alvarez in a sworn statement on January 14, 1958 testified, "When I helped Praxedes in her home she gave me orders that

if anyone came to the door to beg, I was to give them her food—
which meant that she went without any." And in a letter she wrote
later on April 7, 1968 she said, "It is some time that I worked
in Amalia's home and I must say that I have never seen anyone
with so much charity to the poor as Praxedes had. There is a little
village by the name of Reimeses nearby and I know there was
a very poor family there that Praxedes herself used to take food
to. It didn't matter what the weather was like. She did the same
with needy families in Sueros or with the dying." Justa Curieses,
in a sworn statement on November 1, 1957, said, "She was so generous that she went without food to give to the poor. She didn't
have one single enemy. She pardoned everyone and defended the
reputation of those that were absent. She was always busy at home
or in church."

Maria Alonso, in a sworn statement on January 26, 1958 affirmed,
"I know that she was kind to the poor and took food and alms
to those in need. I never heard anyone speak ill of her. She was
very gentle and was always so submissive and obedient."

10. Sworn statement of Gabriel on December 22, 1966 in which he
stated, "My mother always assisted the sick in the town, especially the ones that were gravely ill. She saw to it that they had
the help of the Sacraments. She baptized the infants that were
in danger of death."

11. Works of St. Teresa of Avila. Mansion VII, chapter 1, No. 2.

12. Sworn statement of Ovidio on November 8, 1958 in which he said,
"The poor never left our door without Praxedes giving him an
alms or food, after the example of her mother. Moreover, she gave
room to them, especially to the women. She visited the sick and
the afflicted. She always defended the reputation of the absent.
She always avoided arguments. Everyone respected her." Gabriel,
in a sworn statement on November 14, 1957 said, "I don't think
she ever had an enemy. When some would say that the people
that went to Mass were bad, they would always add, 'except
Praxedes.' "

Celestina, Praxedes' sister, in a sworn statement on November
25, 1957, testified, "She had no enemies and the Socialists themselves adored her. Then when they spoke or discussed religion
they would say that Praxedes was the only true Christian."

13. Sworn statement of Florentina on September 27, 1972.

14. Bishop Segundo Garcia, currently bishop of the Archdiocese of
Burgos, wrote in regard to Praxedes on September 9, 1959, "In order
to be able to evaluate Praxedes' holiness, it is necessary to place
oneself in the tortuous surroundings of an Asturia of hate

and persecution, and inflamed manifestations of the multitudes. Churches and sanctuaries were blown up or burned; the clergy and religious were persecuted from all sides, and numerous calumnies were written in the newspapers—not to mention the sarcasms right to their faces. Think of how this must have affected this gentle, holy widow. She lived in this atmosphere for five years, yet she grew in holiness like a beautiful flower amid this 'red fire,' doing her penances and praying for her brothers and sisters so that God would pour His mercy upon them. She was the prudent woman who carried her lamp lighted, and one could not find in her any doubts, inquietude or the least vacillation. We need such a model of Christian charity, open, generous, quiet, sweet, patient in suffering, steady and full of such delicacy, such as only God's elect possess. It is necessary to make this ordinary woman so full of charity and holiness known, who succeeded in finding the hidden way that leads to God."

15. Sworn statement of Florentina on November 11, 1957, where she affirmed, "My sister proved herself fearless in the practice of her faith and never feared the persecutors of the Church. She ignored the dangers she encountered in the practice of her religion in the open, never hiding in the least."

   Celestina, in another sworn statement on November 13, 1957 added, "Under adverse conditions she overcame all difficulties in order to be able to fulfill her religious obligations."

16. *Priests'* Magazine, No. 275, October, 1972, pp. 30 and 32, affirmed, "Yes, it would be stupendous if one could see in Bernini's glory, not a little nun nor some ecclesiastical personage, but some proletariat saint....And what an honor it would be for Spain to be the nation to present this miracle of grace to the Church. Truly an authentic *sign of our times!"*

17. Father Moises told the following to Father Enrique in an interview in June, 1953, upon his return from the United States, in the Convent of St. Dominic in Oviedo. It was published in the second edition of the biography, *A Holy Mother For Our Times,* Salamanca, 1954.

18. Edelmira Fernandez, who was in charge of selling these calendars, told this in a sworn statement on October 18, 1966.

CHAPTER 27—*A False Calm*

1. *Phil.* 4:8.
2. Sworn statement of Father Jacinto on July 23, 1973.
3. Sworn statement of Florentina Fernandez on January 8, 1967.
4. Sworn statement of Obdulia Iglesias on January 8, 1958.

5. Sworn statement of Marcelino Llaneza on July 25, 1973.
6. Sworn statement of Sister Felisa Canal on January 10, 1967.
7. Declaration of Sister Amparo Fernandez, O.P. on May 12, 1955.
8. *Episodes of the Revolution in October in Asturias.* Work in collaboration. Ed. *The Passionist*, Santander, 1935, p. 4.

CHAPTER 28—*"Like in Russia"*

1. The Revolution in October in Spain. Second Official Edition. Madrid, 1935, pp. 13-15.
2. Carlos Seco Serrano, *General History of Spanish Towns.* Volume VI. *Contemporary Times.* Publications of the Institute Gallach. Barcelona, 1962, p. 97.
3. Published in the periodical *The Socialist* on January 19, 1936.
4. Joaquin Arraras, *History Of The Second Spanish Republic* (Madrid, 1964. p. 535).
5. The same protagonists refer to it in the work, *Episode Of The Revolution In October In Asturias* (Santander, 1935, p. 44). That Praxedes fell on her knees praying for them was testified by Gabriel in a sworn statement on December 22, 1966.
6. *Episodes Of The Revolution In October In Asturias*, ed. cit.
7. Op. cit., p. 10.
8. Sworn statement of Gabriel on December 22, 1966.
9. Official numbers given by the government of Madrid in *The Revolution Of October In Spain*, second edition, official, Madrid, 1935, pp. 36 & 40. The historian Georges Roux added to this that after the revolution was over, there were more than a thousand detained, 20 militants were condemned to death, but only two were executed.
10. Father Angel de la Puente's letter of August 26, 1954.
11. Sworn statement of Antonio de la Uz on December 28, 1965.
12. Sworn statement of Sister Angeles Mellado on January 7, 1958.

CHAPTER 29—*From Here to Heaven*

1. Praxedes' letter of October 27, 1934.
2. *El Sol* of Madrid, October 27, 1934.
3. Sworn statement of Gabriel on December 22, 1973.
4. Sworn statement of Sister Maria Canal on July 23, 1973.
5. *Ibid.*
6. Sworn statement of Obdulia Iglesias on January 14, 1958.
7. Sworn statement of Sister Pilar Vila on December 28, 1957.
8. Milagros herself affirmed in 1964, "When the October Revolution broke out I discussed the unpleasantness of the revolution—but Praxedes never said a word, but humbly kept quiet."
9. Sister Pilar Sanza's letter of February 2, 1958.

10. Praxedes' letter of April 30, 1934, in which she spoke of the destruction of the parish in Seana: "Your grandma says that she would not like to be buried where there is no parish."
11. Sworn statement of Florentina on September 27, 1972.
12. Sworn statement of Sister Amalia Villa on December 28, 1957.
13. Sworn statement of Marcelino Llaneza on December 25, 1973.
14. Sworn statement of Maria Alonso on September 24, 1973.
15. Sworn statement of Maria Dolores Garcia on September 24, 1973.
16. Sworn statement of Edelmira Fernandez on October 18, 1966.
17. Sworn statement of Florentina on March 3, 1965.

CHAPTER 30—*Attentive to the "Sacrament of the Present Moment"*

1. Cf. *Matt.* 6:34.
2. Sworn statement of Paz Vega on November 12, 1967.
3. Sworn statement of Pilar Soro on December 30, 1967.
4. Sworn statement of Sister Pilar Sanza on September 27, 1958.
5. Sworn statement of Teresa Menendez on September 29, 1965.
6. Sworn statement of Leonor Gutierrez on October 18, 1965.
7. Sworn statement of Florentina Fernandez on September 27, 1972.
8. Sworn statement of one who received hospitality from Praxedes, December 27, 1957.
9. Sworn statement of Maxima Suarez on January 26, 1958.
10. Sworn statement of Dolores Alvera.
11. Praxedes' letter of November 6, 1933.

CHAPTER 31—*"Another War Will Come"*

1. Cf. *Col.* 1:23-24.
2. Cf. *Rom.* 9:3.
3. Sworn statement of Florentina Fernandez on March 3, 1966.
4. Sworn statement of Gabriel on December 22, 1966. [Praxedes' attitude here is admittedly somewhat unrealistic and self-contradictory. The Catholic Church teaches that a person may choose the path of non-resistance for himself, but he has an obligation to defend his family or country if they are attacked, and this self-defense may involve violence. One must, however, admire Praxedes' spirit of meekness; moreover, she undoubtedly had a keen realization that all violence, even legitimate self-defense, brings with it many temptations to hatred, revenge and cruelty.]
5. Sworn statement of Lucrecia Garcia on September 12, 1966.
6. Sworn statement of Gabriel on December 22, 1966.
7. Sworn statement of Gabriel on December 22, 1966.
8. Sworn statement of Gabriel on December 22, 1966.
9. Teresa Bolea's letter on January 18, 1976.

10. Sworn statement of Gabriel on December 22, 1966.

11. Sworn statement of Gabriel on December 22, 1966.

CHAPTER 32—*"Like Christ on the Cross"*

1. Published in *History Of The Spanish Crusade*, Madrid, 1941. Vol. IV. pp.100-126, where are found all the details of the attack on Oviedo.

2. Sworn statement of Gabriel on December 22, 1966.

3. Sworn statement of Florentina on March 3, 1966.

4. Sworn statement of Florentina on March 3, 1966.

5. Sworn statement of Florentina on September 27, 1972.

6. Celestino's letter of May 26, 1937, one month before his death.

7. Sworn statement of Florentina on March 3, 1966.

8. Sworn statement of Josefa Garcia on November 11, 1967.

9. Sworn statement of Carmen Martinez on September 12, 1966.

10. Sworn statement of Maximina Suarez on September 12, 1966.

11. Sworn statement of Gabriel on December 22, 1966.

12. *Life and Writings of St. John Berchmans of the Company of Jesus.* Edition of the Apostolate of the Press (Madrid, 1901, p. 297). The saint, holding up his rosary, crucifix and his rule, said, "'These are my weapons."

13. Sworn statement of Consuelo Fernandez on July 7, 1975.

14. Sworn statement of Gabriel on November 14, 1957 and a sworn statement of Florentina on November 14, 1957.

15. Sister Pilar tells us that D. Luciano Fernandez established the Association of Christian Mothers in the chapel of the Fabrica in 1920. Praxedes enrolled on the very day of inauguration.

16. Praxedes' letter of November 6, 1933.

17. Florentina testified to all these phrases in a sworn statement on March 3, 1966.

18. Sworn statement of Florentina on March 3, 1966.

19. Sworn statement of Florentina on March 3, 1966.

20. Paz Ruiz de Moragas' letter Mendoza, Argentina, April 28, 1952.

21. Official publication of the war published on October 7, referring to the day before.

22. Sworn statement of Gabriel on December 22, 1966.

EPILOGUE

1. Feliciano Suarez's letter dated June 23, 1965.

If you have enjoyed this book, consider making your next selection from among the following...

The Four Last Things—Death, Judgment, Hell, Heaven......... 4.50
Little Catechism of the Curé of Ars. St. John Vianney.......... 4.00
The Curé of Ars—Patron St. of Parish Priests. Fr. B. O'Brien.... 3.50
St. Teresa of Ávila. William Thomas Walsh...................15.00
The Rosary and the Crisis of Faith. Msgr. Cirrincione & Nelson. .75
The Secret of the Rosary. St. Louis De Montfort.............. 1.00
Modern Saints—Their Lives & Faces. Ann Ball................10.00
The 12 Steps to Holiness and Salvation. St. Alphonsus.......... 6.00
Eucharistic Miracles. Joan Carroll Cruz.....................10.00
The Incorruptibles. Joan Carroll Cruz....................... 8.00
Raised from the Dead—400 Resurrection Miracles. Fr. Hebert....12.00
Saint Michael and the Angels. Approved Sources............. 3.50
Dolorous Passion of Our Lord. Anne C. Emmerich............10.00
Our Lady of Fatima's Peace Plan from Heaven. Booklet......... .40
Divine Favors Granted to St. Joseph. Pere Binet.............. 3.00
St. Joseph Cafasso—Priest of the Gallows. St. J. Bosco......... 2.00
Catechism of the Council of Trent. McHugh/Callan............15.00
The Sinner's Guide. Ven. Louis of Granada................... 8.00
Padre Pio—The Stigmatist. Fr. Charles Carty.................. 8.50
Why Squander Illness? Frs. Rumble & Carty.................. 1.50
The Sacred Heart and the Priesthood. de la Touche............ 5.00
Fatima—The Great Sign. Francis Johnston................... 6.00
Heliotropium—Conformity of Human Will to Divine............ 8.50
Purgatory Explained. (pocket, unabr.). Fr. Schouppe............5.00
Who Is Padre Pio? Radio Replies Press...................... 1.00
Child's Bible History. Knecht............................... 2.00
The Stigmata and Modern Science. Fr. Charles Carty........... .75
The Life of Christ. 4 Vols. H.B. Anne C. Emmerich...........67.00
The Life of Christ. 4 Vols. P.B. Anne C. Emmerich...........40.00
The Glories of Mary. (pocket, unabr.). St. Alphonsus........... 5.00
Is It a Saint's Name? Fr. William Dunne.................... 1.25
St. Anthony—The Wonder Worker of Padua. Stoddard.......... 2.50
The Precious Blood. Fr. Faber.............................. 7.50
The Holy Shroud & Four Visions. Fr. O'Connell.............. 1.50
Clean Love in Courtship. Fr. Lawrence Lovasik................ 1.50
The Prophecies of St. Malachy. Peter Bander................. 3.00
The History of Antichrist. Rev. P. Huchede.................. 2.00
Douay-Rheims Bible. Leatherbound.........................35.00
St. Catherine of Siena. Alice Curtayne...................... 7.50
Where We Got the Bible. Fr. Henry Graham.................. 3.00
Imitation of the Sacred Heart of Jesus. Fr. Arnoudt............10.00
An Explanation of the Baltimore Catechism. Kinkead........... 8.50
The Way of Divine Love. Sr. Menendez...................... 5.00
The Curé D'Ars. Abbé Francis Trochu......................15.00
Love, Peace and Joy. St. Gertrude/Prévot.................... 4.00

At your bookdealer or direct from the publisher.

Prices guaranteed through December 31, 1988.